BRITAIN'S STEAM
LOCOMOTIVES

Published by Collins
An imprint of HarperCollins Publishers
Westerhill Road, Bishopbriggs, Glasgow G64 2QT
www.harpercollins.co.uk

HarperCollins Publishers
Macken House, 39/40 Mayor Street Upper, Dublin 1, D01 C9W8, Ireland

First edition 2023
© HarperCollins Publishers 2023
Text © Julian Holland

A catalogue record for this book is available from the British Library

ISBN 978-0-00-862279-4

10 9 8 7 6 5 4 3 2 1

Printed in India

If you would like to comment on any aspect of this book,
please contact us at the above address or online.
e-mail: collins.reference@harpercollins.co.uk

collins.co.uk

BRITAIN'S STEAM
LOCOMOTIVES

100 of the best, from *Penydarren* to *Tornado*

JULIAN HOLLAND

Collins

Contents

A replica model of Richard Trevithick's Penydarren in Merthyr Tydfil, South Wales. Built for the Penydarren Ironworks in 1804, this was the first steam railway locomotive in the world (see page 10).

Designed by Henry Ivatt, GNR small-boilered Class 'C1' 4-4-2 No 984 poses for the camera on the East Coast Main Line at Bawtry, 1903 (see page 83).

The Early 20th Century

The 'Big Four'

British Railways

Seen here at Stirling on 16 June 2013, new-build Peppercorn Class 'A1' 4-6-2 No 60163 was completed in 2008. It was named Tornado in honour of RAF Tornado crews flying in the Gulf War (see page 208).

Introduction

It is now more than 200 years since the world's first steam railway locomotive made its maiden voyage along a primitive plateway in South Wales – in 1804, Richard Trevithick's high-pressure steam locomotive successfully hauled a loaded train for a distance of nine miles at an average speed of 2½ mph. Only 25 years later, Robert Stephenson's *Rocket* won the Rainhill Trials in Lancashire with a top speed of nearly 30 mph. With Britain leading the way, the evolution of the steam locomotive continued unabated through the 19th and into the 20th centuries, culminating in Nigel Gresley's streamlined Class 'A4' *Mallard*, which still holds the world speed record for steam railway locomotives after achieving 126 mph in 1938.

Although steam haulage on Britain's nationalised standard-gauge railways ended in 1968, the British public's passion for these moving mechanical monsters lives on – steam haulage on the country's heritage railways and national rail network is a regular feature, with packed trains being hauled by lovingly restored locomotives that were saved from the scrapheap some decades ago.

The most famous is undoubtedly Class 'A3' 4-6-2 No 60103 *Flying Scotsman*, which has recently celebrated its 100th birthday – thousands of people turn out to see this celebrity wherever it goes. Brand new steam locomotives of extinct classes are also being built by dedicated enthusiasts – the first of many is 'A1' Class 4-6-2 *Tornado* which, since its first journey in 2008, has continued to attract admirers wherever it appears. Britain's love affair with steam looks set to continue.

Britain's Steam Locomotives is a fitting memorial to more than two centuries of British steam locomotive design, and traces this fascinating, unfolding story from the early 19th century to the present day. While the locomotives in all their glory are obviously the stars of the show, I interweave the equally fascinating stories of their engineers, ranging from Richard Trevithick, Robert Stephenson, Daniel Gooch and Samuel Waite Johnson to George Jackson Churchward, William Stanier, Nigel Gresley and Robert Riddles. In addition, I have also provided a technical specification for each locomotive (see Explanation of locomotive specifications on page 8), personal trainspotting notes (as below), plus selected features on the works where they were built, and some famous named trains. Let me warn you now that the choice of British steam locomotives found in this book is entirely mine!

Since I was very young, I have had a passion for railways and my memories of watching steam-hauled expresses and goods trains thundering through my hometown of Gloucester, along with Swindon, Basingstoke and Templecombe, as a teenager in the late 1950s and early 1960s are as vivid today as if I had seen them yesterday. Saved by my mother when I went off to art college, my trainspotting notebooks from this period, which I often refer to in this book, offer a personal glimpse of an era slowly fading away into the mists of time.

The end of a glorious era. BR Standard Class '9F' 2-10-0 No 92220 Evening Star on display at the National Railway Museum in York. It was the last steam locomotive to be built by British Railways and it emerged from Swindon Works in 1960. Sadly, it had a very short working life as it was withdrawn in 1965 (see page 223).

Preserved ex-LMS 'Princess Royal' Class 4-6-2 No 6201 Princess Elizabeth storms along the Settle–Carlisle Line at Helwith Bridge with a Railway Touring Company charter train on 20 July 2019. Built at Crewe Works in 1933, this powerful loco was withdrawn in October 1962 (see page 171).

Explanation of locomotive specifications

Wheel arrangement

British locomotive wheel arrangement uses the *Whyte* notation which counts the number of leading wheels, coupled wheels and trailing wheels, all separated by dashes. For example, a 4-6-2 *Pacific* has two leading axles (4 wheels), three driving axles (6 wheels), and one trailing axle (2 wheels). The suffixes following the wheel arrangements denote the following: T = tank; PT = pannier tank; ST = saddle tank; WT = well tank.

BR power classification

The BR classification was based on the original MR/ LMS system, with each locomotive allocated a numerical rating between 0 and 9, signifying its power, followed by a suffix: F (freight) or P (passenger). Mixed traffic locomotives were allocated two classifications, for example a Gresley 'V2' Class 2-6-2 *Prairie* was classified as 7P6F, but the suffix MT (mixed traffic) was used if a locomotive had an equal freight and passenger rating, for example 5MT in the case of a Stanier 'Black Five' 4-6-0.

Cylinders

Cylinders can be placed either inside or outside the locomotive main frames, inside cylinders giving a more stable ride but being more difficult to access and maintain. More powerful locomotives possessed either three cylinders (two outside and one inside) or four (two inside and two outside).

Driving wheels

The diameter measurement of the driving wheels is given in feet and inches. These are powered by the locomotive's pistons and coupled together with side rods (known as coupling rods). Normally one pair of wheels is directly driven by the main rod (connecting rod), which is connected to the end of the piston rod, and the power is transmitted to the other wheels through the side rods.

Tractive effort

This is the pulling or pushing capability of a locomotive – calculated by its mechanical characteristics such as steam pressure, weight, etc. – to accelerate to a given speed, overcoming the aerodynamic forces against the locomotive itself and the drag of its trailing load.

Boiler pressure

The two basic functions of a steam locomotive are the boiler, where steam is raised, and the engine (cylinders, connecting/coupling rods and driving wheels), where the steam is expended. In later designs of locomotive, working steam pressure usually fell within the range of 200–300 pounds per square inch.

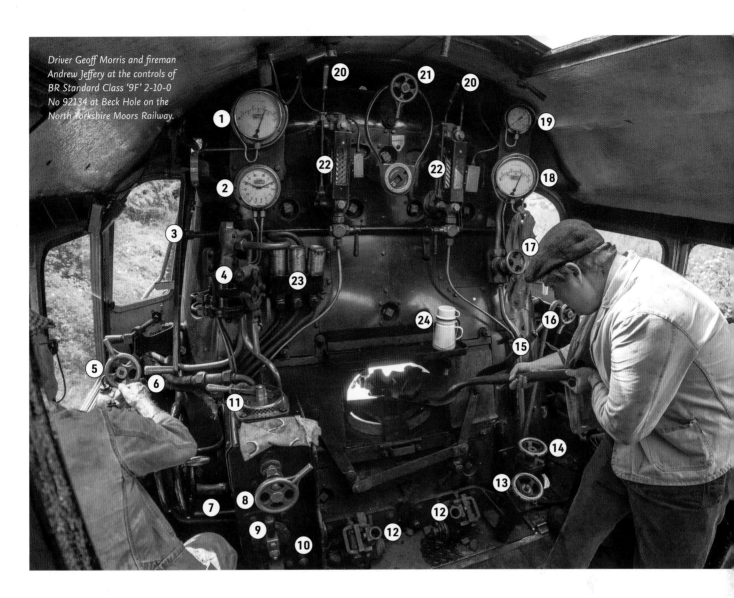

Driver Geoff Morris and fireman Andrew Jeffery at the controls of BR Standard Class '9F' 2-10-0 No 92134 at Beck Hole on the North Yorkshire Moors Railway.

Footplate controls: BR Standard Class '9F' 2-10-0 No 92134

1	Steam chest pressure gauge		**13**	Rear damper
2	Vacuum duplex gauge		**14**	Front damper
3	Whistle		**15**	Firehole door linkage handle
4	Steam-operated independent proportional locomotive brake		**16**	Steam injector feeds
			17	Carriage warming valve
5	Ejector		**18**	Boiler pressure gauge
6	Regulator		**19**	Carriage warming gauge
7	Reverser		**20**	Gauge frame shut-off handles
8	Blower		**21**	Manifold shut-off
9	Sanders		**22**	Gauge frames and boiler water level glasses
10	Vacuum chamber release			
11	Train brake		**23**	Steam brake oil pots
12	Rocker grate lever points		**24**	Yorkshire tea

Trevithick's *Penydarren*

The mineral-mining region of Cornwall was the birthplace, in 1771, of engineer and inventor Richard Trevithick. He went to work at the age of 19 in a local mine, where he soon became a consultant, fascinated by the steam pumping engines that stopped the mines from being flooded.

Richard Trevithick went on to develop the use of high-pressure steam and in 1801 he demonstrated a full-size steam passenger-carrying road carriage on the streets of Camborne. The *Puffing Devil*'s range was limited as it soon ran out of steam, but this was the first time in the world that passengers had been transported by a steam vehicle. In 1802 he had taken out a patent for his high-pressure steam engine – this was first successfully demonstrated as a stationary engine at Coalbrookdale Iron Works in Shropshire.

Trevithick also built a high-pressure stationary steam engine to drive a hammer at the Penydarren

Ironworks in South Wales. The owner of the works suggested to him that the engine could be placed on wheels and driven along his horsedrawn cast-iron L-section plateway. The conversion was completed with the drive being transmitted from the single cylinder to the driving wheels via a flywheel and cogs. The locomotive made its first and only rail journey in 1804, successfully hauling 10 tons of iron and 70 men in five wagons a distance of nearly 10 miles at an average speed of 2½ mph – a world first. Despite this success the locomotive proved too heavy for the cast-iron plateway and it reverted to its original use as a stationary engine. A second Trevithick steam locomotive was built with flanged wheels for the Wylam Colliery near Newcastle in 1805 but it also proved too heavy for the wooden waggonway on which it ran.

In 1808 Trevithick went on to build a circular demonstration steam railway which gave rides to the public in London behind his third locomotive, *Catch Me Who Can*. Despite its novelty value it was not a great success and Trevithick's steam railway locomotive career came to an end. His designs were later improved by John Blenkinsop for his rack-and-pinion Middleton Railway in Leeds (see page 12).

Trevithick's later years saw further developments with his stationary high-pressure steam engines for various uses in industry and inventions such as a steam threshing machine, a steam tug and floating crane, a steam dredger, buoyancy tanks for raising wrecked ships, floating docks and buoys. In 1811, while in partnership with Robert Dickinson, a London merchant, Trevithick was declared bankrupt. He was discharged in 1814. In 1816 he travelled to Peru where he became a consultant engineer for silver and copper mines and explored methods of transporting ore back to England. After travelling to Ecuador and Peru, Trevithick ended up in Costa Rica where he was considering building a steam railway to connect mines with ports. All of this came to nothing and, virtually penniless, he met Robert Stephenson (see page 21) in 1827, who paid for his sea journey back to England.

His final years in England were spent as a poverty-stricken inventor and, as the creator of the world's first working steam railway locomotive, he died penniless in Dartford, Kent in 1833.

A replica of Richard Trevithick's Penydarren 1804 tramway locomotive on display in the National Waterfront Museum, Swansea.

Specification

Builder	Richard Trevithick
Wheel arrangement	four-wheel
Build date	1804
Cylinders	1 outside

John Blenkinsop's *Salamanca*

Born in County Durham in 1783, John Blenkinsop served his apprenticeship in Northumberland coal mines until 1808, when he became the agent to the owner of collieries on the Middleton Estate near Leeds. A horsedrawn waggonway had already opened in the mid-18th century to convey coal from the mines to Leeds. Known as the Middleton Railway, it was the first railway in Britain to be authorised by an Act of Parliament, and in 1807 the wooden rails on the railway were replaced by stronger iron edge rails.

Following his appointment to the Middleton Collieries, Blenkinsop lost no time in designing a steam railway locomotive to haul the coal trains. While Trevithick's 1805 locomotive for the Wylam Colliery provided much inspiration, Blenkinsop wanted a more powerful machine capable of hauling much heavier loads. His six-wheeled design, named *Salamanca*, was a marked improvement on the early Trevithick locomotives, weighing in at 5 tons and with innovative features such as twin double-acting cylinders driving geared cog wheels which engaged with a rack rail. The first two locomotives were built by Matthew Murray of Holbeck in 1812 and proved an immediate success. More followed in 1813 and 1814, and others were built for collieries in Lancashire and Newcastle. These were the world's first practical steam railway locomotives and stayed in service until the 1830s, by which time the rack-and-pinion system had become obsolete following the introduction of the now-familiar rolled iron rail and improved adhesion locomotives. Blenkinsop died in Leeds in 1831 and is buried at Rothwell Parish Church.

A model of *Salamanca*, made by Matthew Murray in 1811, is in the Leeds Industrial Museum.

Specification

Builder	Matthew Murray
Wheel arrangement	six-wheel rack
Build date	1812
Cylinders	2 outside

19th-century engraving of John Blenkinsop's rack-and-pinion steam locomotive, Salamanca. Built by Matthew Murray in 1812, it successfully hauled coal wagons from Middleton Colliery to Leeds.

William Hedley's *Puffing Billy*

When the young William Hedley became a colliery manager at Wylam Colliery in the mid-1790s, coal from the mine was being transported to staithes on the River Tyne along a 5-mile horsedrawn wooden waggonway. In 1805 Hedley, who had been born in nearby Newcastle upon Tyne in 1773, briefly tried steam haulage after Richard Trevithick's second steam railway locomotive was fitted with flanged wheels to run on the wooden rails. The locomotive was too heavy for the flimsy trackwork and the experiment soon ended.

Hedley replaced the wooden rails in 1808 with cast-iron L-section plate rails and set about designing a steam locomotive with his foreman, Timothy Hackworth (see page 16). The initial design, based on Trevithick's single-cylinder locomotive, was not a success. Undeterred by this failure the pair built a second engine, again with flangeless wheels to run on the L-section track, but this time incorporating John Blenkinsop's two-cylinder feature as used on the Middleton Railway (see page 12). There the similarity ended as adhesion was used instead of the rack-and-pinion system employed on the latter railway.

As originally built in 1813, Hedley's *Puffing Billy* was a cumbersome 8-ton, eight-wheeled locomotive driven from the pistons by a complicated system of pivoting beams, rods, crankshaft and gears – but it worked, albeit at a maximum speed of 5 mph. The cast-iron plateway continually broke under its weight so Hedley modified the loco to spread the weight more evenly. Along with a sister engine named *Wylam Dilly*, the locomotive continued to operate in this form until 1830, when it was converted into a four-wheeler with flanged wheels to run on newly laid iron edge rail track. Amazingly these two archaic steam locomotives stayed in service until 1862. William Hedley died in 1843.

The original *Puffing Billy* in its final form can be seen at the Science Museum in London, while *Wylam Dilly* now resides in the National Museum of Scotland in Edinburgh. They are the world's oldest surviving steam railway locomotives. A working replica of *Puffing Billy* was built by Alan Keef Ltd in 2006 for Beamish – The Living Museum of the North, in County Durham.

Specification

Builders	William Hedley and Timothy Hackworth
Wheel arrangement	eight-wheel/four-wheel
Build date	1813
Cylinders	2 outside
Driving wheels	3 ft 3 in
Boiler pressure	50 psi
Number built	2

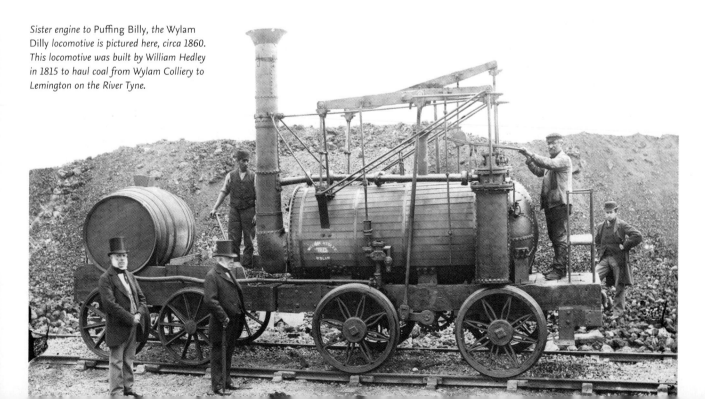

Sister engine to Puffing Billy, *the* Wylam Dilly *locomotive is pictured here, circa 1860. This locomotive was built by William Hedley in 1815 to haul coal from Wylam Colliery to Lemington on the River Tyne.*

Following the success of his early colliery railways and steam locomotives, George Stephenson was appointed Chief Engineer of the Stockton & Darlington Railway (S&DR) in 1821. A year later Parliamentary approval was given for this new 25-mile route, the use of 'moveable engines' and the carrying of passengers. Orders for the first steam locomotives were soon placed with Robert Stephenson & Co by the S&DR.

The new railway was to be built to the gauge of 4 ft 8 in, which Stephenson had already used for his colliery railways at Killingworth and Hetton. With an extra ½ inch added to reduce friction on curves this was soon adopted as the standard gauge for the majority of railways around the world, and remains so today.

On 27 September 1825 and watched by thousands of people, George Stephenson's *Locomotion No. 1* hauled a passenger-carrying steam train on a public railway for the first time in the world. Around 500 passengers on this first train were carried in the railway's only passenger coach (*The Experiment*) and in 21 converted coal wagons. *Locomotion No. 1* was built at Stephenson's new locomotive works in Newcastle and featured, for the first time, driving wheels connected by coupling rods instead of gears. T-section wrought-iron rails, connected by 'fishplates' at 15 ft intervals, were laid on sturdy stone blocks designed to take the weight of heavily loaded coal trains.

The new line was an immediate success and finally proved the viability of steam railways. Apart from the inaugural run on opening day, passengers were still carried in horsedrawn coaches until steam-hauled passenger trains were introduced in 1833. *Locomotion No. 1* was retired in 1841 when it became a stationary steam engine until being preserved in 1857. Following many years on display at Darlington Bank Top station it was moved to the Head of Steam Museum in Darlington, then to the National Railway Museum in Shildon, County Durham. It has now returned to the Head of Steam – Darlington Railway Museum, awaiting the 200th anniversary of the Stockton & Darlington Railway.

A working replica of the locomotive was built in 1975 and is currently based at Locomotion, the railway museum in Shildon, County Durham.

Specification

Builder	Robert Stephenson & Co
Wheel arrangement	0-4-0
Build date	1825
Cylinders	2 outside
Driving wheels	4 ft 0 in
Tractive effort	1,900 lbs
Boiler pressure	50 psi
Number built	1

George Stephenson

George Stephenson was born of illiterate parents in Wylam, Northumberland in 1781. His father worked as a fireman for the Wylam Colliery stationary pumping engine. Opened in 1748 to transport coal from the colliery down to the River Tyne, the Wylam Waggonway passed close to George's home and as a young man he would have seen his first steam locomotive. At the age of 14 he went to work with his father at the colliery where he learnt to control the steam-powered winding gear. Intent on improving himself, George also attended night classes to learn the '3 Rs'.

In 1802 George was promoted to colliery engineman and later that year married local girl Frances Henderson. Their son, Robert (later to become an important railway engineer in his own right, see page 21), was born a year later. In 1808 he was appointed as engineman at Killingworth Colliery, northeast of Newcastle, where on his days off he would take apart and put back together the stationary steam engines. His growing knowledge of steam engines was recognised by the colliery owners who appointed him as enginewright at Killingworth in 1812, where he was responsible for maintaining and repairing the colliery's stationary steam engines.

Working replica of George Stephenson's Locomotion No. 1 on the Pockerley Waggonway at Beamish – The Living Museum of the North.

Following William Hedley and Timothy Hackworth's successful introduction of their locomotive *Puffing Billy* (see page 13) at Wylam Colliery in 1813, George went on to build his first steam locomotive. Named *Blücher* after the Prussian general who later fought at the Battle of Waterloo, it was built in a colliery workshop behind his house in 1814 and in many respects was similar to Blenkinsop's machines on the Middleton Railway (see page 12) but, importantly, its flanged wheels ran on normal edge rails without the use of rack-and-pinion. It was a great success and could haul 30 tons of coal uphill at 4 mph, and was the first practical locomotive of its type in the world. George went on to build a number of these locomotives for use at Killingworth, Hetton Colliery and the Kilmarnock & Troon Railway.

In 1820, Stephenson was appointed to build a railway linking Hetton Colliery to staithes on the River Wear in County Durham. The 8-mile line was a combination of gravity inclines and locomotive-hauled sections, becoming the first railway in the world not to use horsepower. Built to a gauge of 4 ft 8 in – the same that George had used at Killingworth – it was opened in 1822 and remained operational until 1959.

George Stephenson's greatest triumphs were yet to come. In 1822 he was appointed Chief Engineer of the Stockton & Darlington Railway. He also opened a locomotive works in Newcastle, jointly with S&DR director Edward Pease, and installed his son Robert as managing director. After his success with the S&DR – on opening in 1825 it was the world's first public railway to use steam locomotives – Stephenson went on to engineer the world's first intercity railway, the Liverpool & Manchester Railway (see page 18), which opened in 1830.

Following his successes in Britain, George Stephenson was inundated with requests from railway promoters, including the developers of the early American railroads, who ordered their first locomotives from his factory in Newcastle. As a civil engineer he worked with his former assistant Joseph Locke on the building of the Grand Junction Railway and was Chief Engineer for several English railways including the Manchester & Leeds, the York & North Midland and the North Midland. While tunnelling for the latter company he discovered rich seams of coal in Derbyshire and went into business with railway promoters George Hudson and Joseph Sanders opening coal mines, ironworks and limestone quarries around Chesterfield.

Stephenson spent his latter years living in Tapton House near Chesterfield and ran a small farm where he experimented in stock breeding and the speeding up of fattening chickens. He died on 12 August 1848.

The Northumbrian village of Wylam was the birthplace of another steam locomotive engineer, Timothy Hackworth, who was born five years after George Stephenson in 1786. Following in his father's footsteps, Hackworth became a boilermaker at Wylam Colliery in 1807. Working closely with William Hedley (see page 13), he played a major part in the design, construction and the continuing maintenance of *Puffing Billy* (see page 13), which was built in 1813.

In 1825, Hackworth was appointed Locomotive Superintendent of the new Stockton & Darlington Railway. While in that post he made important modifications to Stephenson's locomotives by realigning the steam blastpipe, thus resulting in a marked improvement in locomotive performance. Built by Robert Stephenson & Co in 1827 for the S&DR, the 0-6-0 *Royal George* incorporated many of Hackworth's ideas, and subsequent locomotives built at Newcastle all featured his innovative blastpipes.

Hackworth also entered his own locomotive, the *Sans Pareil*, for the Rainhill Trials on the Liverpool & Manchester Railway in 1829 (see page 19). Although not the winner, his locomotive, featuring vertical cylinders and a blastpipe, performed well before breaking down with a broken cylinder.

While Locomotive Superintendent of the S&DR, Hackworth also went into business with his son, John, building steam locomotives at Shildon, the western terminus of the railway. Their output included the first steam locomotive to run in Russia in 1836 and one of the first to run in Canada, in 1838.

Hackworth continued to work on the development of steam locomotives until shortly before his death in 1850. His former home at Shildon is now a museum.

Specification

Builder	Robert Stephenson & Co
Wheel arrangement	0-6-0
Build date	1827
Cylinders	2 outside
Number built	1

Timothy Hackworth's Royal George, *built for the Stockton & Darlington Railway in 1827.*

While the Liverpool & Manchester Railway (L&MR) was being built, a competition was organised by the directors of the company to find out if locomotives were more suitable for hauling their trains than stationary steam engines. At this early stage in their development steam locomotives often proved unreliable – even until 1833 the Stockton & Darlington Railway continued to rely on horsepower to haul its passenger trains.

The competition took place over six days in October 1829 at Rainhill on a 1½-mile section of level track that had already been completed. The company offered a prize of £500 to the winner. Performing in front of a panel of distinguished officials, each locomotive had to satisfy the rather complicated conditions on weight and load set by the organisers. They were required to make ten return trips without refuelling, equivalent to travelling the 35 miles between Liverpool and Manchester, at an average speed of not less than 10 mph and with 30 miles performed at top speed. After this gruelling test the locomotives then had to repeat the process, equivalent to a return journey from Manchester to Liverpool.

The organisers set a severe weight limit: 4½ tons for a four-wheeled locomotive or 6 tons for a six-wheeled locomotive. This effectively barred any existing locomotives already in service, such as the 8-ton *Locomotion No. 1* on the Stockton & Darlington Railway (see page 14).

The competition caught the imagination of the British public and attracted ten entries, although five of these, such as a perpetual motion machine, were purely flights of fancy existing only on paper. The five entries that succeeded in starting the competition were themselves a very mixed bunch and they all gradually fell by the wayside as the competition progressed, except for one.

First to withdraw was a horse-powered machine called *Cycloped*. Designed by Thomas Brandreth of Liverpool, who was also a director of the L&MR, it was powered by a horse walking on a continuous treadmill, which soon became unstuck when the horse fell through the floor. The next unsuccessful candidate was Timothy Burstall's steam locomotive *Perseverence* which was damaged en route to Rainhill from Scotland. Burstall managed to repair it in time for its trials on the sixth and

final day but it could only achieve 6 mph. Despite this he was awarded a consolation prize by the organisers for his endeavours in the face of adversity.

The third locomotive to withdraw was Timothy Hackworth's *Sans Pareil*. While a more serious competitor, it was overweight and its steam technology was already obsolete. Employing vertical cylinders driving two pairs of connected driving wheels, it lacked the more modern fire-tube boiler of the eventual winner, Stephenson's *Rocket*, for it consumed prodigious amounts of fuel and eventually had to be withdrawn due to a cracked cylinder. Despite these failures the L&MR bought the locomotive and after several careers it ended up as a stationary boiler before being presented to the Patent Office Museum in 1864. It is currently on display at Locomotion, the museum in Shildon, County Durham.

The penultimate steam competitor was a bit of a lightweight. Built by John Ericsson and John Braithwaite – better known for their horse-drawn fire engines fitted with steam pumps – the *Novelty* was an 0-2-2 well tank (i.e. carrying its water supply in a well between the wheels) capable of raising steam very quickly and incorporating some novel features including a copper firebox and mechanical blower. Fitted with two vertical cylinders it was also fast and achieved an astonishing 28 mph on the first day of

A working replica of Robert Stephenson's Rocket, hauling examples of Liverpool & Manchester Railway passenger coaches, makes its way sedately along the Great Central Railway during a visit in 2010.

the competition. Unfortunately the locomotive then experienced several failures with its blower and water feed pipe and was forced to withdraw.

The ultimate winner of the Rainhill Trials was Robert Stephenson's 0-2-2 *Rocket*. Built by his locomotive building company in Newcastle it featured many ground-breaking innovations that kick-started Britain's railway revolution and the evolution of steam locomotive technology. This winning locomotive combined a single pair of driving wheels that provided much greater adhesion than a 0-4-0 type. They were driven directly by a pair of pistons in angled cylinders, unlike the unwieldy upright cylinders employed in earlier locomotives. The *Rocket* was also fitted with a separate firebox, a multi-tube boiler and a blastpipe, all resulting in significantly reduced fuel consumption.

The *Rocket* was the only locomotive to successfully complete the trials, averaging 12 mph while hauling a load of 13 tons at a top speed of nearly 30 mph. It was declared the winner and went on to work on the L&MR between 1830 and 1834. Robert Stephenson was also contracted to build further locomotives for the railway, including the *Northumbrian* which was fitted with horizontal cylinders and drew the inaugural train on opening day in 1830. Later locomotives such as the 2-2-0 *Planet* (see page 20) were fitted with horizontal inside cylinders mounted between the frames at the front.

After retiring from the L&MR in 1834, *Rocket*, the world famous locomotive, went on to more humble duties working on Lord Carlisle's Railway, a colliery line in Cumberland, before being presented to the Patent Office Museum in 1862. It is now preserved in its later, much-modified state at the Science Museum in London.

Specification

Builder	Robert Stephenson & Co
Wheel arrangement	0-2-2
Build date	1829
Cylinders	2 outside
Driving wheels	4 ft 8½ in
Tractive effort	825 lbs
Boiler pressure	50 psi
Number built	1

Designed by Robert Stephenson and built in 1830, the groundbreaking 2-2-0 *Planet* was the ninth locomotive built for the Liverpool & Manchester Railway and was the first steam locomotive in the world to have a steam dome, inside cylinders and buffers and couplings. It set a new record in 1830 when it travelled from Liverpool to Manchester in one hour. The success of this locomotive led to six more being ordered from Robert Stephenson & Co in Newcastle, the first time that steam locomotive types were mass produced.

Planet was rebuilt in 1833 and withdrawn around 1841. A working replica was built in 1992 at the Science and Industry Museum in Manchester.

Specification

Builder	Robert Stephenson & Co
Wheel arrangement	2-2-0
Build date	1830
Cylinders	2 inside
Driving wheels	5 ft 0 in
Number built	7

A working replica of Robert Stephenson's Planet locomotive in Pickering station, North Yorkshire Moors Railway.

Robert Stephenson

Born near Wallsend on Tyneside in 1803, Robert Stephenson was the only son of railway pioneer George Stephenson and received the education that his father had missed out on. He began his apprenticeship at Killingworth Colliery, before joining his father and Edward Pease in 1823 when they founded the world's first railway locomotive works, Robert Stephenson & Co, in Newcastle. However, Robert departed for South America the following year where he worked as a mining engineer in Colombia until 1827. Returning to Newcastle, he took over the running of the company and played a major part in the design of the *Rocket* (see page 19) which won the Rainhill Trials on the Liverpool & Manchester Railway in 1829. The following year he designed the *Planet*, a groundbreaking 2-2-0 locomotive that was the first in the world to have inside cylinders and a steam dome.

In 1833 Robert's career took a different direction when he was appointed Chief Engineer of the newly authorised London & Birmingham Railway, the first main line to serve London. From then on he excelled as a railway engineer and, in particular, as a bridge designer. In Britain the most famous examples of his work are the High Level Bridge in Newcastle, the Royal Border Bridge at Berwick-upon-Tweed and the Britannia tubular bridge in North Wales (since rebuilt). Further afield his skills as a railway and bridge builder also took him to France, Switzerland, Spain, Egypt and Canada.

In later years Stephenson became a Member of Parliament and on his death in 1859 he was buried with full honours in Westminster Abbey.

A 1:8 scale model of Robert Stephenson's Planet. The full-size locomotive was built for the Liverpool & Manchester Railway in 1830.

GWR 'Iron Duke' Class 4-2-2

A development of the earlier 'Firefly' Class 2-2-2, the Great Western Railway (GWR) broad-gauge (7 ft 0¼ in) 'Iron Duke' Class 4-2-2 was also designed by Daniel Gooch. Thirty members of the class were built at Swindon Works between 1847 and 1855. The leading wheels were not a bogie but set inflexibly within the frame. A 2-2-2 prototype, *Great Western*, was built with 8-ft-0-in-diameter driving wheels in 1846 but it suffered damage to its leading axle soon after entering service and was rebuilt as a 4-2-2 'Iron Duke' Class.

'Iron Duke' locomotives did not have numbers but were named rather randomly after Middle Eastern rulers, Greek mythological characters, Scottish nobility, Isambard Kingdom Brunel's steamships and Crimean war battles.

With their enormous single driving wheels, the class was well known for its speed when hauling the 'Flying Dutchman', the GWR's premier train between Paddington and Exeter via Bristol, with speeds in excess of 70 mph common at that time.

In 1870 three members of the class were rebuilt with new boilers and frames. These formed the basis for the new 'Rover' Class 4-2-2s which were built between 1871 and 1888. This was the last class of broad-gauge passenger locomotives built by the GWR – *Bulkeley* had the dubious honour of hauling the last broad-gauge passenger train on the main line in 1892.

Withdrawals of the 'Iron Duke' Class started in 1870 and continued until 1884 when the last survivor, *Lord of the Isles*, was preserved at Swindon Works. During this time it was exhibited at Edinburgh, Chicago and Earl's Court. Despite this stay of execution this famous locomotive was eventually scrapped in 1906. All that remains now is the pair of 8-ft-0-in driving wheels which can be seen at STEAM – Museum of the Great Western Railway, Swindon.

A working replica of *Iron Duke* was built in 1985 to celebrate the 150th anniversary of the Great Western Railway. It is currently a static exhibit at the Didcot Railway Centre.

Specification

Builder	Swindon Works
Wheel arrangement	4-2-2
Build dates	1847–1855
Cylinders	2 inside
Driving wheels	8 ft 0 in
Tractive effort	8,100 lbs
Boiler pressure	100–115 psi
Number built	30

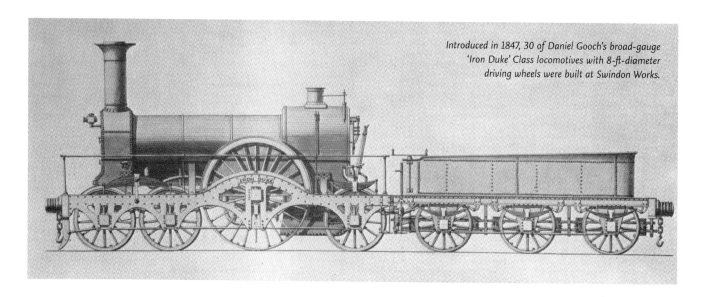

Introduced in 1847, 30 of Daniel Gooch's broad-gauge 'Iron Duke' Class locomotives with 8-ft-diameter driving wheels were built at Swindon Works.

Daniel Gooch

Great Western Railway (1837–1864)

The youngest of three brothers, Daniel Gooch was born in Northumberland in 1816. He trained as an engineer at Robert Stephenson's Vulcan Foundry in Warrington and on the new London & Birmingham Railway. In 1837 (at the age of 21) he was appointed Superintendent of Locomotive Engines for Isambard Kingdom Brunel's fledgling broad-gauge Great Western Railway. His first locomotive design was the 'Firefly' Class 2-2-2 which were introduced in 1840 – these were Gooch's development of the earlier 'Star' Class 2-2-2 which had been built for the GWR by Robert Stephenson. At this time the GWR did not have its own locomotive works so Gooch's first engines were built by a whole range of locomotive builders such as Nasmyth, Gaskell & Co and Fenton, Murray & Jackson.

Gooch's next step was to set up the GWR's own locomotive works and in 1840 he had decided on a greenfield site near the village of Swindon in Wiltshire, roughly midway between Paddington and Bristol. Gooch's first broad-gauge locomotive to be built at Swindon, the first 'Iron Duke' Class 4-2-2, emerged from the Works in 1847. With their 8-ft-diameter driving wheels and a speed of 80 mph, these magnificent machines (albeit with modifications) remained in service until just before the end of the broad gauge in 1892.

Gooch remained in his post as Superintendent of Locomotives until 1864 when he resigned. The following year he was Chief Engineer during the laying of the first trans-Atlantic telegraph cable from Brunel's SS *Great Eastern*, and was appointed Chairman of the GWR at a time when the company was in financial difficulties. While on board the *Great Eastern* out in the Atlantic he was also elected as Conservative MP for Cricklade, a seat he held for 20 years. In 1866 he was created a Baronet for the laying of the trans-Atlantic telegraph cable.

Gooch's strong chairmanship of the GWR continued until his death in 1889.

This working replica of Daniel Gooch's 7-ft-gauge locomotive Iron Duke *was built to celebrate the 150th anniversary of the Great Western Railway.*

LNWR 'DX Goods' Class 0-6-0 / 1870 'Special Tank' 0-6-0ST

Designed by John Ramsbottom for the London & North Western Railway (LNWR), the 'DX Goods' Class had 943 members, making it the single largest mass-produced class of steam locomotives ever built in Britain. They were built at Crewe Works between 1858 and 1874, with 54 being named briefly until their nameplates were transferred to new passenger locomotives. Those built under Ramsbottom's successor, Francis Webb (see page 46) sported such luxuries as cabs. Webb also rebuilt 500 of the 'DX' with a new boiler (150 psi) and vacuum brakes as 'Special DX' locomotives for hauling passenger trains. The versatile and reliable 'DXs' were found right across the large LNWR network from North Wales to northwest England and from the Midlands to London.

Of the 943 locomotives built at Crewe, 857 were for the LNWR and 86 were built for the Lancashire & Yorkshire Railway. In addition, 278 0-6-0ST versions with smaller driving wheels were built between 1870 and 1880 as LNWR 'Special Tanks', with five surviving into British Railways' ownership in 1948. Four of these locomotives were in departmental stock as Carriage Department shunters at Wolverton Works and one at Crewe Works. They had all been withdrawn by 1959.

Although mass withdrawals of the 'DX Goods' occurred in the early 20th century, 88 examples passed into London Midland & Scottish Railway's ownership in 1923. By 1930 this ground-breaking class was extinct. None were preserved, surely a major oversight at that time.

Three of the former LNWR 'Special Tanks', including CD7, seen here on 10 October 1954 outside Wolverton Works, where they were employed as Carriage Department shunters.

Specification

Locomotive	'DX Goods'
Builder	Crewe Works
Wheel arrangement	0-6-0
Build dates	1858–1874
Cylinders	2 inside
Driving wheels	5 ft 2 in
Tractive effort	11,410 lbs
Boiler pressure	120 psi
Number built	943

Locomotive	'Special Tank'
Builder	Crewe Works
Wheel arrangement	0-6-0ST
Build dates	1870–1880
Cylinders	2 inside
Driving wheels	4 ft 5½ in
Tractive effort	17,005 lbs
Boiler pressure	150 psi
Number built	278

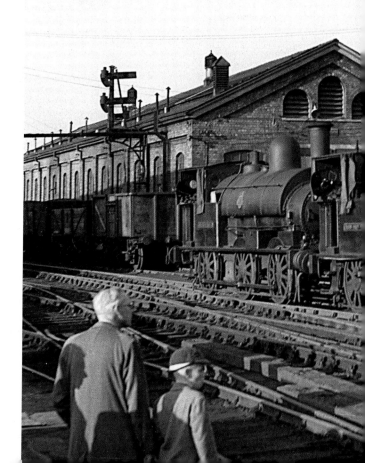

John Ramsbottom

London & North Western Railway (1857–1871)

The son of a cotton mill owner, John Ramsbottom was born in Todmorden, Lancashire, in 1814. He first learnt about steam engines in his father's mill and at the local mechanics institute and, in 1839, went to work at the Atlas Works of locomotive builders Sharp, Roberts & Co in Manchester. Here, his boss, Charles Beyer (co-founder of Beyer, Peacock & Co in 1854) was so impressed with his skills that he recommended the young Ramsbottom to the management of the newly opened Manchester & Birmingham Railway (M&BR) – he was appointed as Locomotive Superintendent in 1842. The M&BR became part of the London & North Western Railway in 1846 and by 1857 Ramsbottom had risen to the position of Locomotive Superintendent at Crewe. Over the next 14 years a succession of successful locomotive types were turned out at Crewe, including nearly 1,000 of his standard 'DX' 0-6-0 goods engines, 60 of the 2-2-2 'Lady of the Lake' Class (see page 27) and 260 of his 0-6-0 'Special Tank' Class. Examples of the latter class remained in service until 1959.

Also a prolific inventor, by 1880 Ramsbottom had accumulated 36 patents to his name including locomotive safety valves, locomotive hoists and water scoops. He retired from the LNWR in 1871 and died in 1897.

Crewe Works

On its formation in 1923 the London Midland & Scottish Railway (LMS) inherited several large railway works from its constituent companies. By far the largest was at Crewe in Cheshire, which had been established on a greenfield site at an important railway junction in 1843 by the Grand Junction Railway. By the early 20th century the population of this railway town had grown to 40,000, with 8,000 being directly employed in the Works. Under successive Chief Mechanical Engineers (CMEs) – John Ramsbottom, Francis Webb, George Whale, Charles Bowen-Cooke, H. P. M. Beames and George Hughes – it went on to become the main locomotive works for the London & North Western Railway and by 1923 had built over 6,000 new and rebuilt locomotives.

In 1932 William Stanier was appointed CME of the LMS and Crewe went on to build some of the most successful steam locomotive types in Britain – these included Stanier's 'Black Five' and 'Jubilee' 4-6-0s, 'Princess Royal' and 'Coronation' 4-6-2s and '8F' 2-8-0s. Following nationalisation in 1948, Crewe went on to build many British Railways standard class locomotives including 'Britannia' and 'Clan' 4-6-2s and '9F' 2-10-0s. The 7,331st and last steam locomotive to be built at Crewe was BR Standard Class '9F' 2-10-0 No 92250, which emerged from the workshops in December 1958. Diesel-electric and diesel-hydraulic locomotive building continued until 1990, by which time Crewe had built over 8,000 locomotives and at its peak had employed 20,000 workers.

1859 LNWR 'Lady of the Lake' Class 2-2-2

Built primarily to haul fast 'Irish Mail' trains between Holyhead and Euston, the 'Lady of the Lake' Class 2-2-2s were designed by John Ramsbottom (see page 25) for the London & North Western Railway. A total of 60 locomotives were built at Crewe Works between 1859 and 1865 and they were the first class in Britain to be fitted with a water scoop – the first water troughs were installed at Mochdre on the LNWR's Chester to Holyhead line in 1860. Their large single driving wheels of 7 ft 6 in gained them the reputation of being very speedy.

In 1862, No 531 *Lady of the Lake* was exhibited at the International Exhibition in London and was awarded a bronze prize. Although this loco gave its name to the class, No 184 *Problem* was the first to be built. In addition to hauling the 'Irish Mails', the class was also employed on express passenger trains between Crewe, Liverpool and Manchester. Ramsbottom's successor, Francis Webb, rebuilt the class several times between 1873 and 1897 adding a roof to the cab, fitted steam brakes, enlarged boilers and fireboxes, and enclosed driving wheel splashers. Thus reborn, the class went on to act as pilot engines for heavy express trains, often at speeds approaching 80 mph.

The double-heading of LNWR trains became redundant when new and more powerful 4-4-0s were introduced in the early 20th century. The single-wheelers such as the 'Lady of the Lake' Class soon became redundant and were withdrawn. The entire class became extinct in 1907 and, sadly, no example of these graceful and speedy locomotives was saved for preservation.

A 1:8 scale model of the LNWR 2-2-2 Lady of the Lake express passenger locomotive. It is shown here in the condition as rebuilt in 1876.

Specification

Builder	Crewe Works
Wheel arrangement	2-2-2
Build dates	1859–1865
Cylinders	2 outside
Driving wheels	7 ft 6 in
Boiler pressure	120 psi
Number built	60

MR '156' Class 2-4-0

The Midland Railway's '156' Class 2-4-0s were designed by Matthew Kirtley to haul express passenger trains on its main line from the Midlands to King's Cross station, then jointly shared with the Great Northern Railway. It was only in 1868 that the Midland Railway (MR) had its own new terminus at adjoining St Pancras.

A total of 29 locomotives of the Class '156' were built at Derby Works between 1866 and 1874. Overall, Kirtley was responsible for the building of eight classes with this wheel arrangement, totalling 145 locomotives, between 1862 and 1874. The Class '156' was rebuilt by Kirtley's successor, Samuel Johnson (see page 45), between 1873 and the early 20th century. However, the introduction of Johnson's more powerful 4-4-0s in 1876 soon led to the 2-4-0s being downgraded to secondary duties.

Twenty-one locomotives of this class survived into London Midland & Scottish Railway's ownership in 1923 but by then they were performing more menial tasks. Although an attempt to preserve one of these major milestone locos failed in 1930, it fell to No 158A (LMS No 20002), built in 1866, to have the honour of being rescued at the last minute – it was withdrawn in 1947 after acting as station pilot at the ex-Midland Railway's Nottingham station and restored at Derby Works, where it stayed for many years. It is now part of the National Collection and currently resides as a static exhibit at Barrow Hill Roundhouse.

Matthew Kirtley

Midland Railway (1844–1873)

Matthew Kirtley was born in Tanfield, County Durham, in 1813 and commenced his railway career at the age of 13 by becoming a fireman on the newly opened Stockton & Darlington Railway. After stints as an engine driver on the Liverpool & Manchester Railway and the London & Birmingham Railway he was appointed Locomotive Foreman of the Birmingham & Derby Junction Railway (B&DJR) in 1839, rising to Locomotive Superintendent in 1841. The B&DJR formed part of the Midland Railway in 1844 and Kirtley became its Locomotive Superintendent based at its headquarters in Derby.

During his 30 years at Derby, Kirtley expanded the Works and by 1851 it had started to build locomotives, the first of which were the 2-2-2 'Jenny Lind' type. Over the succeeding years Kirtley designed eight classes of 2-4-0 express passenger locos and two large classes (totalling 552 locos) of 0-6-0 goods locos – eleven of these outside-frame locos survived into the 1940s. Kirtley died in office in 1873.

Still sporting its LMS number, ex-MR '156' Class 2-4-0 No 20155 is seen here at Nottingham on 3 June 1950. The loco was the last survivor of its class, being withdrawn at the end of October that year. The loco's British Railways number of 58020 was never applied.

Specification

Builder	Derby Works
Wheel arrangement	2-4-0
Build dates	1866–1874
Cylinders	2 inside
Driving wheels	6 ft 2½ in
Tractive effort	12,340 lbs
Boiler pressure	140 psi
Number built	29

Preserved MR '156' Class 2-4-0 No 158A is seen here at Wirksworth in 1961. This fine locomotive is part of the National Collection and currently resides at Barrow Hill Roundhouse.

GWR Class '517' 0-4-2T

A total of 156 Class '517' 0-4-2Ts were built in thirteen batches at Great Western Railway's Wolverhampton Works between 1868 and 1885. Designed by George Armstrong for working local passenger trains, there were many differences within the class. For example, there were two different wheelbases ranging from 13 ft 7 in to 15 ft 0 in, earlier examples had saddle tanks while later ones had side tanks, and there were also variations to the boilers. The later locos with enclosed cabs and large coal bunkers were the direct ancestors of Charles Collett's '4800' Class (from 1946 '1400' Class) 0-4-2Ts.

The class was first concentrated on hauling local passenger trains in the west Midlands but in the early 20th century many were converted to push-pull operation and thus became more widely spread throughout the GWR network. Withdrawal of the unconverted locomotives began in 1904 although many of the push-pull members survived into the 1930s. The last three survivors were withdrawn in 1949 and no example of this class has been preserved.

Specification

Builder	Wolverhampton Works
Wheel arrangement	0-4-2T
Build dates	1868–1885
Cylinders	2 inside
Driving wheels	5 ft 0 in – 5 ft 2 in
Tractive effort	12,635–14,780 lbs
Boiler pressure	150–165 psi
Number built	156

GWR Class '517' 0-4-2T No 558 with an auto coach and cattle wagons at Weymouth, circa 1930.

Wolverhampton Stafford Road Works

First opened as a locomotive maintenance facility by the Shrewsbury & Birmingham Railway in 1849, the Stafford Road railway works in Wolverhampton became the main northern standard-gauge workshop under Joseph Armstrong of the Great Western Railway in 1854. Joseph was promoted to Swindon in 1864 and he was replaced by his brother, George. At Stafford Road both brothers enjoyed much autonomy from Swindon, and even locomotive liveries were different.

During George's tenure, as well as standardising the numerous variety of locomotives taken over by the GWR, the Works produced many long-lived standard-gauge Class '517' 0-4-2 tanks and 0-6-0 saddle tanks. The end of the broad gauge in 1892 led to all GWR standard-gauge locomotive building being moved to Swindon and, after producing 800 locomotives, the Works ceased new construction in 1908. However, locomotive repairs and overhauls continued until 1964, when the Works finally closed.

George Armstrong

Great Western Railway, Stafford Road Works, Wolverhampton (1864–1896)

George Armstrong, younger brother of Joseph (see page 32), was born in 1822 and grew up near Newcastle upon Tyne. After an apprenticeship working with stationary steam colliery engines, he and his brother were taken on as engineers in 1840 for the newly opened Hull & Selby Railway where they worked as assistants to the Locomotive Engineer, John Gray. Gray was appointed Locomotive Superintendent of the London, Brighton & South Coast Railway in 1846 and George followed him down to Brighton. His next move was to France where he worked on the building of the Chemin de Fer du Nord before returning to Britain during the 1848 French Revolution.

George then became a driver for the Shrewsbury & Chester Railway (S&CR), where his brother was Assistant Locomotive Superintendent, and rose to the rank of locomotive foreman. In 1854 the standard-gauge S&CR was amalgamated with the broad-gauge Great Western Railway and George, along with his brother, moved to Wolverhampton where the GWR had set up its standard-gauge locomotive works. George became assistant to his brother who had been appointed the company's standard-gauge Locomotive Superintendent at the Stafford Road Works and, when Joseph was promoted to take over at Swindon in 1864, George stepped into his brother's shoes.

During his long reign at Stafford Road, George was virtually left to his own devices by his brother at Swindon and was responsible for the efficient building, rebuilding and repair of many types of saddle and side tank locomotives including 155 of the '517' Class 0-4-2 tanks, 130 '850' Class 0-6-0 saddle tanks, 60 '1016' Class 0-6-0 saddle tanks and 120 '1901' Class 0-6-0 saddle tanks. George had so much autonomy that even the Wolverhampton livery was different to the Swindon livery. He retired in 1896 after 33 years at the top and died, a single man, in 1901.

GWR Class '517' 0-4-2T No 1154 at Ebbw Junction, Newport in July 1933.

Joseph Armstrong

Great Western Railway, Stafford Road Works, Wolverhampton (1854–1864)
Great Western Railway, Swindon (1864–1877)

Joseph Armstrong was born in Cumberland in 1816 and grew up near Newcastle upon Tyne, within sight of the Wylam Waggonway, stamping ground of William Hedley's *Puffing Billy* (see page 13). He first gained experience of steam engines while being apprenticed at Walbottle Colliery and later worked as a driver on the Liverpool & Manchester Railway. After following his brother George Armstrong (see page 32) to the Hull & Selby Railway in 1840, Joseph went on to become Assistant Locomotive Superintendent on the Shrewsbury & Chester Railway in 1847, followed by promotion to Locomotive Superintendent six years later. Following amalgamation of the S&CR with the Great Western Railway in 1854, Joseph was appointed Locomotive Superintendent of that company's standard-gauge fleet at Wolverhampton where, from 1859, GWR standard-gauge locomotives were built.

Down in Swindon, Daniel Gooch (see page 23) resigned in 1864 and Joseph was appointed to replace him, with the new title of Locomotive, Carriage & Wagon Superintendent. During his tenure at the heart of 'God's Wonderful Railway', Joseph made his mark by being both paternalistic and strict with his workforce. A Methodist lay preacher, he also involved himself in the life of the fast-expanding railway town of Swindon.

As a locomotive designer he led a double life, producing both broad-gauge and standard-gauge locomotives until his sudden death in 1877. Probably the most famous of his locomotives were the highly successful 'Metro' '455' Class 2-4-0 tanks that could be seen all over the system on suburban trains and the 310 '388' Class 0-6-0 goods engines, the latter the precursor of the famous 'Dean Goods' (see page 52). On his death he was succeeded by his brother's protégé at Wolverhampton, William Dean (see page 52).

GWR 2-4-0T 'Metro Tank' No 3596 at Southall in 1931.

1868 GWR Class '455' ('Metro Tank') 2-4-0T

Designed by Joseph Armstrong for working local passenger trains on the Great Western Railway, the standard-gauge Class '455' 2-4-0Ts were built at Swindon Works between 1868 and 1899. The first 60 were built primarily for West London suburban passenger services which included operating on the underground section of the Metropolitan Railway, hence the nickname of the class, 'Metro Tanks'. Armstrong's successor, William Dean, was so impressed by the 'Metros' that a further 80 were built at Swindon under his watch between 1881 and 1899.

There were many variations within the class, including length of wheelbase, size of boiler, side tanks and coal bunkers. The earlier examples had no cabs but these were added later. For working on the Metropolitan Railway some members were also fitted with condensing apparatus. This was removed once electrification of the railway was completed in 1907. In the early 20th century some were converted for push-pull autotrain working, as were some of the Class '517' (see page 30).

The 'Metros' not only continued to haul suburban services from Paddington but were also found in the West Country, South Wales and the West Midlands.

Although withdrawals of some of the earlier members started in 1900, others continued into old age in the 1930s. Ten of the last batches built under William Dean survived into British Railways' ownership in 1948 but all had been withdrawn by the end of 1949. No member of this highly successful and long-lived class was preserved.

Specification

Builder	Swindon Works
Wheel arrangement	2-4-0T
Build dates	1868–1899
Cylinders	2 inside
Driving wheels	5 ft 0 in
Tractive effort	13,900 lbs
Boiler pressure	165 psi
Number built	140
BR numbering	3561–3600 (with gaps due to pre-1948 withdrawals)

One of the last surviving GWR 2-4-0T 'Metro Tanks', No 3582 is seen here at Fowey on 23 July 1948. Built at Swindon in 1899, it was withdrawn from St Blazey shed (83E) in November 1949.

Ffestiniog Railway 'Double Fairlie' *Little Wonder* 0-4-4-0T

Robert Fairlie's articulated 0-4-4-0T *Little Wonder*, which he designed for the Ffestiniog Railway (FR) in 1869, was built by George England. It was an outstanding success and, in trials attended by many foreign dignitaries, demonstrated its remarkable capabilities by hauling 112 slate wagons weighing over 200 tons up the steeply graded railway from Porthmadog to Blaenau Ffestiniog at an average speed of 12½ mph. This success led to other articulated steam locomotives, known as 'Double Fairlies', being built for the railway by another locomotive manufacturer and also by the FR at their Boston Lodge Works.

Despite its success, this pioneering locomotive had reliability issues and was withdrawn in 1882. However, five other 'Double Fairlies' are still very much alive and kicking on the Ffestiniog Railway, as follows:

- No 8 *James Spooner*. Built by the Avonside Engine Company in 1872. Withdrawn in 1930. A replica of this locomotive is being built at Boston Lodge.
- No 10 *Merddin Emrys*. Built at Boston Lodge in 1879 and still in service.
- No 3 *Livingston Thompson*. Built at Boston Lodge in 1885 and still in service.
- No 11 *Earl of Merioneth*. Built at Boston Lodge in 1979 and still in service.
- No 12 *David Lloyd George*. Built at Boston Lodge in 1992 and still in service.

Specification

Builder	George England
Wheel arrangement	0-4-4-0T
Gauge	1 ft 11½ in
Build date	1869
Cylinders	4 outside
Driving wheels	2 ft 4 in
Tractive effort	8,595 lbs
Boiler pressure	160 psi
Number built	1

Built in 1879, Ffestiniog Railway 'Double Fairlie' Merddin Emrys hauls a train of slate wagons at Ddaullt Spiral on 4 November 2013.

Robert Francis Fairlie

Londonderry & Coleraine Railway (1852–1855)
Bombay, Baroda & Central India Railway
(1856–1859)

Born in Glasgow in 1830, the Scottish engineer Robert Francis Fairlie trained at Crewe Works and Swindon Works. In 1852 he was appointed Locomotive Superintendent of the Londonderry & Coleraine Railway in the north of Ireland. In 1856 he was appointed Locomotive Superintendent of the Bombay, Baroda & Central India Railway before returning to Britain in 1859 where he became a railway engineering consultant. Fairlie's claim to fame is his invention of the double-bogie articulated steam locomotive, designed for sharply curved narrow-gauge railways in mountainous regions.

Built for the Ffestiniog Railway in North Wales in 1869 by George England, Fairlie's first successful locomotive of this type was named *Little Wonder*. In 1870 a series of live demonstrations of this locomotive's capabilities was held on the Ffestiniog Railway with invited guests from the world's railways in attendance. Following the trials, Fairlie received many orders and commissions and by 1876 there were 43 railways around the world operating his patent locomotives. Robert Fairlie died on 31 July 1885 and is buried at West Norwood Cemetery in Lambeth, London.

Built in 1992, Ffestiniog Railway 'Double Fairlie' David Lloyd George heads a train of vintage coaches at Campbells Platform on 1 November 2015.

GNR Class 'A2' ('Stirling Single') 4-2-2

With their enormous 8-ft-1-in driving wheels, the Class 'A2' ('Stirling Singles') are one of most iconic and beautiful of 19th-century British steam locomotives. They were designed by Patrick Stirling to haul Great Northern Railway (GNR) express passenger trains between King's Cross and York. While previously working at the Glasgow & South Western Railway, Stirling had designed a series of 2-2-2s. His GNR 4-2-2s were a development of these, with a four-wheel front bogie for greater stability. With domeless boilers, the 'Stirling Singles' were built at Doncaster Works in three batches, in 1870, 1884 and 1894, with the last two batches an improvement on the earlier version. In service they were exceptionally fast with a top speed of 85 mph on lightly loaded trains. They were also involved in the 'Railway Race to the North' in 1888 and 1895, when one of the locos averaged nearly 65 mph over a distance of 82 miles.

By the end of the 19th century the 'Stirling Singles' were being displaced on the King's Cross to York expresses by Henry Ivatt's new 'Klondyke' 4-4-2s (see page 83). About this time, several 'Stirling Singles' were rebuilt by Ivatt with domed boilers. However, withdrawals began in 1899 with the last examples being retired in 1916. One is preserved – No 1, the first of the class, is currently a static exhibit at the National Railway Museum in York. Having been withdrawn in 1907 it was steamed again in 1938 to work some enthusiasts' specials. It was once again brought back to life from 1981 to 1985, when it operated on the Great Central Railway and the North Yorkshire Moors Railway.

Specification

Builder	Doncaster Works
Wheel arrangement	4-2-2
Build dates	1870–1895
Cylinders	2 outside
Driving wheels	8 ft 1 in
Tractive effort	11,129 lbs (1870)
	12,719 lbs (1884)
	15,680 lbs (1894)
Boiler pressure	140 psi (1870)
	160 psi (1884)
	170 psi (1894)
Number built	53

Preserved GNR 'Stirling Single' No 1 was brought back to life in the early 1980s. Here it is seen crossing the viaduct across Swithland Reservoir on the Great Central Railway. This historic locomotive is currently on display at the National Railway Museum in York.

Doncaster Works

Doncaster Works was opened by the Great Northern Railway in 1853. Under Locomotive Superintendents Patrick Stirling and Henry Ivatt, the Works (nicknamed 'The Plant') built many iconic steam locomotives such as the 'Stirling Singles' and 'Ivatt Atlantics'. In 1923 the Works became the principal locomotive workshops of the newly formed London & North Eastern Railway.

Under the LNER's Chief Mechanical Engineer, Nigel Gresley, the Works went on to build some of the finest and most graceful steam locomotives in the world. During the 1930s, Doncaster turned out Gresley's 'A3' and 'A4' 4-6-2s and the highly successful 'V2' 2-6-2s. Following Gresley's death in 1941 the Works built Thompson 'A2/2' 4-6-2s and many of the Peppercorn Class 'A1' 4-6-2s, the latter built during the British Railways era. The post-war years also saw production of BR standard locomotives. The last to be built, BR Standard Class '4' 2-6-0 No 76114, being shopped out in October 1957, by which time Doncaster had built 2,228 steam locomotives. Diesel-electric and electric locomotive building continued until 1987.

Patrick Stirling

Glasgow & South Western Railway (1853–1866)
Great Northern Railway (1866–1895)

Patrick Stirling was born in Kilmarnock in 1820. He served his apprenticeship at Blackness Foundry, manufacturers of mill and textile machinery, in Dundee before working for Neilson's Locomotive Works in Glasgow, where he became foreman. In the late 1840s he became Superintendent of the Caledonian & Dumbartonshire Junction Railway, which opened for traffic in 1850. In 1853, Stirling was appointed Locomotive Superintendent of the Glasgow & South Western Railway which, in the following year, moved its locomotive works from Glasgow to Kilmarnock. Here, Stirling designed fifteen locomotive classes, the majority of which were of the 2-2-2 and 0-4-2 wheel arrangement, featuring his trademark domeless boilers.

In 1866, Stirling moved to Doncaster where he was appointed Locomotive Superintendent of the Great Northern Railway. During his 30 years in this post he produced many classic locomotive designs of which his 4-2-2 'Stirling Singles' are the most famous, giving outstanding performances on the GNR main line from King's Cross to York during the 'Railway Race to the North'. Fifty-three of these locos were built at Doncaster between 1870 and 1895 and No 1 is now preserved at the National Railway Museum in York. A total of 28 different classes of locomotive were designed by Stirling until his death in office in 1895 at the age of 75.

William Stroudley

London, Brighton & South Coast Railway (1870–1889)

Born in Oxfordshire in 1833, William Stroudley was apprenticed at the age of 14 to the engineering company of John Inshaw in Birmingham where he gained experience on steam engines. In 1854 Stroudley moved to the GWR's Swindon Works as a trainee locomotive engineer under Daniel Gooch, before working for the Great Northern Railway at Peterborough. A move to Scotland came in 1861 when he was appointed Works Manager at the Edinburgh & Glasgow Railway's Cowlairs Works in Glasgow. Four years later he moved to Inverness where he was appointed as Locomotive and Carriage Superintendent at the Highland Railway's Lochgorm Works – due to financial constraints he was only able to design one locomotive class there, the diminutive 0-6-0ST being the forerunner of his later 'Terrier' locos for the London, Brighton & South Coast Railway (LB&SCR).

Stroudley's final move came in 1870 when he was appointed Locomotive Superintendent of the LB&SCR at its Brighton Works following the resignation of John Craven. During his tenure there he designed many successful and graceful locomotive classes ranging from the 'A1' Class 0-6-0Ts, or 'Terriers' as they became known – 50 of these were built, with some remaining in service until 1963 – the 125 'D1' Class 0-4-2T suburban passenger locos and the 80 'E1' Class 0-6-0T goods locos. Without doubt the high point of his career, the 36 'B1' Class 0-4-2 (see page 48) express passenger locomotives were the mainstay of the London to Brighton services – they were mostly named after politicians and were nicknamed 'Gladstones' after the first to enter service in 1882. Sadly, Stroudley died from bronchitis while exhibiting one of these fine locomotives at the Paris Exhibition in 1889. He was succeeded at Brighton by R. J. Billinton (see page 69).

LB&SCR Class 'A1'/'A1X' ('Terrier') 0-6-0T

Nicknamed 'Terriers', 50 of the diminutive Class 'A1' 0-6-0Ts were built at Brighton Works between 1872 and 1880. They were designed by William Stroudley to haul commuter trains on the London, Brighton & South Coast Railway's busy suburban routes that radiated out from London Bridge and Victoria termini. The locomotives were originally named after London boroughs that were served by these trains. One of the locos, No 40, was exhibited at the 1878 Paris Exhibition where it won a gold medal for its high quality of workmanship. As the commuter trains became heavier the Class 'A1s' were displaced by more powerful 'D1' Class tank locomotives. However, the reliability of the 'A1' meant that they found work on LB&SCR branch lines or as goods shunters.

Between 1898 and 1905 many members of the class were withdrawn, with the majority being sold to new owners such as the Isle of Wight Central Railway, Kent & East Sussex Railway, London & South Western Railway and the civil engineering contractor Pauling & Co. Others found work as departmental locomotives at Brighton Works and Lancing Carriage Works. Many of those that remained were converted to push-pull working for operating on branch lines.

Sixteen of the remaining LB&SCR locomotives were rebuilt by Stroudley's successor, Douglas Marsh, as the heavier and more powerful Class 'A1X' between 1911 and 1919. Five locos were sold to the Government in 1918 for work on a military establishment in Scotland – three of these later found a home on the Shropshire & Montgomeryshire Railway.

A total of 24 'Terriers' passed into Southern Railway's ownership in 1923. Two were later sold to the Weston, Clevedon & Portishead Railway – on its closure in 1940 these locomotives passed into Great Western Railway stock.

On nationalisation in 1948 a total of 15 'Terriers' (all 'A1X' except for one 'A1') passed into British Railways' ownership. Apart from use as departmental locomotives, their duties were by now confined to working on the weight-restricted Kent & East Sussex Railway and the Havant to Hayling Island branch lines. The former closed in 1961 but the latter, with its severely weight-restricted bridge over Langstone Harbour, remained profitable. Despite this the line closed on 3 November 1963, a victim of Dr Beeching's 'Axe', and the last 'Terriers' were withdrawn.

A total of nine 'Terriers' have been preserved in England and one in Canada, where it is on static display at the Canadian Railway Museum in Saint-Constant, Québec. In England, examples are found at the Isle of Wight Steam Railway, Spa Valley Railway, Bluebell Railway, Kent & East Sussex Railway, Bressingham Steam Museum and the National Railway Museum in York.

On the last day of services, immaculately clean ex-LB&SCR Class 'A1X' 0-6-0T No 32636 waits to depart from Havant for Hayling Island on 3 November 1963. This veteran locomotive was built at Brighton Works in 1872 and withdrawn from Eastleigh shed (71A) in January 1964. It has since been preserved on the Bluebell Railway.

Specification

Builder	Brighton Works
Wheel arrangement	0-6-0T
Build dates	1872–1880 (16 rebuilt as 'A1X' 1911–1919)
BR power classification	0P
Cylinders	2 inside
Driving wheels	4 ft 0 in
Tractive effort	7,650 lbs ('A1') 10,695 lbs ('A1X')
Boiler pressure	150 psi
Number built	50 (16 rebuilt as 'A1X')
BR numbering	32635–32678 (with gaps due to withdrawals), DS 377, DS 680, DS 681

NER Class '901' 2-4-0

The North Eastern Railway's (NER's) Class '901' 2-4-0s were designed by Edward Fletcher to haul express passenger trains on the East Coast Main Line (ECML) between York, Newcastle and Edinburgh. From 1872 to 1882 a total of 35 were built at the NER's Gateshead Works and 10 each by Beyer, Peacock & Co and Neilson & Co. Ten of the earlier locomotives were rebuilt with larger cylinders from 1884. In the 1890s new standard steel boilers were also fitted to the class. Initially the class were allocated to York and Gateshead depots to haul the ECML expresses – as these trains got heavier they were often seen double-heading in pairs.

By the end of the 1880s the Class '901s' had been displaced by more powerful locos and were relegated to secondary duties such as the stopping passenger trains across the Pennines between Darlington and Tebay/Penrith, the line between Scarborough and Hull, and as station pilots at York and Newcastle.

Withdrawals started just before World War I and by 1923 a total of 45 had been retired. This left ten locomotives that passed into London & North Eastern Railway's (LNER's) ownership, with most of these employed hauling the stopping passenger trains between Darlington, Barnard Castle, Stainmore, Kirkby Stephen and Tebay or Penrith. The last '901' Class was withdrawn in 1925.

Fortunately one of Fletcher's iconic Class '901' (LNER Class 'E6') has been preserved – built at Gateshead Works in 1875, No 910 was withdrawn in 1925. It was then restored to take its place in the 100th-anniversary procession of the Stockton & Darlington Railway in that year. No 910 is now part of the National Collection and is currently on loan to the Stainmore Railway at Kirkby Stephen East station.

Preserved NER Class '901' 2-4-0 No 910 took part in the Shildon Cavalcade at the end of August 1975 – this was the 150th anniversary of the opening of the Stockton & Darlington Railway (see page 14).

Specification

Builders	Gateshead Works (35)
	Beyer, Peacock & Co (10)
	Neilson & Co (10)
Wheel arrangement	2-4-0T
Build dates	1872–1882
Cylinders	2 inside
Driving wheels	7 ft 0 in
Tractive effort	12,590 lbs
Boiler pressure	160 psi
Number built	55

Edward Fletcher

North Eastern Railway (1854–1883)

Edward Fletcher, born in Northumberland in 1807, was apprenticed to George Stephenson (see pages 14–15) during the building of the 'Rocket' for the Liverpool & Manchester Railway, and assisted him during the construction of George Hudson's York & North Midland Railway. In 1845 he became Locomotive Superintendent of the Newcastle & Darlington Junction Railway, which subsequently became one of the four founding railway companies of the North Eastern Railway in 1854. Fletcher became the new company's Locomotive Superintendent, a position he held until his retirement (at the grand old age of 75) in 1882. He died in 1889. Fletcher's main claims to fame were his Class 'G6' 0-4-4 passenger tank locomotives, Class '901' 2-4-0 express locos and the '1001' Class 0-6-0 freight locos.

London & South Western Railway's (LSWR's) Chief Engineer, Joseph Beattie, designed the Class '0298' well tank locomotives for suburban passenger services in southwest London. Eighty-two locomotives were built by Beyer, Peacock & Co of Manchester between 1863 and 1875 and a further three at the LSWR's works at Nine Elms in 1872. Five of the later locomotives were named *Phoenix*, *Osprey*, *Comet*, *Pluto* and *Firefly*. Towards the end of the 19th century the Class '0298s' were displaced by more powerful locos for the London suburban services and sent to engine sheds further afield. Consequently, 31 examples were rebuilt with tenders to increase water capacity. Apart from three locomotives, withdrawals began in 1888 and continued until 1899.

The remaining three locos were transferred to the Bodmin & Wenford Railway in Cornwall in 1895, where their short wheelbases allowed them to work on the sharply curved line. There they hauled china clay trains down from Wenford Bridge to Bodmin until 1962 when they were replaced by ex-GWR '1366' Class dock tank locos. At that time the three '0298s' were the oldest class of steam locomotives then operating in Britain.

After withdrawal in 1962, two of the locos, Nos 30585 and 30587, were saved for preservation. The former is owned by the Quainton Railway Society and is based at the Buckinghamshire Railway Centre at Quainton Road station and the latter by the National Railway Museum in York.

Veteran preserved ex-LSWR Class '0298' 2-4-0 well tank, with a short goods train, chugs its way along the Dean Forest Railway at Upper Forge on 6 July 2016.

Specification

Builders	Beyer, Peacock & Co (82)
	Nine Elms Works (3)
Wheel arrangement	2-4-0WT
Build dates	1863–1875
BR power classification	0P
Cylinders	2 outside
Driving wheels	5 ft 7 in
Tractive effort	11,500 lbs
Boiler pressure	160 psi
Number built	85
BR numbering	30585–30587

Joseph Hamilton Beattie

London & South Western Railway (1850–1871)

Joseph Beattie was born in Belfast in 1808 and trained as an architect. He moved to England in 1835 where he became assistant to the engineer Joseph Locke during the building of the Grand Junction Railway and the London & Southampton Railway (later to become the London & South Western Railway). Following completion of the latter line in 1840 Beattie was appointed Superintendent at the Nine Elms Carriage and Wagon Works (see page 67), becoming Chief Locomotive Engineer in 1850. During his tenure at Nine Elms, Beattie was responsible for the development of the 2-4-0 locomotive for express work and the 2-4-0 well tank – three of the latter locos (later classified as the '0298' Class) remained in service for British Railways until 1962.

Joseph Beattie died suddenly in 1871 and was succeeded by his son, William, as Locomotive Engineer for the London & South Western Railway.

MR Class '2F' and '3F' Goods 0-6-0

One of the most numerous classes of steam locomotives in Britain, the Midland Railway's '2F' and '3F' goods locomotives were designed by Samuel Johnson and his successor Richard Deeley (see page 96). A total of 935 locos of both classes were built at Derby Works and seven locomotive suppliers between 1875 and 1908 – they became the railway's highly successful standard goods engine, seen at work right across the railway's network into the 1960s. The later locos had larger diameter boilers and a longer firebox, thus increasing their tractive effort.

In addition to working on the Midland Railway, a total of sixteen were sold to the Midland & Great Northern Joint Railway in two batches in 1896 and 1899 respectively. These later became London & North Eastern Railway stock as Class 'J40' and Class 'J41', withdrawn between 1936 and 1944. Ten locos were sold to the Somerset & Dorset Joint Railway in 1896 and 1902 and these later became London Midland & Scottish Railway stock.

Although withdrawals of the '3Fs' started in 1925, several hundred survived into British Railways' ownership in 1948. One hundred of these were still in service in the summer of 1961. The '2Fs' were renumbered by BR into a new class numbered 58114 to 58310 – there were 32 survivors in 1948. The last survivors of these two once-numerous classes were withdrawn in 1964. Regrettably no examples of either class have been preserved.

Samuel Waite Johnson

Edinburgh & Glasgow Railway (1864–1866)
Great Eastern Railway (1866–1873)
Midland Railway (1873–1904)

Samuel Johnson was born near Leeds in 1831 and began his apprenticeship with local locomotive builders E. B. Wilson & Co, makers of the famous 'Jenny Lind' 2-2-2 of 1847. In 1859, Johnson was appointed Acting Locomotive Superintendent of the Manchester, Sheffield & Lincolnshire Railway and five years later as Locomotive Superintendent of the Edinburgh & Glasgow Railway. In 1866, he was appointed Locomotive Superintendent of the Great Eastern Railway at Stratford Works where he designed several 'firsts' in Britain including a 4-4-0 with inside cylinders and inside frame and a 0-4-4T.

Johnson's final move was to Derby where he was appointed Locomotive Superintendent of the Midland Railway in 1873, a post he held for 31 years. During his tenure he was responsible for the introduction of many successful locomotive types of which the most famous are his beautiful 4-2-2 'Spinners' (see page 72) introduced in 1896 (one is preserved at the National Railway Museum) and the '1000' Class 4-4-0 three-cylinder compounds (see page 96) introduced in 1902 (No 1000 is also preserved). However his standard 0-6-0 goods loco really stood the test of time with a total of 935 being built, many of which survived into the British Railways (BR) era in the early 1960s. After an illustrious career, Johnson retired from Derby in 1904 and died in 1912.

One of ten Class '3F' 0-6-0s built for the Somerset & Dorset Joint Railway, No 43194 departs from Evercreech Junction on 11 July 1959. Built at Derby Works in 1896, this locomotive was withdrawn from Templecombe shed (71H/82G) at the end of 1960.

I can well remember seeing '3Fs', along with ex-MR Deeley 0-4-0Ts Nos 41535 and 41537, on the High Orchard branch line close to my childhood home in Gloucester when I was a trainspotter in the early 1960s. My very first trainspotting notebook records '2F' No 58165 seen at Gloucester Eastgate in, I believe, 1958. On a visit to Derby Works and shed on 1 November 1961 I also spotted Class '2F' No 58143 along with Class '3Fs' Nos 43389, 43623, 43453, 43496, 43608 and 43687.

Specification

Builders	Derby Works (160)
	Neilson & Co (290)
	Dubs & Co (150)
	Kitson & Co (120)
	Sharp, Stewart & Co (85)
	Beyer, Peacock & Co (80)
	Robert Stephenson & Co (30)
	Vulcan Foundry (20)
Wheel arrangement	0-6-0
Build dates	1875–1908
BR power classification	2F and 3F
Cylinders	2 inside
Driving wheels	4 ft 10½ in ('2F') / 5ft 2½ in ('3F')
Tractive effort	18,185 lbs ('2F') / 21,240 lbs ('3F')
Boiler pressure	140 psi ('2F') / 175 psi ('3F')
Number built	935
BR numbering	43185–43837 (3F) / 58114–58310 (2F) with gaps for withdrawals

LNWR 'Coal Tank' Class 0-6-2T

The London & North Western Railway's rugged mixed traffic 0-6-2T 'Coal Tanks' were a side tank version of the simple and reliable standard 0-6-0 'Coal Engine' of which the LNWR had built a total of 499. Maids of all work, both classes were designed by Francis Webb and built at Crewe Works. The cheaply produced 'Coal Tanks' had the same H-spoked cast iron wheels as the 'Coal Engines' and also had low running costs. Their only fault, and it was a big one, was that their brakes were appalling, a fact which precluded them from hauling heavy unbraked goods trains.

By the time of the 'Big Four Grouping' in 1923 only eight examples had been withdrawn, thus 292 passed into London Midland & Scottish Railway's ownership. Withdrawals continued through the 1930s and '40s until 64 'Coal Tanks' passed into British Railways' ownership in 1948. The final withdrawals took place in 1958 but not before the last survivor, No 58926, took part in a Stephenson Locomotive Society 'last train' over the steeply graded Head of the Valleys line between Abergavenny and Merthyr Tydfil on 5 January.

Built in 1888, No 58296 is now preserved and owned by the National Trust. It is cared for by the Bahamas Locomotive Society at the Keighley & Worth Valley Railway.

Specification

Builder	Crewe Works
Wheel arrangement	0-6-2T
Build dates	1881–1897
BR power classification	2F
Cylinders	2 inside
Driving wheels	4 ft 5½ in
Tractive effort	16,530 lbs
Boiler pressure	150 psi
Number built	300
BR numbering	58880–58937

Ex-LNWR 'Coal Tank' 0-6-2T No 58880 at Shrewsbury shed in the early 1950s. Built at Crewe works in 1882, this locomotive was withdrawn from Swansea Victoria shed in 1954.

The last surviving ex-LNWR 'Coal Tank' 0-6-2T No 58926 at Abergavenny Junction on 5 January 1958, prior to hauling the last train on the Head of the Valleys route that ran between Abergavenny and Merthyr.

Francis William Webb

London & North Western Railway (1871–1903)

Francis Webb was born near Stafford in 1836 and started his apprenticeship with the London & North Western Railway at Crewe Works in 1851. Following this he worked his way up the LNWR ladder, becoming a draughtsman, Chief Draughtsman, Works Manager and Chief Assistant to the Locomotive Superintendent, John Ramsbottom (see page 25). The latter retired in 1871 and Webb stepped into his shoes and became Chief Mechanical Engineer, a position he held for over 30 years. During this period Webb designed 35 locomotive classes, many of them three- or four-cylinder compounds, which were built in huge numbers for Britain's 'Premier Line' at Crewe. The most numerous were his 500 0-6-0 'Coal Engines' introduced in 1873, 220 2-4-2Ts introduced in 1879, 310 0-6-0 'Cauliflowers' introduced in 1880, 300 0-6-2T 'Coal Tanks' introduced in 1881, 500 0-6-0 'Special DXs' introduced in 1881, 166 2-4-0 'Renewed Precedents' (see page 58) introduced in 1887, and 170 0-8-0 four-cylinder compound heavy goods.

Also a prolific inventor with around 50 patents to his name, Webb resigned from the LNWR in 1903 and died in 1906.

1882 LB&SCR Class 'B1' ('Gladstones') 0-4-2

Thirty-six of the elegant Class 'B1' 0-4-2s were built at London, Brighton & South Coast Railway's Brighton Works between 1882 and 1891. They were designed by William Stroudley (see page 38) to haul the London Victoria to Brighton express passenger trains, a job they excelled at until displaced by Stroudley's successor Robert Billinton's (see page 69) more powerful Class 'B4' 4-4-0s at the beginning of the 20th century. The 'B1s' were named after British politicians, LB&SCR railway dignitaries or destinations of the railway. They were nicknamed 'Gladstones' after the first to be built, No 214 *Gladstone*. No 189 *Edward Blount* received a gold medal when exhibited at the 1889 Paris Exhibition – sadly, William Stroudley died in Paris at the same time.

Apart from two examples (No 199 *Samuel Laing* and No 190 *Arthur Otway*) the names of the 'Gladstones' were removed in 1906. By now relegated to secondary passenger duties, withdrawals began in 1910 and by 1914 ten had been taken out of service and scrapped. At the 'Big Four Grouping' of 1923 the remaining 26 locomotives passed into Southern Railway's ownership. Withdrawals restarted in 1925 with the last, No 172 (once named *Littlehampton*), being withdrawn in 1933.

The first of the class, No 214 *Gladstone*, was preserved as early as 1927 and is currently a static exhibit at the National Railway Museum in York.

Sporting the regalia of the royal train, preserved ex-LB&SCR Class 'B1' 0-4-2 No 214 Gladstone is currently a static exhibit at the National Railway Museum in York.

Specification

Builder	Brighton Works
Wheel arrangement	0-4-2
Build dates	1882–1891
Cylinders	2 inside
Driving wheels	6 ft 6 in
Tractive effort	14,155 lbs
Boiler pressure	140–150 psi
Number built	36

Brighton Works

Down on the south coast at Brighton, the London & Brighton Railway's works had been established as early as 1840. Built on a rather cramped and restricted site, it then became the main works facility for the London, Brighton & South Coast Railway in 1847. However, by the early 20th century the Works had become very inefficient, with huge backlogs in construction and repair, a situation which persisted until 1912 when the Carriage and Wagon Works were relocated to Lancing, thus freeing up desperately needed space at Brighton.

Although threatened with closure in the early 1930s, Brighton continued to build locomotives under Southern Railway and later British Railways management – by 1957, when production ceased, it had built more than 1,200 steam locomotives including 100 of Bulleid's 'West Country' and 'Battle of Britain' 4-6-2s. His ill-fated 'Leader' Class, together with a number of BR Standard Class '4' 4-6-0s and Class '4' 2-6-4Ts, were also built at Brighton Works in the latter years. The last and 1,211th locomotive to be built was No 80154, which emerged from the workshops on 26 March 1957.

Following closure, part of the workshop was utilised for the building of Isetta bubble cars until 1964.

Ex-LB&SCR Class 'B1' 0-4-2 No B172 is seen here at New Cross in October 1929.

1882 LSWR Class '0415' 4-4-2T

The London & South Western Railway's Class '0415' radial tank locomotives were designed by William Adams for intensive suburban passenger work in southwest London. A total of 71 were built by four different locomotive builders between 1882 and 1885. From 1897 they were replaced by Drummond's more powerful 'M7' Class 0-4-4Ts (see page 78), however their short wheelbase enabled them to work on sharply curved branch lines, which was the saving grace for a few members of the class.

Withdrawals started in 1916 – one was sold to the East Kent Light Railway in 1923 and the rest of the class, with the exception of two, were withdrawn by 1928. The two exceptions were allocated to Exmouth Junction shed in Exeter for working the Axminster to Lyme Regis branch line – their short wheelbases were ideal for this sharply curved line. In 1946 they were joined by a third which was bought back from the East Kent Light Railway.

These remaining Class '0415' locomotives became Nos 30582–30584 on nationalisation of Britain's railways in 1948. They continued their activities on the Lyme Regis branch until 1961 when they were replaced by newer Ivatt Class '2' 2-6-2Ts. Nos 30582 and 30584 were subsequently scrapped but No 30583 was saved for preservation by the Bluebell Railway in East Sussex, where it is currently a static exhibit.

Specification

Builders	Robert Stephenson & Co (28)
	Dubs & Co (20)
	Neilson & Co (11)
	Beyer, Peacock & Co (12)
Wheel arrangement	4-4-2T
Build dates	1882–1885
BR power classification	1P
Cylinders	2 outside
Driving wheels	5 ft 7 in
Tractive effort	14,919 lbs
Boiler pressure	160 psi
Number built	71
BR numbering	30582–30584

Ex-LSWR Class '0415' 4-4-2T No 30582 at Axminster with a train for Lyme Regis in the summer of 1960. Built in 1885, this veteran locomotive was withdrawn from Exmouth Junction shed (72A) in July 1961.

William Adams

East & West India Docks & Birmingham Junction Railway (1854–1858)
North London Railway (1858–1873)
Great Eastern Railway (1873–1878)
London & South Western Railway (1878–1895)

William Adams was born in Limehouse, London, in 1823. Following apprenticeships in the design of dockyards and steam engines, he worked in Italy installing steam marine engines in naval ships. On his return to England in 1852 Adams became a railway surveyor before being appointed Locomotive Engineer for the East & West India Docks & Birmingham Junction Railway, which became the North London Railway (NLR) in 1858. As Locomotive Engineer of the NLR he designed a series of 4-4-0 tank locomotives which were built at the company's

workshops in Bow. In 1873 he became Locomotive Superintendent of the Great Eastern Railway (GER) at Stratford where he designed a series of tank engines and 4-4-0 and 2-6-0 (the first in Britain) classes of locomotive. However, his main claim to fame at the GER was the modernising of Stratford Works.

Adams' third and final move as Locomotive Superintendent was to the London & South Western Railway's works at Nine Elms in 1878. During his seventeen years there he designed eight classes of 4-4-0 express locomotives and 0-4-2 'Jubilees' as well as six classes of tank locomotives – of the latter, his most famous and long-lived were the 4-4-2 radial tanks, the last three of which remained in service on the Lyme Regis branch until 1961. He also supervised the move of the Carriage and Wagon Works from Nine Elms to Eastleigh in 1891. Adams retired in 1895 and died in Putney in 1904.

Ex-LSWR Class '0415' 4-4-2T No 30582 has just arrived at Lyme Regis with a train from Axminster on 11 September 1959.

1883 GWR Class '2301' ('Dean Goods') 0-6-0

Breaking with past GWR tradition, the '2301' Class 0-6-0 freight locomotives were built with inside frames. Designed by William Dean, 260 were built at Swindon Works between 1883 and 1899. Due to their light axle loads they were well suited for working on GWR branch lines in England and Wales. Twenty were rebuilt as '3901' Class 2-6-2Ts in 1907.

In 1917, 62 class '2301s' were shipped by the Railway Operating Division (ROD) to northern France for war work and a year later sixteen were sent to Greece. Not all of them returned. In the early years of World War II, 100 were requisitioned by the War Department and shipped to France. Trapped there by the invading Germans, many did not make it back home until after hostilities ended, while others were eventually shipped to China. At the end of the war 30 were returned to Britain and scrapped.

A total of 54 Class '2301' locos passed into the newly nationalised British Railways in 1948. Replaced by new Ivatt Class '2' 2-6-0s locos, they were slowly withdrawn. The last survivor, No 2538, was retired from Oswestry shed (89D) in 1957. Fortunately one example, No 2516, also late of Oswestry shed, has been preserved and is currently on static display at STEAM – Museum of the Great Western Railway, Swindon.

Specification

Builder	Swindon Works
Wheel arrangement	0-6-0
Build dates	1883–1899
Cylinders	2 inside
Driving wheels	5 ft 2 in
Tractive effort	17,120 lbs
Boiler pressure	180 psi
Number built	260
BR numbering	2301–2360, 2381–2580 (many already withdrawn before 1948)

Soon-to-be-preserved GWR Class '2301' 0-6-0 No 2516 and sister engine No 2538 at Merthyr shed on 12 May 1956. The latter loco was the last member of this class to be withdrawn, from Oswestry shed (89D) in May 1957.

GWR Class '2301' 0-6-0 No 2516 outside Swindon Works prior to preservation in 1956. Built in 1897, this locomotive is now on static display at STEAM – Museum of the Great Western Railway in Swindon.

William Dean

Great Western Railway (1877–1902)

The son of a soap factory manager, William Dean was born in London in 1840 and, following his education, became an apprentice engineer under Joseph Armstrong (see page 32) at the Great Western Railway's Stafford Road Works in Wolverhampton. In 1863 Dean was appointed as Armstrong's Chief Assistant – a year later Armstrong was appointed as the GWR's Chief Locomotive Engineer at Swindon Works following the retirement of Daniel Gooch (see page 23). At Wolverhampton George Armstrong (see page 31) replaced his brother Joseph and Dean was promoted to manager of the works. Dean's rise up the corporate ladder continued in 1868 when he was appointed as Joseph Armstrong's Chief Assistant at Swindon.

Joseph Armstrong's sudden death in 1877 saw Dean catapulted into the top post at Swindon and over the next 25 years he was responsible for designing many successful locomotive classes for the GWR including the '3300' Class 4-4-0 'Bulldog' (see page 88), the '3252' Class 4-4-0 'Duke', the '2600' Class 2-6-0 'Aberdare' and his long-lived '2301' Class 0-6-0 'Dean Goods'. During his time at Swindon, Dean had successfully overseen the smooth transition from broad gauge to standard gauge, a process that was completed in 1892. Following several years of illness Dean retired in 1902 – to be succeeded by G. J. Churchward (see page 99) – and died three years later in Folkestone.

Thomas William Worsdell

Great Eastern Railway (1882–1885)
North Eastern Railway (1885–1890)

Thomas Worsdell was born in Liverpool in 1838. He was apprenticed at the London & North Western Railway's Crewe Works before joining the Pennsylvania Railroad in the USA as a locomotive engineer in 1865. Six years later Worsdell returned to Crewe where he worked under Francis Webb (see page 46) before being appointed Locomotive Superintendent of the Great Eastern Railway in 1882. During his sojourn at Stratford he introduced five classes of locomotive including 289 0-6-0s (later Class 'J15'), some of which remained in service until 1962, and 160 2-4-2Ts (later Class 'F4'), nicknamed 'Gobblers' for their high coal consumption, the last of which was withdrawn in 1956.

In 1885, Worsdell was appointed Locomotive Superintendent of the North Eastern Railway and over the next six years introduced fifteen different classes of locomotive, many of them compounds which were later rebuilt as simple engines by his successors. He retired in 1890 and died in 1916.

Preserved ex-GER Class 'J15' 0-6-0 No 65462 at work on the Gloucestershire Warwickshire Railway on 5 January 2008.

1883 GER Class 'Y14' (LNER Class 'J15') 0-6-0

The Class 'Y14' (LNER Class 'J15') 0-6-0s were highly successful and versatile freight locomotives designed by Thomas Worsdell for the Great Eastern Railway. They were also pressed into service hauling troop trains and, in the summer months, excursion trains. They were built in 26 batches at Stratford Works between 1883 and 1913 with an additional batch of nineteen locomotives built by Sharp, Stewart & Co of Manchester in 1884. They were easy to maintain and their low axle weight allowed them to operate over the whole of the GER network.

The GER also set a world record (which still stands today) with one of these locos in 1891. The company built one at Stratford Works in 9 hours 47 minutes. Painted only in grey primer, it then ran 5,000 miles hauling coal trains between London and Cambridgeshire before returning to the works for servicing and the application of its company livery.

During World War I the Railway Operating Division (ROD) requisitioned 43 of these locomotives which were shipped to northern France for war work. All were repatriated back to Britain at the end of hostilities. On the 'Big Four Grouping' in 1923 there were still 272 Class 'J15s' spread around East Anglia and London with the majority based at Stratford, Cambridge, Norwich and Ipswich. In World War II a few locomotives were temporarily transferred to South Yorkshire to assist with hauling coal trains.

On nationalisation in 1948, 127 of this already veteran class had miraculously survived into British Railways' ownership. Withdrawals continued until the last four survivors were retired in 1962. Fortunately, one example of a 'J15' has been preserved – built in 1912, No 65462 was withdrawn on 16 September 1962. It is owned by the Midland & Great Northern Joint Railway Society and is currently based on the North Norfolk Railway.

I was lucky to spot four 'J15s' – Nos 65361, 65460, 65476 and 65469 – at Stratford Works and shed (30A) when on a visit on 4 September 1962. They were all on 'death row' as the first three were all withdrawn at the end of that month and No 65469 had just been withdrawn.

Specification

Builders	Stratford Works (270)
	Sharp, Stewart & Co (19)
Wheel arrangement	0-6-0
Build dates	1883–1913
BR power classification	1P2F
Cylinders	2 inside
Driving wheels	4 ft 11 in
Tractive effort	16,940 lbs
Boiler pressure	160 psi
Number built	289
BR numbering	65361–65478 (as in summer 1961, many already withdrawn within this sequence)

Class 'J15' 0-6-0 No 65440 at Stratford shed (30A) in August 1959. Built at Stratford Works in 1900, this veteran locomotive was withdrawn from Stratford shed in October 1960.

L&YR Class '21' 0-4-0ST

John Aspinall's short-wheelbase 0-4-0 saddle tanks were specifically designed to operate on the sharply curved dock and industrial branch lines of the Lancashire & Yorkshire Railway (L&YR). The first three were built by Vulcan Foundry and delivered in 1886. These had a 6-ft wheelbase, a boiler pressure of 140 psi and a tractive effort of 10,060 lbs. A further 57 locomotives were subsequently built at Horwich Works between 1891 and 1910. These had a wheelbase of 5 ft 9 in, a boiler pressure of 160 psi and a tractive effort of 11,492 lbs.

Nicknamed 'Pugs', the Class '21' were initially allocated to docks and industrial sidings in Fleetwood, Preston, Liverpool, Salford and Goole. Under London Midland & Scottish Railway ownership they became more widely dispersed, serving also in Bristol, Bangor, Crewe, Derby and Widnes. By 1938 a total of 37 members had been withdrawn, with six of these being sold to private owners for use on their sidings. The remaining 23 passed into British Railways' ownership in 1948. Although withdrawals continued from 1957, a member of this class, No 51218, even found its way in the 1960s to Swansea East Dock shed (87E) for working on the local docks network. By 1961 there were only ten remaining members at work six were withdrawn in 1962, three in 1963 and the final one, No 51218, in 1964.

Two members of this class have been preserved. LMS No 11243 (built in 1910) was withdrawn in 1931 and sold firstly to Mowlem & Co and then to United Glass Bottle Manufacturers. It was bought from the latter company by the Lancashire & Yorkshire Railway Trust in 1967. It is currently being restored at the East Lancashire Railway.

Late of Swansea East Dock shed where I saw it in 1963, No 51218 (built in 1901) was bought from British Railways and has spent the last 58 years operating on the Keighley & Worth Valley Railway.

Specification

Builders	Vulcan Foundry (3)
	Horwich Works (57)
Wheel arrangement	0-4-0ST
Build dates	1886 (3),
	1891–1910 (57)
BR power classification	0F
Cylinders	2 outside
Driving wheels	3 ft 0 in
Tractive effort	10,060/11,492 lbs
Boiler pressure	140 /160 psi
Number built	60
BR numbering	51202–51253 (many already withdrawn prior to 1948)

The final shed allocation of ex-L&YR Class '21' 0-4-0ST No 51218 was at Swansea East Dock (87D). It is seen here on 27 October 1963. Withdrawn in September 1964, it has since been preserved and can be seen at the Keighley & Worth Valley Railway.

John Aspinall

Lancashire & Yorkshire Railway (Chief Mechanical Engineer 1886–1899, General Manager 1899–1919)

John Aspinall was born in Liverpool in 1851. At the age of 17 he started his apprenticeship with the London & North Western Railway at Crewe. In 1875 he became Works Manager at the Inchicore Works of the Great Southern & Western Railway in Ireland, becoming Locomotive Superintendent in 1882. Aspinall was subsequently appointed Chief Mechanical Engineer of the Lancashire & Yorkshire

Railway in 1886 where, at Horwich, he was responsible for the design and building of over 300 2-4-2 tank locos, 60 diminutive 0-4-0 saddle tanks, 230 0-6-0 saddle tanks (converted from 0-6-0 goods locos) and nearly 500 0-6-0 freight locos. All of these four classes were long-lived, with many surviving well into the BR era. Aspinall went on to become General Manager of the L&YR in 1899, introducing Britain's first mainline electric trains in the Liverpool area between 1904 and 1913. Also serving as president of the Institute of Civil Engineers and the Institute of Mechanical Engineers, Aspinall died in 1937 at the age of 85.

Built in 1910, preserved ex-L&YR Class '21' 0-4-0ST No 51231 (aka 11243) at the erstwhile Steamport museum at Southport, a museum that had been based at the former BR motive power depot, which closed in 1966. Steamport was subsequently closed in 2000, with exhibits being moved to the Ribble Steam Railway at Preston. No 11243 is currently under restoration at the East Lancashire Railway.

1887 LNWR 'Improved Precedent' Class 2-4-0

Later nicknamed 'Jumbos', the London & North Western Railway's 'Improved Precedent' Class 2-4-0s were designed by Francis Webb (see page 46) to haul heavy express passenger trains on the West Coast Main Line between Euston and Carlisle. It is widely accepted that this was his most outstanding design of locomotive. The class was a development of Webb's 'Precedent' Class 2-4-0s of which 70 had been built, with eight of these later being rebuilt as 'Improved Precedents'.

Built at Crewe Works, the numbering and names of the 158 'Improved Precedents' was random, with these being taken from withdrawn locomotives – the first to be built in 1887 was No 271 *Minotaur* and the last, in 1901, was No 861 *Amazon*. In 1895, No 790 *Hardwick* set a new speed record when it travelled from Crewe to Carlisle at an average speed of just over 67 mph while taking part in the 'Railway Race to the North' – its top speed was 90 mph – an achievement that remained unsurpassed until 1936. Another member of this class, No 955 *Charles Dickens*, worked between Euston and Manchester for twenty years and in doing so clocked up over 2 million miles – this feat has never been accomplished by a British steam locomotive since.

Although withdrawals commenced in 1905, 76 of the class survived to pass into the ownership of the new London Midland & Scottish Railway in the 'Big Four Grouping' of 1923. By then they had been relegated to more humble duties. Withdrawals continued through the 1920s and into the '30s until renumbered No 5001 *Snowdon* became the last survivor. It was withdrawn in 1934.

Built as a 'Precedent' Class in 1873, No 790 *Hardwick* was later rebuilt as an 'Improved Precedent' in 1892. It was withdrawn in 1932 and stored at Crewe Works until being put on display at the new Museum of British Transport at Clapham in 1962. It was returned to steam in 1975 and took part in the 150th anniversary of the Stockton & Darlington Railway at Shildon before spending the next seven years hauling enthusiasts' specials. It is currently on static display at the National Railway Museum in York.

Specification

Builder	Crewe Works
Wheel arrangement	2-4-0
Build dates	1887–1901
Cylinders	2 inside
Driving wheels	6 ft 9 in
Tractive effort	10,918 lbs
Boiler pressure	150 psi
Number built	158

ABOVE AND BELOW: *Built in 1873, preserved ex-LNWR 'Improved Precedent' 2-4-0 No 790 Hardwick was withdrawn in 1932 and returned to steam in 1975.*

1888 NBR Class 'C' (LNER Class 'J36') 0-6-0

The North British Railway's Class 'C' (LNER Class 'J36') 0-6-0s were a long-lived freight locomotive seen all over the railway's network. Designed by Matthew Holmes, a total of 168 were built between 1888 and 1900 at Cowlairs Works (138), Sharp, Stewart & Co (15) and Neilson & Co (15). Also designated Class 'C' were the 32 locomotives of Dugald Drummond's (see page 78) 0-6-0s which were built between 1876 and 1877. These were rebuilt between 1898 and 1903 to match Holmes' locomotives although they passed into LNER's ownership in 1923 as Class 'J32'.

While the original boiler pressure of this class was 140 psi, this was increased to 165 psi between 1913 and 1923 when the class was rebuilt with larger boilers.

During World War I, 25 of this class were shipped to northern France by the Railway Operating Division.

They all returned safely after the war and were subsequently named after wartime generals and battles – the names were painted on the mid-driving wheel splasher. On the 'Big Four Grouping' in 1923, all 168 locomotives passed into LNER's ownership where they were designated Class 'J36'. While withdrawals had already started in the 1930s and 1940s, a total of 123 Class 'J36s' passed into the new British Railways on nationalisation in 1948. Withdrawals continued at a steady pace during the 1950s and early 1960s until the last two survivors, Nos 65288 and 65345, were retired in June 1967 when they became the last BR operating steam locomotives in Scotland. My trainspotting notebook for 23 August 1966 records the former in steam at Dunfermline shed (62C) and the latter at Thornton shed (62A).

Matthew Holmes

North British Railway (1882–1903)

Matthew Holmes was born in Paisley in 1844 and joined the Edinburgh & Glasgow Railway in 1859, eventually rising to the post of Locomotive Superintendent for the Edinburgh-based North British Railway (NBR) in 1882. During his long tenure at Cowlairs Works, Holmes designed his famous

Class 'C' 0-6-0 (LNER Class 'J36') – 168 were built, most of them at Cowlairs, with some examples remaining in service until the end of steam in Scotland in 1967. He also designed the Class 'M' 4-4-0 (LNER Class 'D31') with some examples surviving until 1952. Holmes retired in June 1903 and died a few weeks later. As a mark of respect to a much-loved man, his funeral train was hauled from Lenzie to Haymarket by one of his own engines.

Built at the end of 1891, one named example that served in France during World War I, No 65243 *Maude*, was withdrawn from Bathgate shed (64F) in 1966 and bought for preservation by the Scottish Railway Preservation Society. The locomotive is currently on static display at the Museum of Scottish Railways in Bo'ness.

Ex-NBR Class 'J36' 0-6-0 No 65225 is seen here in ex-works condition at Inverurie Works in the mid-1950s. Built in 1891, this loco was withdrawn from Bathgate (64F) in October 1957.

Built in 1897, ex-NBR Class 'J36' 0-6-0 No 65288 was a veteran survivor. It is seen here in steam at Dunfermline shed (62C) on 23 August 1966. It was finally withdrawn in June 1967.

Specification

Builders	Cowlairs Works (138)
	Sharp, Stewart & Co (15)
	Neilson & Co (15)
Wheel arrangement	0-6-0
Build dates	1888–1900
BR power classification	2F
Cylinders	2 inside
Driving wheels	5 ft 0 in
Tractive effort	19,690 lbs
Boiler pressure	140 psi / 165 psi
Number built	168 (+ 32 rebuilt from earlier Drummond locos)
BR numbering	65210–65346

L&YR Class '5'/'6' 2-4-2T

The highly successful Class '5' and later more powerful Class '6' 2-4-2 radial tank locomotives were built in great numbers over a period of 25 years. Designed by John Aspinall (see page 57) for the Lancashire & Yorkshire Railway, they were to be seen in action hauling stopping passenger trains across the network west of the Pennines. In 1909 it was reckoned that these locomotives made up 56% of the L&YR's total passenger mileage

The Class '5s' were built under three L&YR Chief Mechanical Engineers: Aspinall from 1889 to 1899, Henry Hoy from 1899 to 1904 and George Hughes (see pages 150–151) from 1905 to 1911. The locomotives had modifications to the coal bunker and water capacity, the length of the frame and to the firebox. The later Class '6' locomotives included 44 rebuilds of Class '5s' and had superheating, longer smokeboxes on Belpaire boilers and an increased

cylinder bore – these final modifications increased the tractive effort to 24,585 lbs and the weight to 66 tons. Some of these locos were later fitted for push-pull operations.

One of these locomotives, later numbered as BR No 46762, was sold to the Wirral Railway in 1921, surviving into the British Railways era as No 46762 before being withdrawn in 1952. A total of 110 Class '5s' and a further fourteen of Class '6' survived to join the newly nationalised British Railways in 1948. All of Class '6' had been withdrawn by 1952, and by 1961 only Nos 50746 and 50850 remained of Class '5'. Both based at Southport shed, the former was withdrawn in February 1961 and the latter in November of that year.

One example of an L&YR Class '5' has been preserved – built in 1889, No 50621 was withdrawn in 1954 and is now in the National Collection at the National Railway Museum in York.

Specification

Builder	Horwich Works
Wheel arrangement	2-4-2T
Build dates	1889–1911 (Class '5') / 1911–1914 (Class '6')
BR power classification	2P (Class '5') / 3P (Class '6')
Cylinders	2 inside
Driving wheels	5 ft 8 in
Tractive effort	16,848–19,496 lbs (Class '5') / 24,585 lbs (Class '6')
Boiler pressure	160–180 psi (Class '5') / 180 psi (Class '6')
Number built	310 (Class '5') / 64 (Class '6', including 44 rebuilds)
BR numbering	Class '5': 46762, 50621–50953 / Class '6': within the range 50835–50953

Ex-L&YR Class '6' 2-4-2T No 10939 is seen here at Accrington in May 1935.

Built at Horwich Works in 1892, ex-L&YR Class '5' 2-4-2T No 50650 in ex-works condition at Horwich on 15 May 1949. This loco was withdrawn in October 1956.

Horwich Works

By the end of the 19th century Horwich, in Lancashire, was one of the youngest railway towns to come into existence. When the Lancashire & Yorkshire Railway's mechanical engineering works were established at Horwich in 1887 the population of the small town was under 4,000; by 1904 it was 16,000, of which around 10,500 were dependent on the employment provided by the railway company. Under L&YR ownership the Works had built 1,000 steam locomotives by 1907.

Under LMS and BR management the Works continued to build steam locomotives including 70 of the Hughes 'Crab' 2-6-0s, 72 of the Ivatt Class '4' 2-6-0s and 120 of the Stanier 'Black Five' 4-6-0s. Locomotive building ceased in 1957. Horwich Works continued to overhaul steam locomotives until May 1964 when the last, Stanier Class '8F' 2-8-0 No 48756, was outshopped. In 1969 the Works became part of British Rail Engineering and continued to repair rolling stock until its complete closure at the end of 1983.

Built at Horwich Works in 1890, ex-L&YR Class '27' 0-6-0 No 52093 at Crewe Works on 8 April 1962. One of the last two surviving Class '27s', it was withdrawn at the end of September that year.

L&YR Class '27' 0-6-0

Designed by John Aspinall (see page 57) for the Lancashire & Yorkshire Railway, the Class '27' 0-6-0s were robust and simple freight locomotives that stood the test of time. They were built in great numbers at Horwich Works between 1889 and 1918, with many surviving until the early 1960s. By the end of the 19th century over 400 had been built and this continued under Aspinall's successors, Henry Hoy and George Hughes (see pages 150–151) – the latter adding superheating to the new locomotives still being built under his watch. Many locos were also rebuilt with Belpaire boilers and extended smokeboxes from 1911.

During World War I over 30 of the Class '27s' were shipped by the Railway Operating Division (ROD) of the Royal Engineers to northern France for war work – they all were subsequently repatriated safely. Around 300 locomotives passed into the ownership of the new London Midland & Scottish Railway in 1923, their simplicity and usefulness being much admired by their new owners. On nationalisation in 1948, 235 locomotives passed into British Railways' ownership and by the summer of 1962 there were still sixteen on the books – I remember seeing Nos 52093 and 52312 at Crewe Works when I visited in the spring of that year – these last survivors were all withdrawn later that year.

One Class '27', No 52322, has been preserved and currently can be seen in action on the East Lancashire Railway. Built at Horwich Works in 1895, this loco was withdrawn from Lees Oldham shed in 1960 and purchased privately from BR.

Specification

Builder	Horwich Works
Wheel arrangement	0-6-0
Build dates	1889–1918
BR power classification	3F
Cylinders	2 inside
Driving wheels	5 ft 1 in
Tractive effort	21,130 lbs
Boiler pressure	180 psi
Number built	484
BR numbering	52088–52529 (with gaps due to withdrawals)

Built at Horwich Works in 1896, preserved ex-L&YR Class '27' 0-6-0 No 52322 at work on the Embsay & Bolton Abbey Steam Railway on 8 September 2022.

The Class 'O2' 0-4-4T locomotives were designed by William Adams (see page 51) for working intensive suburban commuter services on the London & South Western Railway's routes in southwest London. Replacing the less powerful Class 'O298' well tanks (see page 42) and with their small diameter driving wheels, they were ideally suited for this task. However, they had a short reign on these services as they began to be gradually replaced by even more powerful Class 'M7' 0-4-4Ts (see page 78) from 1897. The 'O2s' then became widely dispersed throughout the LSWR network where they were well suited to branch line duties. All 60 of the 'O2s' survived into Southern Railway's ownership in 1923 but electrification and the introduction of more powerful types led to the first withdrawals in the 1930s. A few examples were fitted for push-pull operations.

As they became redundant on the mainland, a total of 23 Class 'O2' locos were shipped to the Isle of Wight between 1923 and 1949. Replacing ageing LB&SCR Class 'E1' 0-6-0Ts, they were fitted with Westinghouse air brakes, renumbered W14 to W36 and named after towns and villages on the island. While the last mainland examples had all been withdrawn by 1962, the Isle of Wight locos continued in service until the end of 1966, by which time most of the island lines had been closed – the last survivor, Ryde to Shanklin, was electrified with redundant London Underground stock and reopened in March 1967. I was fortunate to pay a visit to the island on 2 October 1965 and to enjoy a ride from Ryde Pier Head behind veteran 'O2s', No 31 *Chale* to Ventnor and No 26 *Whitwell* to Cowes.

All but one of the Isle of Wight locomotives were subsequently scrapped. The survivor, W24 *Calbourne*, was saved for preservation by the Isle of Wight Steam Railway and is currently in service on that railway's reopened route between Wootton and Smallbrook Junction.

Specification

Builder	Nine Elms Works
Wheel arrangement	0-4-4T
Build dates	1889–1896
BR power classification	0P
Cylinders	2 inside
Driving wheels	4 ft 8 in
Tractive effort	17,235 lbs
Boiler pressure	160 psi
Number built	60
BR numbering	30177–30236 mainland / W14–W36 Isle of Wight

A trio of ex-LSWR Class 'O2' 0-4-4Ts receive attention at the Isle of Wight's Ryde shed (70H) on 2 October 1965. In the centre is No 14 Fishbourne and on the right is No 24 Calbourne in immaculate unlined 'ex-works' condition.

Nine Elms Works

The original railway works at Nine Elms in Battersea were opened by the London & South Western Railway in 1839. Due to restricted space the Works was rebuilt on a nearby larger site in 1865. The site of the original Works then became Nine Elms motive power depot which remained operational, serving Waterloo station, until 1967. New Covent Garden Market was then built on the site. The second Nine Elms Works then went on to build steam locomotives to the designs of Joseph Hamilton Beattie, William Beattie, William Adams and Dugald Drummond. These included the long-lived Class '0298' 2-4-0 WTs, Class '0415' 4-4-2 radial tanks, Class 'O2' and 'M7' 0-4-4 tanks and Class 'T9' 4-4-0s. By the early 20th century over 700 locomotives had been constructed at the Works, which by then employed about 2,500 people.

However, it had been obvious since the end of the 19th century that further expansion of Nine Elms Works was not possible. Subsequently the LSWR moved its locomotive construction and repair facility to a new site at Eastleigh in Hampshire (see page 137), a process which was completed by 1910.

Ex-LSWR Class 'O2' 0-4-4T No 20 Shanklin at the head of a train at Ryde in 1964.

Built at Vulcan Foundry in 1900, ex-LB&SCR Class 'C2X' 0-6-0 No 536 on shed somewhere in the south of England. This loco was withdrawn from Three Bridges shed (75E) in March 1961.

Built by Vulcan Foundry in 1894, ex-LB&SCR Class 'C2' 0-6-0 No 450 at Fratton shed in the 1930s. This loco was rebuilt as a 'C2X' in 1910 and withdrawn from Norwood Junction (75C) in October 1961.

LB&SCR Class 'C2'/'C2X' 0-6-0

Vulcan Foundry in Newton-le-Willows, Lancashire, built a total of 55 Class 'C2' 0-6-0s between 1893 and 1902. They were designed by Robert Billinton to haul heavy goods trains for the London, Brighton & South Coast Railway. The class was highly reliable and capable of a good turn of speed, which attribute suited them also for hauling passenger trains.

To enable the class to haul heavier freight trains, Billinton's successor, Douglas Marsh (see page 111), rebuilt a Class 'C2' with a larger diameter boiler and an extended smokebox in 1908. The results were so good that a further 29 had been rebuilt in the same way by 1912 and a further three by 1922. These more powerful locos received the classification of 'C2X'. All of the 'C2' and 'C2X' locos passed into Southern Railway's ownership in 1923 and a further nine 'C2s' had been rebuilt by 1925. A downturn in freight traffic during the 1930s led to the withdrawal of seven of the original 'C2s' between 1935 and 1937 and further withdrawals would have followed but for the onset of World War II. The urgent need for heavy freight locos led to the rebuilding of four of the remaining 'C2s' from 1939 to 1940 – the remaining survivors of Class 'C2' were all withdrawn by 1950.

All of the Class 'C2Xs' survived into British Railways' ownership in 1948. Withdrawals began in 1957 with the final examples, Nos 32523 and 32535, being taken out of service in February 1962. Sadly, none of these long-lived work horses were preserved.

Specification

Builder	Vulcan Foundry
Wheel arrangement	0-6-0
Build dates	1893–1902
BR power classification	2F
Cylinders	2 inside
Driving wheels	5 ft 0 in
Tractive effort	18,050 lbs ('C2') / 19,175 lbs ('C2X')
Boiler pressure	160 psi ('C2') / 170 psi ('C2X')
Number built	55
BR numbering	32434–32451, 32521–32554 with gaps due to earlier withdrawals

Robert John Billinton

London, Brighton & South Coast Railway (1890–1904)

Born in Wakefield, Yorkshire, in 1845, Robert Billinton served his apprenticeship at William Fairbairn's engineering company in Manchester followed by employment between 1863 and 1870 at several large engineering firms and manufacturers of steam locomotives in Yorkshire. In 1870 he moved to Brighton where he became assistant to William Stroudley (see page 38), the newly appointed Locomotive Superintendent of the London, Brighton & South Coast Railway. In 1874 Robert moved again, this time to Derby where he became assistant to Samuel Johnson (see page 45), the Chief Mechanical Engineer of the Midland Railway.

William Stroudley died in 1889 and Billinton was appointed as his successor at Brighton. During his tenure as Locomotive, Carriage, Wagon & Marine Superintendent, Robert Billinton designed many successful steam locomotive types ('B' Class 4-4-0, 'C2' Class 0-6-0, 'D' Class 0-4-4T, and numerous 'E' Class 0-6-2T) and steel-framed coaching stock for the LB&SCR. He died suddenly in 1904 and was succeeded by Douglas Marsh (see page 111).

HR 'Jones Goods' Class 4-6-0

When introduced in 1894, the Highland Railway's (HR's) 'Jones Goods' were not only the first class in Britain with a 4-6-0 wheel arrangement (a design that originated in the USA) but they were also the most powerful mainline locomotives in the country. Designed by David Jones, fifteen of these locomotives were built by Sharp, Stewart & Co of Glasgow in 1894. Although intended primarily as freight locos they were often pressed into passenger service, especially during the busy tourist season in the summer months. With their small driving wheels they were highly successful in hauling heavy freight or passenger trains over the Highland Railway's steeply graded mainline network.

The 'Jones Goods' class all passed to the London Midland & Scottish Railway on the 'Big Four Grouping' in 1923. Withdrawals started in 1929, with the last example being retired in 1940. The first locomotive, No 103 (LMS No 17916), was saved for preservation when it was withdrawn in 1934. This famous loco was restored to full working order in 1959 and over the next six years was much in demand for hauling enthusiasts' special trains in Scotland. I spotted No 103 at Dawsholm Shed (65D) while on a mega trainspotting trip to Glasgow and Edinburgh on 29 March 1964. In 1965 it was retired and moved to Glasgow Transport Museum in Kelvin Hall. It has since been moved to the Riverside Museum in Glasgow where it is on static display.

Soon after being restored to full working order, preserved ex-HR 'Jones Goods' 4-6-0 No 103 just fits on the turntable at Inverness shed (60A) in 1959.

Specification

Builder	Sharp, Stewart & Co
Wheel arrangement	4-6-0
Build date	1894
Cylinders	2 outside
Driving wheels	5 ft 3 in
Tractive effort	24,555 lbs
Boiler pressure	175 psi
Number built	15

David Jones

Highland Railway (1870–1896)

David Jones was born in Manchester in 1834 and was apprenticed at the London & North Western Railway's Crewe Works. In 1855 he joined what was to become the Highland Railway at Lochgorm Works, Inverness, later working as an assistant to William Stroudley (see page 38) and Dugald Drummond (see page 78) before being appointed Locomotive Superintendent in 1870. Jones designed five classes of 4-4-0 locomotives for the Highland Railway, culminating in the 'Loch' Class which was introduced in 1896, with two examples remaining in service for BR until 1950. However, he is most famous for his 4-6-0 'Jones Goods', the first loco built with this wheel arrangement in Britain, which was introduced in 1894. Fortunately, the first of the class, No 103, was saved for preservation in 1934 and now resides in the new Riverside Museum in Glasgow. Jones retired in 1896 and died in 1906.

MR Class '115' ('Spinner') 4-2-2

The Midland Railway's Class '115' was the third of four classes of single-wheel express passenger locomotives designed by Samuel Waite Johnson (see page 45). Although single-wheel locomotives were generally considered to be past their 'sell-by date' by then, a steam-powered sanding device invented by the MR's Francis Holt greatly improved the adhesion of larger diameter wheels on wet and slippery rails. The first single wheeler with a diameter of 7 ft 4 in was built at Derby Works in 1887 and subsequent classes had progressively larger driving wheels until the Class '115' was introduced in 1896 with 7 ft 9½ in wheels. They were a common sight on the MR main line out of St Pancras, hauling express passenger trains at speeds of up to 90 mph, their whirring driving wheels earning them the nickname 'Spinners'. In the first years of the 20th century they were used on heavier trains, as pilot engines for the new Class '1000' Compound 4-4-0s (see page 97). Twelve Class '115s' passed into LMS's ownership in 1923 but by 1927 only three remained in service. The last survivor, No 673, was withdrawn the following year and preserved.

Kept at Derby Works as a static exhibit for many years, No 673 was restored to working order in 1976 and took part in the 150th anniversary cavalcade of the Rainhill Trials in May 1980. It is now a static exhibit at the National Railway Museum in York.

Specification

Builder	Derby Works
Wheel arrangement	4-2-2
Build dates	1896–1897 (5), 1899 (10)
Cylinders	2 inside
Driving wheels	7 ft 9½ in
Tractive effort	15,279 lbs
Boiler pressure	170 psi
Number built	15

The elegant lines of the Midland Railway's 4-2-2 'Spinners' are shown to good effect in this early 20th century photograph of No 622.

Derby Works

Established in 1844, the Midland Railway's locomotive works at Derby built many fine and long-lived steam locomotives under Locomotive & Carriage Superintendents Matthew Kirtley and Samuel Johnson, Locomotive Superintendent Richard Deeley and Chief Mechanical Engineer Henry Fowler.

In 1923 the Works came under the control of London Midland & Scottish Railway. While the majority of the LMS's larger engines were built at Crewe, Derby Works went on to build large numbers of tank locomotives and, during World War II, a large batch of Stanier 'Black Five' 4-6-0s. Steam locomotive building and overhauls continued until 1957 when the 2,941st locomotive, BR Standard Class '5' 4-6-0 No 73154, rolled off the production line on 30 June.

Large numbers of diesel-electric locomotives were also built between 1958 and 1962 while the adjacent Carriage & Wagon Works at Litchurch Lane made some of the first diesel multiple units, the Derby Lightweights, in Britain. While the main works closed in 1990, the latter, now under private ownership, continues to make rolling stock.

Preserved MR 4-2-2 'Spinner' No 673, seen here at the Midland Railway Centre at Butterley in 1978, was restored to full working order in 1976. It is currently a static exhibit at the National Railway Museum in York.

CR Class '721' ('Dunalastair I-IV') 4-4-0

Designed to haul heavy passenger trains at speed on the Caledonian Railway's (CR's) main lines, the fifteen 'Dunalastair' Class (Class '721') 4-4-0s were designed by John McIntosh and introduced in 1896. Their ability to maintain high speeds with heavy loads on steeply graded track was legendary, so doing away with double-heading, a feat accomplished by the fitting of a large boiler operating at, what was then, a high pressure. Built at St Rollox Works, so successful was the first batch that a second batch of fifteen locomotives ('766' Class) was built the following year – some of these were rebuilt with superheaters in 1914. A third batch of sixteen locos ('900' Class) was built in 1899 and 1900 – again, some were rebuilt with superheaters between 1914 and 1918. A final batch of nineteen locomotives ('140' Class) was built between 1904 and 1910, some being rebuilt with superheaters between 1915 and 1917.

McIntosh's 'Dunalastair' was a highly influential locomotive class, with his ideas of large boilers and superheating being taken up by many British railway companies – even the Belgian State Railways built six classes of locomotives similar to the 'Dunalastair' design.

All of the 'Dunalastairs' survived into London Midland & Scottish Railway's ownership in 1923. Withdrawals began in 1930 and by 1947 only one of the original four batches survived – No 54363 was finally withdrawn from Aviemore shed in October 1948. The last of the rebuilds, No 54439, survived until 1958 when it was withdrawn in August from Wick shed. Unfortunately no example of this pioneering class was preserved.

Specification

Builder	St Rollox Works
Wheel arrangement	4-4-0
Build dates	1896 (I) / 1897 (II) / 1899–1900 (III) / 1904–1910 (IV)
BR power classification	2P (rebuilds 3P)
Cylinders	2 inside
Driving wheels	6 ft 6 in
Tractive effort	15,100 lbs (I) / 17,900 lbs (II) / 18,411 lbs (III + IV)
Boiler pressure	160 psi (I) / 175 psi (II) / 180 psi (III + IV)
Number built	15 (I) / 15 (II) / 16 (III) / 19 (IV)
BR numbering	54363, 54434, 54438–54439

John Farqharson McIntosh

Caledonian Railway (1895–1914)

A labourer's son, John McIntosh was born near Brechin, Scotland, in 1846 and by 1860 had started an apprenticeship with the Scottish North Eastern Railway at Arbroath before becoming a driver in 1867, by which time the railway had been absorbed by the Caledonian Railway. A 'Caley' man through and through, McIntosh worked his way up to become Locomotive Running Superintendent and, in 1895, was appointed Locomotive Superintendent at St Rollox works in Glasgow.

McIntosh's reign at St Rollox was marked by a series of over twenty locomotive designs which included the superb 4-4-0 'Dunalastairs' and the 4-6-0 'Cardeans' and 'Oban Bogies', while his '2P' 0-4-4Ts and '2F' and '3F' 0-6-0 freight locos continued in service with BR into the 1960s. Honoured by King George V in 1911, he retired in 1914 and died in 1918.

Seen at Stirling shed and carrying LMS number 14332, this ex-CR 'Dunalastair II' 4-4-0 was built at St Rollox Works in 1897. It was withdrawn in July 1946.

Designed by Robert Billinton (see page 97), the London, Brighton & South Coast Railway's Class 'E4' 0-6-2 radial tanks were built for local passenger and freight duties, a task they performed admirably for 60 years. The 'E4' was a development of William Stroudley's Class 'E3', the first of which had been built just after his untimely death in December 1889, with increased boiler pressure and larger diameter driving wheels.

A total of 75 'E4s' were built at Brighton Works between 1897 and 1903. Some members were named after places and geographical features found in the LB&SCR's sphere of operation. In 1909 four locomotives were rebuilt by Douglas Marsh (see page 111) with larger boilers and were reclassified Class 'E4X'. During World War I the Railway Operating Division (ROD) of the Royal Engineers requisitioned thirteen of the locos and shipped them to northern France for war work – they all returned safely to England in 1919.

All of the class passed into Southern Railway's ownership in 1923 and all but one survived into the British Railways era from 1948 – the exception was No 2483 *Hellingly*, which was destroyed in a Luftwaffe air raid in 1942. Withdrawals began in 1955 and continued until 1964. Fortunately one example, No 32473, was preserved and is permanently based on the Bluebell Railway in East Sussex. Built at Brighton Works in 1898, this loco was originally named *Birch Grove*, and was withdrawn in 1962. In its latter operational years it was based at Nine Elms shed and employed on empty coaching stock duties at Waterloo station.

Specification

Builder	Brighton Works
Wheel arrangement	0-6-2T
Build dates	1897–1903
BR power classification	2MT
Cylinders	2 inside
Driving wheels	5 ft 0 in
Tractive effort	18,050 lbs ('E4') / 19,175 lbs ('E4X')
Boiler pressure	160 psi ('E4') / 170 psi ('E4X')
Number built	75
BR numbering	32463–32520, 32556–32566, 32577–32582

Built at Brighton Works in 1900, ex-LB&SCR Class 'E4' 0-6-2T No 498 is pictured here at West Croydon, circa 1930s. Serving with the Railway Operating Division in France from 1917 to 1919, it survived into British Railways' ownership and was withdrawn in November 1961.

Replacing the less powerful Class 'O298' (see page 42) and Class 'O2' (see page 66) locomotives, the Class 'M7' 0-4-4Ts were designed by Dugald Drummond to haul intensive commuter passenger trains on the London & South Western Railway's network in southwest London. A total of 105 were built between 1897 and 1911, the last batch at the new LSWR works at Eastleigh. There were a number of variations to the design, including differences in the length of the frame. At 60 tons, this was the heaviest class of its type to be built in Britain.

Thirty-one of these highly successful locomotives were fitted with a rudimentary push-pull apparatus from 1912 onwards, but this was changed to a more modern compressed air system in the 1930s. In addition to their London suburban duties, the 'M7s'

became a familiar sight hauling stopping trains on the main lines and branch lines around southern England.

Withdrawals started in 1957 and by 1963 there were only thirteen examples remaining, notably at Bournemouth for working the Swanage branch line. I can well remember while on holiday in Swanage in August 1961 spotting Nos 30010, 30031, 30105, 30107, 30108, 30112, 30328 and 30379 working the branch line trains to Wareham and Bournemouth during my week there.

Final withdrawals of this classic class took place in 1964 although two were saved for preservation. Built in 1897, No 30245 is part of the National Collection and is currently a static exhibit at the National Railway Museum in York. No 30053 spent 20 years at Steamtown in Vermont, USA, before being repatriated in 1987. It is currently based at the Swanage Railway.

Dugald Drummond

North British Railway (1875–1882)
Caledonian Railway (1882–1890)
London & South Western Railway (1895–1912)

Born in Ardrossan in 1840, Dugald Drummond went on to become one of the most prolific and successful steam locomotive designers of his time. Following an engineering apprenticeship in Glasgow, Drummond first worked as a boilerman for the civil engineer Thomas Brassey at Birkenhead before gaining employment at the Cowlairs Works of the Edinburgh & Glasgow Railway in 1864. He later moved to Inverness where he worked as a foreman under William Stroudley (see page 38) at the Highland Railway's Lochgorm Works. In 1870 Stroudley was appointed Locomotive Superintendent for the London, Brighton & South Coast Railway at Brighton Works and Drummond went with him.

In 1875 Drummond moved back to Scotland to take the post of Locomotive Superintendent for the North British Railway and was involved as an expert witness during the official inquiry into the Tay Bridge disaster of 1879. While at Cowlairs Works, Drummond designed seven classes of locomotive ranging from 0-6-0s and

2-2-2s to 4-4-0s and 0-4-2Ts, the majority of which remained in service through to the LNER era.

Drummond's next move was to the Caledonian Railway where he was Locomotive Superintendent from 1882 to 1890. Here he designed nine classes of locomotive, many of which survived into the BR era – his '294' Class 0-6-0 Standard Goods locos of 1883 were still being used in Scotland in the early 1960s, as were some of his '264' Class 0-4-0 saddle tanks.

From 1890 Drummond opened two locomotive engineering works, the first in Australia and the second in Glasgow, but he returned to railway company employment in 1895 when he was appointed Locomotive Engineer for the London & South Western Railway. Drummond oversaw the move of the LSWR's locomotive works from Nine Elms to Eastleigh in 1909. Before his death in 1912, he designed over twenty different classes of locomotive, ranging from the unusual 'E10' Class 4-2-2-0 to the famous 'T9' Class 4-4-0s, or 'Greyhounds' as they became known. In addition to the latter class his '700' Class 0-6-0s and 'M7' Class 0-4-4Ts provided sterling service for both the Southern Railway and for British Railways, until their demise in the early 1960s.

Built in 1905, ex-LSWR Class 'M7' 0-4-4T No 30050 awaits its next turn of duty to Swanage at Bournemouth shed (71B), circa 1960. This loco was withdrawn in January 1962.

Specification

Builders	Nine Elms Works (95)
	Eastleigh Works (10)
Wheel arrangement	0-4-4T
Build dates	1897–1911
BR power classification	2P
Cylinders	2 inside
Driving wheels	5 ft 7 in
Tractive effort	16,933–17,235 lbs
Boiler pressure	150–175 psi
Number built	105
BR numbering	random groups within 30XXX series

Preserved ex-LSWR Class 'M7' 0-4-4T No 30053 heads into Corfe Castle station on the Swanage Railway, 12 June 2008. Built at Nine Elms in 1905, this loco was withdrawn in May 1964.

GNR Class 'J13' (LNER Class 'J52') 0-6-0ST

Introduced in 1897 as shunting locomotives for large marshalling yards, the Great Northern Railway's Class 'J13' 0-6-0 saddle tanks were Henry Ivatt's development of Patrick Stirling's (see page 37) Class 'J14', of which 52 were built with a domeless boiler between 1892 and 1897. The very similar 'J13s' were built with a domed boiler, with some being fitted with condensing apparatus for working on the underground Metropolitan Railway in London. Forty-eight Class 'J14s' were rebuilt as Class 'J13' from 1922 onwards.

In 1923 the GNR became one of the constituent companies of the new London & North Eastern Railway and the Class 'J13' was reclassified as 'J52' – there were two variations: 'J52/1' was for rebuilt locos and 'J52/2' for the original types. This long-lived class of locomotive survived more-or-less intact into the British Railways era – 48 'J52/1s' and 85 'J52/2s' passed to BR in 1948. Mass withdrawals started in 1950 and continued until 1961 when the last survivors, Nos 68869 and 68875, together with departmental locomotives No 7 (68858) and No 9 (68840), were withdrawn.

One class 'J52' was preserved. Built by Sharp, Stewart & Co in 1899, No 68846 latterly worked at King's Cross shed, shunting larger engines around the depot until withdrawal in 1959. It was purchased directly from BR by Captain W. G. Smith and, after restoration in GNR apple green livery, was used to haul enthusiasts' trains around southern England. The loco was donated to the National Railway Museum in York in 1980, where it is currently on static display.

Specification

Builders	Doncaster Works (50)
	Robert Stephenson & Co (10)
	Sharp, Stewart & Co (25)
Wheel arrangement	0-6-0ST
Build dates	1897–1909
BR power classification	3F
Cylinders	2 inside
Driving wheels	4 ft 8 in
Tractive effort	21,735 lbs
Boiler pressure	170 psi
Number built	85 (+ 48 rebuilds)
BR numbering	68757–68889

Ex-GNR Class 'J52' 0-6-0ST No 68835 trundles through Doncaster station with a goods train, circa 1950. Built by Sharp, Stewart & Co in 1900, this loco was withdrawn from Doncaster shed (36A) in February 1958.

Henry Alfred Ivatt

Great Northern Railway (1895–1911)

Henry Ivatt was born near Ely in 1851 and started his apprenticeship under John Ramsbottom (see page 25) at the London & North Western Railway's Crewe Works in 1868. Ivatt went on to become a fireman and locomotive shed foreman with the LNWR before being appointed as Locomotive Engineer for the Great Southern & Western Railway at their Inchicore Works in Dublin in 1886. While in Ireland he patented the famous carriage window-opening device operated by a leather strap, which stayed in service through to BR days in the 1960s.

In 1895, Ivatt was appointed Locomotive Superintendent of the Great Northern Railway at Doncaster Works. His 'Klondyke Atlantic' 4-4-2 locos of 1898 (see page 83) were the first of this wheel arrangement to be built in Britain and proved to be capable of high speeds with heavy loads along the East Coast Main Line between King's Cross and York. The first to be built, *Henry Oakley*, is now preserved at the National Railway Museum, York. With later modifications by Nigel Gresley (see page 159) the last examples remained in service until 1945. The longest-surviving Ivatt design for the GNR were the Class 'J13' (LNER Class 'J52') 0-6-0 saddle tanks, introduced in 1897, several of which remained in service for BR until 1961. Henry Ivatt retired in 1911 and died in 1923.

Built by Sharp, Stewart & Co in 1899, preserved ex-GNR Class 'J52' 0-6-0ST No 1247 is seen here at the Keighley & Worth Valley Railway in August 1965. As BR No 68846, it was withdrawn from King's Cross shed (34A) in 1959 before being bought by Captain W. G. Smith for preservation.

The LNER's large-boilered Class 'C1' 4-4-2 No 2817 at Doncaster Works on 13 June 1950. Built at Doncaster Works in 1904, this loco had been officially withdrawn from Sheffield Darnall shed by the time this photo was taken.

Seen here at Doncaster Works, preserved small-boilered ex-GNR class 'C1' 4-4-2 No 990 Henry Oakley is currently on static display at the National Railway Museum in York.

GNR small- and large-boilered Class 'C1' (LNER Class 'C1'/'C2') 4-4-2

Developed from the American wheel arrangement of 4-4-2 (or 'Atlantic') that had been introduced in 1888, the first locomotive of this class was built in record time at Doncaster Works. No 990 *Henry Oakley* was also the first of this type to be built in Britain. The small-boilered (4 ft 8 in diameter) Class 'C1' 4-4-2 was designed by Henry Ivatt (see page 81) for express passenger duties on the Great Northern Railway and nicknamed 'Klondykes' after the famous gold rush in Canada in 1897. Entering service on the East Coast Main Line in 1900, the small-boilered 'Klondykes' were fast locomotives, almost too fast for this route. Between 1909 and 1925 the 22 locos of this class were fitted with superheaters, which resulted in a boiler pressure reduction from 170 to 160 psi.

Somewhat confusingly, the small-boilered Class 'C1' was reclassified by the LNER in 1923 as Class 'C2'. The large-boilered versions (see below) then became Class 'C1'.

Following on from the success of the small-boilered 'C1', Henry Ivatt developed a large-boilered (5 ft 6 in diameter) version, of which 94 were built at Doncaster Works between 1902 and 1910. There were several versions including four-cylinder compounds (including one built by Vulcan Foundry in 1905), superheating and one that had a steam-powered booster engine on the trailing axle.

Like their small-boilered cousins, these locomotives were capable of 90 mph and remained in charge of East Coast Main Line expresses until gradually displaced by new Gresley Class 'A1' 4-6-2s in the 1920s. They continued on lighter passenger duties for the LNER with the first withdrawals taking place in 1944. In 1948 there were seventeen survivors that made it through to British Railways' ownership. These had all been withdrawn by 1950 with the last, No 62822, hauling a special last train from King's Cross to Doncaster in late November 1950.

The first of the small-boilered versions to be built, (LNER Class 'C2') No 990 *Henry Oakley*, has been preserved. It is part of the National Collection and is on static display at the National Railway Museum in York. Withdrawn in 1950, pioneer large-boilered version (LNER Class 'C1') No 251 has also been preserved as part of the National Collection and is currently on loan to Danum Gallery, Library & Museum in Doncaster.

Specification

Locomotive	Small boilered
Builder	Doncaster Works
Wheel arrangement	4-4-2
Build dates	1898–1903
Cylinders	2 outside
Driving wheels	6 ft 8 in
Tractive effort	14,728 lbs
Boiler pressure	160 psi
Number built	22

Locomotive	Large boilered
Builder	Doncaster Works
Wheel arrangement	4-4-2
Build dates	1902–1910
BR power classification	2P
Cylinders	2 outside
	4 (2 outside, 2 inside) – Nos 1300, 3292 and 3279
Driving wheels	6 ft 8 in
Tractive effort	13,808–17,340 lbs
	21,326 lbs (No 3292 compound)
	21,128 lbs (No 3279)
	22,100 lbs (No 1300)
Boiler pressure	170 psi (saturated)
	150 psi (superheated)
	200 psi (Nos 3292 and 1300)
Number built	94
BR numbering	62808–62885 (gaps due to pre-1948 withdrawals)

Built as passenger locomotives, the Highland Railway's 'Ben' Class 4-4-0s were designated 'small' and 'large', the difference being the size of their boilers and boiler pressure. They were built in four batches: eight of the small type were built by Dübs & Co of Glasgow between 1898 and 1899; nine of the small type were built at the HR's Lochgorm Works in Inverness between 1899 and 1901; three of the small type were built by the North British Locomotive Company (NBL) of Glasgow in 1906; and all six of the large type were also built by the NBL between 1908 and 1909.

All 26 locomotives passed into the ownership of the London Midland & Scottish Railway in 1923. Withdrawals started in 1931 and by 1937 all the large 'Bens' had been taken out of service. Ten examples passed into British Railways' ownership on nationalisation in 1948, although seven were soon withdrawn and never carried their BR numbers. The remaining three, all from the first batch built by Dübs & Co – No 54404 *Ben Clebrig*, No 54399 *Ben Wyvis* and No 54398 *Ben Alder* – were withdrawn in 1950, 1952 and 1953 respectively.

No 54398 *Ben Alder* was set aside for preservation and stored at various locations including Dawsholm and Boat of Garten sheds – I remember seeing this loco in Dawsholm shed (65D) on 29 March 1964. However, it was not to be as this historic locomotive was sent to be scrapped at Motherwell Machinery & Scrap at Wishaw at the end of May 1966.

Specification

Builders	Dübs & Co (8 small)
	Lochgorm Works (9 small)
	North British Locomotive Co
	(3 small, 6 large)
Wheel arrangement	4-4-0
Build dates	1898–1906 (small),
	1908–1909 (large)
BR power classification	2P
Cylinders	2 inside
Driving wheels	6 ft 0 in
Tractive effort	17,890 lbs
Boiler pressure	175 psi (small),
	180 psi (large)
Number built	20 (small), 6 (large)
BR numbering	54397–54410
	(some withdrawn
	before 1948)

TOP RIGHT: *Ex-HR 'Ben' Class 4-4-0 No 54398* Ben Alder *is seen here at Lochgorm Works, Inverness, in September 1953, shortly after the loco was withdrawn. Built by Dübs & Co in 1898, it was destined for preservation but was sadly scrapped in 1966.*

Peter Drummond

Highland Railway (1896–1911)
Glasgow & South Western Railway (1912–1918)

The younger brother of Dugald Drummond (see page 78), Peter Drummond was born in 1850 and became Locomotive Superintendent at the Highland Railway's Lochgorm Works in 1896. During his fifteen years there he designed four classes of locomotive of which the most well known are the 'Ben' Class 4-4-0s. Out of a total of twenty of these delightful engines, nine were built at Lochgorm while the rest were built by Dübs & Co and North British Locomotive Company in Glasgow. Amazingly, ten survived into the BR era, with the last, 'Ben Alder', being at first saved for preservation but then scrapped.

Peter Drummond left the Highland Railway in 1911 to become Locomotive Superintendent of the Glasgow & South Western Railway (G&SWR), a post he held until his death in 1918. The last example of his G&SWR 2-6-0 locomotives, known as 'Austrian Goods', just failed to survive into BR ownership as it was scrapped in 1947.

*Ex-HR 'Ben' Class 4-4-0 No 14404 Ben Clebrig was
photographed at Forres station in June 1934. Built by
Dübs & Co in 1899, this loco was withdrawn from
Wick shed (60D) in October 1950.*

NER Class 'E1' (LNER Class 'J72') 0-6-0T

The North Eastern Railway's highly successful Class 'E1' (LNER Class 'J72') 0-6-0Ts had the unique distinction of being built without any major modifications during the pre-grouping, 'Big Four Grouping' and British Railways eras. Designed by Wilson Worsdell as a shunting and station pilot locomotive, the Class 'E1' was a development of the Class 'E' 0-6-0T which was designed by Wilson's brother, Thomas Worsdell (see page 54).

The locomotives were built in six batches, spread over a period of 53 years:

- 1898–1899 Darlington Works (20)
- 1914 Darlington Works (20)
- 1920 Darlington Works (10)
- 1922 Armstrong Whitworth & Co of Newcastle (25)
- 1925 Doncaster Works (10)
- 1949–1951 Darlington Works (28).

The 'E1s' were reclassified as 'J72' by the LNER at the time of the 'Big Four Grouping' in 1923. So successful were they that all survived into the British Railways period. They could be seen at work across northeastern England and further afield at former LNER depots such as Ipswich, Wrexham, Aberdeen Kittybrewster and Glasgow Eastfield.

The first withdrawals took place in 1958 when they began to be displaced by new diesel shunters. In their latter years they are well remembered as station pilots at Newcastle Central station, their apple green paintwork adding some colour to the murky scene. The last example was withdrawn in 1964 but two (Nos 69005 and 69023) became departmental locos Nos 58 and 59 respectively, used to de-ice wagons and points. No 58 was withdrawn in 1967 and scrapped, while No 59 was sold for preservation in 1966. One of the British Railways batch built in 1951, it is owned by the North Eastern Locomotive Preservation Group and is currently being overhauled at Darlington.

Specification

Builders	Darlington Works (78)
	Armstrong Whitworth & Co (25)
	Doncaster Works (10)
Wheel arrangement	0-6-0T
Build dates	1898–1951
BR power classification	2F
Cylinders	2 inside
Driving wheels	4 ft 1¼ in
Tractive effort	16,760 lbs
Boiler pressure	140 psi
Number built	113
BR numbering	68670–68754, 69001–69028 (as in summer 1961, many already withdrawn from the first sequence)

Ex-NER Class 'J72' 0-6-0T No 68677 on shunting duties at York on 21 July 1958. Built at Darlington Works in 1900, this loco was withdrawn from York shed (50A) in October 1961.

Wilson Worsdell

North Eastern Railway (1890–1910)

The younger brother of Thomas Worsdell (see page 54), Wilson Worsdell was born in Crewe in 1850 and followed in his brother's footsteps as an apprentice at the LNWR's Crewe Works before he moved to the USA where he worked as an engineer for the Pennsylvania Railroad until 1871. After a further period at Crewe Works, Wilson was appointed Assistant Locomotive Superintendent of the North Eastern Railway in 1883 before taking over from his brother as Locomotive Superintendent in 1890.

Wilson Worsdell's time at the NER was marked by his introduction of 27 different classes of locomotive including the powerful 'V' Class (later Class 'C6') 4-4-2 'Atlantics', and 'S' and 'S1' Class (later Class 'B13' and 'B14') 4-6-0s which gave such outstanding performances on Anglo-Scottish expresses between York and Newcastle. Another of his designs, the diminutive 'E1' Class (later Class 'J72') 0-6-0T introduced in 1898, was very long-lived, with some examples surviving as station pilot at Newcastle Central until 1964.

After a long and illustrious career at the NER, Wilson Worsdell retired in 1910 and died in 1920.

Painted in a cheerful apple green livery, ex-NER Class 'J72' 0-6-0T No 68723 goes about its job as station pilot at Newcastle Central station in 1961. Built by Armstrong Whitworth in 1922, this loco was withdrawn from Gateshead shed (52A) in September 1963.

1899 GWR '3300' Class ('Bulldog' and 'Bird' Classes) 4-4-0

The 'Bulldog' and 'Bird', or '3300', Class 4-4-0s were designed by William Dean (see page 53) for hauling passenger trains on the Great Western Railway. A total of 136 were built at Swindon between 1899 and 1910, plus another twenty which were rebuilt from the 'Duke' Class. The class were inside cylinder double-framed locomotives although initially there were variations to the boiler – up until 1903 most were built with parallel boilers, but from then on the class was fitted with GWR Standard No 2 tapered boilers. There were also variations to the frames, with the first 41 locomotives having curved frames and the rest having straight frames. Somewhat confusingly it was only in 1906 that the class became known as the 'Bulldog' Class, when the locomotive of that name, No 3312, was rebuilt with the same type of boiler. From 1906 to 1909 eighteen members of the 'Duke' Class were rebuilt as 'Bulldogs', when they were also fitted with the same No 2 tapered boiler.

As a move towards simplifying the haphazard GWR locomotive numbering system, all of the 'Bulldog' and 'Bird' Classes were collected together in the series 3300–3455 and became the '3300' Class in 1912 – until then this series had also contained members of four other classes. Naming of the class was complicated as it included names of Greek and Roman gods and mythical creatures, planets, politicians, high-ranking military, the King, West Country rivers, towns and cities served by the GWR, and countries of the British Empire. About half of the names were removed in 1930 while some of those locomotives later rebuilt as 'Earl' Class never received names. The names of towns and cities were also removed at this time as they caused confusion with passengers believing that was their destination.

Withdrawals of the 'Bulldog' Class (Nos 3300–3440) commenced in 1929 and continued during the 1930s and '40s. Thirty survived into British Railways' ownership in 1948 while the last two, No 3406 *Calcutta* and No 3377 *Penzance*, were withdrawn in January and March 1951 respectively.

All of the 'Bird' Class (Nos 3441–3455) survived into British Railways' ownership in 1948. Withdrawals commenced soon after and the last six were taken out of service in 1951.

Sadly, no members of the 'Bulldog' or 'Bird' Classes were preserved although the frames of preserved 'Earl' Class No 9017 *Earl of Berkeley* once belonged to 'Bulldog' Class No 3425.

GWR '3300'/'Bird' Class 4-4-0 No 3453 Seagull *hauling a passenger train on a single-track route somewhere in the West Country, circa 1920s. Built at Swindon in 1910, this loco was withdrawn from Reading shed (81D) in November 1951.*

GWR '3300'/'Bird' Class 4-4-0 No 3446 Goldfinch at Swindon shed in 1937. This elegant loco was
built at Swindon Works in 1909 and withdrawn from Worcester shed (85A) in December 1948.

Specification

Builder	Swindon Works
Wheel arrangement	4-4-0
Build dates	1899–1910
Cylinders	2 inside
Driving wheels	5 ft 8 in
Tractive effort	21,060 lbs
Boiler pressure	200 psi
Number built	121 ('Bulldog' Class), 15 ('Bird' Class), + 20 rebuilds
BR numbering	3335–3440 (with many gaps due to earlier withdrawals)

Built for express passenger work in southwest England, the London & South Western Railway's Class 'T9' 4-4-0s were nicknamed 'Greyhounds' for their speed – 80+ mph – and reliability. Designed by Dugald Drummond (see page 78), a total of 66 were built in eight batches between 1899 and 1901. Construction was shared between the LSWR's Nine Elms Works and the Glasgow locomotive builder Dübs & Co. The final batch was fitted as new with enlarged eight-wheel tenders as there were no water troughs on the LSWR – eventually all the 'T9s' were fitted with these.

Between 1912 and 1922 all of the class were fitted with superheaters, and by 1929 they had all received a stovepipe chimney, an increased cylinder bore and enlarged smokebox.

Popular with footplate crews, the 'T9s' were used on expresses on the LSWR main line from Waterloo to Exeter and Plymouth via Salisbury. All 66 Class 'T9s' survived through Southern Railway ownership into the British Railways era. The first withdrawals began in 1951, by which time the locomotives had been relegated to lighter duties on the so-called 'Withered Arm' network west of Exeter. Withdrawals continued at a slow pace until 1959, when ten of the class were retired, followed by one in 1960, twelve in 1961 and the final member, No 30120, in 1963. The latter locomotive was saved for preservation by the National Railway Museum and has since been active on the Mid-Hants Railway, Swanage Railway, Bluebell Railway and the Bodmin & Wenford Railway. It is currently at the Swanage Railway awaiting an overhaul.

Specification

Builders	Nine Elms Works (35)
	Dübs & Co (31)
Wheel arrangement	4-4-0
Build dates	1899–1901
BR power classification	3P
Cylinders	2 inside
Driving wheels	6 ft 7 in
Tractive effort	17,670 lbs
Boiler pressure	175 psi
Number built	66
BR numbering	random groups within 30XXX series

Ex-LSWR Class 'T9' 4-4-0 No 30707 at Bournemouth shed (71B) on 15 June 1960. Built by Dübs & Co in 1899, this 'Greyhound' was withdrawn from Bournemouth shed in March 1961.

Preserved ex-LSWR Class 'T9' 4-4-0 No 30120 hauls a demonstration goods train on the Bodmin & Wenford Railway in Cornwall, 10 October 2012.

Two preserved ex-LSWR stalwarts of the 19th century are seen here at Norchard on the Dean Forest Railway on 6 July 2016. On the left is Class '0298' 2-4-0WT (see page 42) No 30587 while on the right is Class 'T9' 4-4-0 (see page 90) No 30120.

Nicknamed 'Claud Hamilton', two similar classes of inside-cylinder 4-4-0 express passenger locomotives were designed by James Holden for the Great Eastern Railway (GER). These were GER Classes 'S46' and 'D56' (LNER Classes 'D14' and 'D15'). Also included in the 'Claud Hamilton' family were the later Class 'H88' (LNER Class 'D16') 4-4-0s which were designed by Stephen Holden's successor at Stratford Works, Alfred Hill. These were nicknamed 'Super Clauds' as they were fitted with a superheater, larger boiler and a Belpaire firebox.

This family of locomotive classes got their nickname from the prototype, Class 'S46' ('D14') No 1900 *Claud Hamilton* which emerged from Stratford Works in 1900 and which was named after the then chairman of the GER. This handsome loco was exhibited at the Paris Exposition of that year with a livery of GER blue with red lining and connecting rods, a polished steel smokebox door and a copper-capped chimney. Unusually, all of the locomotives of this class were originally built as oil-burners, with the fuel being supplied as a by-product from the GER's gasworks. They had all been converted to coal-burning by 1911.

Forty-one of the Class 'S46' were built at Stratford Works between 1900 and 1903, 70 of the improved Class 'D56' between 1903 and 1911 and ten of the Class 'H88' 'Super Clauds' in 1923. There were also many variations within these three classes both by the GER and its successor the London & North Eastern Railway – the latter classified them as Classes 'D14', 'D15', 'D15/1', 'D15/2', 'D16', 'D16/1', 'D16/2' and 'D16/3', the last of these being later rebuilds by Nigel Gresley for the LNER.

The 'Claud Hamiltons' performed beyond expectations on the Great Eastern Main Line between Liverpool Street and Norwich. They held sway on that route until gradually displaced by Stephen Holden's larger and more powerful Class 'S69' (LNER 'B12') 4-6-0s which were introduced in 1911 (see page 114).

From 1923 two of the new 'Super Clauds' were kept in tip-top condition specifically for hauling the royal train between Wolferton (for Sandringham) and King's Cross. They carried the LNER livery of apple green with polished connecting rods.

By the 1940s these locos had been relegated to more mundane duties. Withdrawals of the 'Claud Hamiltons' started in 1945, with the last four examples being taken out of service in 1960. None were saved for preservation but a new-build replica of Class 'D16/2' No 8783 *Phoenix* is currently under construction at Whitwell & Reepham Station in Norfolk.

James Holden

Great Eastern Railway (1885–1907)

James Holden was born in Whitstable in 1837 and went on to an apprenticeship under his uncle, Edward Fletcher, who was then Locomotive Superintendent of the North Eastern Railway. In 1865 Holden moved to the Great Western Railway where he first became Superintendent of the GWR workshops in Chester before becoming Chief Assistant to William Dean (see page 53) at Swindon. After twenty years at the GWR he was appointed Locomotive Superintendent of the Great Eastern Railway at its Stratford Works.

During his 23 years at Stratford, Holden modernised the locomotive works, introduced the standardisation of locomotive parts and designed and introduced over twenty different classes of locomotive. Probably the most famous of these are the 'Claud Hamilton' 4-4-0s, introduced in 1900, which were the mainstay of express motive power out of Liverpool Street until the 1930s, the Class 'T19' 2-4-0s, the 'S56' Class 0-6-0Ts (LNER Class 'J69') and Class 'G58' (LNER Class 'J17') 0-6-0, which both remained in service for nearly 60 years, and the unique Class 'A55' 0-10-0 'Decapod'. Introduced in 1902, the loco was built to prove the rapid acceleration of steam locos on suburban services in response to a

Ex-LNER 'Claud Hamilton' 4-4-0 No 62613 at Ipswich station south end on 12 July 1959. Built at Stratford Works in 1923, this locomotive was withdrawn from March shed (31B) in October 1960.

proposed new electric railway. Although in tests it exceeded all expectations, the loco remained a one-off and was converted to a 0-8-0 tender engine in 1906.

The increasing cost of coal led Holden to experiment with an oil-burning locomotive as early as 1893. Known as 'Petrolea', the converted Class 'T19' 2-4-0 was the first of over a hundred oil-burners subsequently built for the GER.

The paternalistic Holden held sway at Stratford Works until 1907 when his son, Stephen (see page 114), took over the post. James Holden died in 1925.

Specification

Builder	Stratford Works
Wheel arrangement	4-4-0
Build dates	1900–1923
BR power classification	3P/1F
Cylinders	2 inside
Driving wheels	7 ft 0 in
Tractive effort	17,095 lbs
Boiler pressure	180 psi
Number built	121
BR numbering	62500–62620 (11 withdrawn before receiving their BR number)

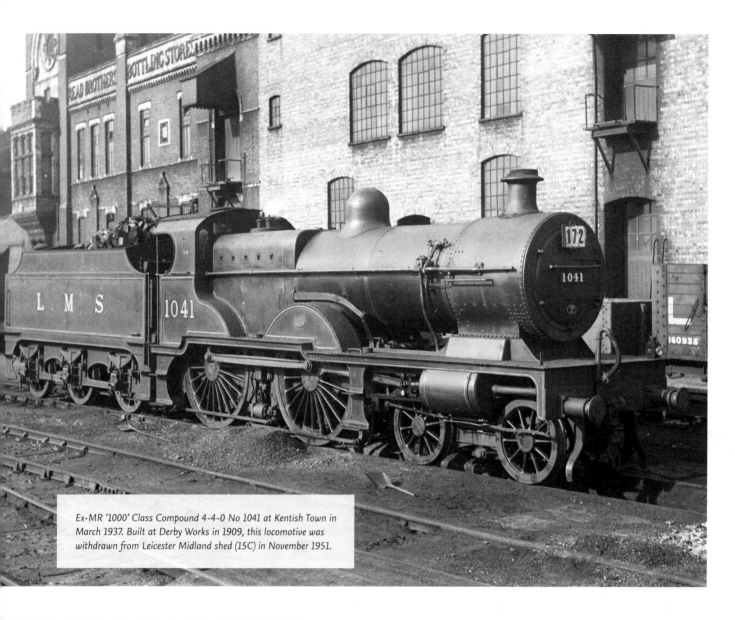

Ex-MR '1000' Class Compound 4-4-0 No 1041 at Kentish Town in March 1937. Built at Derby Works in 1909, this locomotive was withdrawn from Leicester Midland shed (15C) in November 1951.

Richard Mountford Deeley

Midland Railway (1904–1909)

Richard Deeley was born in Chester in 1855 and started his apprenticeship at the Midland Railway's Derby Works in 1875. Under the watchful eye of the MR's Locomotive Superintendent, Samuel Johnson (see page 45), Deeley slowly worked his way up the promotion ladder at Derby: Head of Testing Department in 1890; Inspector of Boilers, Engines & Machines in 1893; Works Manager in 1902; and Chief Electrical Engineer and Assistant Locomotive Superintendent in 1903. Johnson finally retired at the

beginning of 1904 and Deeley was then promoted to Locomotive Superintendent of the Midland Railway.

During his six years in this post Deeley patented an improved valve gear and further developed the compound steam engine as originally developed by the Scottish engineer, Walter Smith. The result was the highly successful class of three-cylinder Midland Compound 4-4-0 locomotives and the rebuilt Johnson-designed 4-4-0s. Sadly, Deeley hit the proverbial buffer stop when the Midland management refused to allow the building of larger engines and he resigned in 1909. Deeley continued to work as an engineer and by the time of his death in 1944 had fifteen patents to his name.

MR '1000' Class Compound 4-4-0

Designed by Samuel Johnson (see page 45) for the Midland Railway in 1902, the first five 3-cylinder '1000' Class Compound 4-4-0s were highly successful express passenger locomotives. Johnson's successor, Richard Deeley, then modified and simplified the design – 30 of these were built at Derby between 1905 and 1907 and a further ten in 1908–1909. Seen all over the Midland Railway's mainline network, including the demanding Settle–Carlisle Line, they often had to be double-headed when hauling heavy passenger trains, a result of the MR's short-sighted 'small engine' policy. The original Johnson locos were rebuilt as Deeley compounds with superheating from 1914 to 1919. The rest of the class was superheated from 1919 onwards.

As a result of their success, the MR's successor, the London Midland & Scottish Railway, built a further 195 of the Class '1000' Compound between 1924 and 1932 – some were built at Derby while others came from Horwich Works, North British Locomotive Company and Vulcan Foundry. They were virtually identical to the Midland Railway's locos except that they had smaller (6 ft 9 in) driving wheels and were superheated as built with a lower boiler pressure (200 psi).

Poor maintenance during World War II led to the original locomotives' downfall, with the first eight being withdrawn in 1948, followed by five in 1949, four in 1950, seventeen in 1951, ten in 1952 and the final one in 1953. No 41000 (1000) was withdrawn in 1951 and has been preserved. It is currently on static display at Barrow Hill Roundhouse.

Built in 1902, preserved ex-MR '1000' Class Compound 4-4-0 No 1000 waits to depart from Gloucester Eastgate on 27 May 1961 with a Gloucestershire Railway Society special to Derby Works.

The last of the class was No 41025 of my local Gloucester Barnwood shed (85E). I have a record in my first trainspotting notebook of a later Fowler Compound No 41078 (built in 1924) seen at Gloucester Eastgate in 1958 shortly before it was withdrawn from Saltley shed (21A) at the end of August that year.

Nearly three years later, on 27 May 1961, I was up bright and early, ready for a wonderful trip behind restored Midland Railway compound 4-4-0 No 1000. Organised by the Gloucestershire Railway Society, we first travelled from Gloucester Eastgate to Derby via Ashchurch, Evesham, Redditch, King's Norton and Castle Bromwich. After a visit to Derby Works we went on to Loughborough for a visit to Brush Traction where I was lucky enough to have a cab ride in the brand new D5800 along the test line within the site – this loco (31270) is now preserved on Peak Rail. We then travelled back on a circuitous route via Oakham, Corby, Wellingborough and Northampton, then on the Stratford-upon-Avon & Midland Junction Railway route from Blisworth to Stratford-upon-Avon, before finally returning to Gloucester via Honeybourne and Cheltenham. What a great day!

Specification

Builder	Derby Works
Wheel arrangement	4-4-0
Build dates	1902–1909
Cylinders	3 (2 outside low pressure, 1 inside high pressure)
Driving wheels	7 ft 0 in
Tractive effort	21,840 lbs
Boiler pressure	220 psi
Number built	45
BR numbering	41000–41044

GWR '2900' ('Saint') Class 4-6-0

G.J. Churchward's '2900' or 'Saint' Class 4-6-0s were highly successful two-cylinder passenger locomotives introduced by the GWR in 1902. Their final design set revolutionary standards for all future 4-6-0 types in Britain and remained in service until the last examples were withdrawn in 1953.

Before the mass production at Swindon Works of the '2900' Class, Churchward built three prototypes, each one with design differences. Heavily influenced by American and French boiler design the first, No 100, was built in 1902 initially with a parallel boiler with a pressure of 200 psi, before being rebuilt in 1910 with a superheated tapered boiler. It was later renumbered 2900 and named *William Dean*.

The second prototype, No 98, was built in 1903 with design differences including a tapered boiler, shorter wheelbase and modified valve gear. It was reboiled in 1906 with an increased pressure of 225 psi. It was named *Ernest Cunard* in 1907, finally received a superheated boiler in 1911, and was renumbered 2998 in 1913.

The third prototype, No 171, was also built in 1903 with a 225 psi boiler. The following year it was named *Albion* and converted to 4-4-2 to compare performance with the French de Glehn 4-4-2 Compound, but reverted back to a 4-6-0 in 1907. It received a superheated boiler in 1910 and was renumbered 2971 in 1912.

Incorporating the best design elements from the three prototypes, the main production run at Swindon began in 1905 and continued until 1913. However, there were four main variations to be found in what became generally known as the '2900' or 'Saint' Class:

- Nineteen further locomotives of a similar design to prototype No 171 were ordered at Swindon in 1905, some named after characters in Sir Walter Scott's novels (for example, *Ivanhoe*) and others named after GWR directors (for example, *Viscount Churchill*). Thirteen of these were built as 4-4-2s but converted to 4-6-0s in 1913. These locomotives were renumbered 2972–2990 in 1912.
- Named after historical, poetical and mythological ladies (for example, *Lady Macbeth*), the 'Ladies' sub-class of ten locomotives had individual differences, especially with the boiler and smokebox length, and were later fitted with No 3 superheaters.
- Named after Saints (for example, *Saint Catherine*), this sub-class of twenty locomotives had improvements to their appearance under the cab and above the cylinders. No 2925 *Saint Martin* was rebuilt with 6-ft driving wheels in 1924 as the prototype 'Hall' Class 4-6-0, designed by Charles Collett (see page 138).
- Built between 1911 and 1913, the last sub-class of 25 locomotives were the 'Courts' (e.g. *Taplow Court*).

The '2900' Class were excellent performers, hauling express passenger trains on the GWR network until they began to be displaced by the new and more powerful 'Castle' Class 4-6-0s (see page 139) from 1923 onwards. From then on, the '2900' Class began to be used for humbler duties hauling stopping passenger trains, although their usefulness as a mixed-traffic locomotive was impaired by the 6-ft-8½-in driving wheels. The later 'Hall' Class 4-6-0s with smaller driving wheels ticked all those boxes!

Withdrawals were spread over many years with the first four being taken out of service in 1931 and the last four in 1953. No example was saved for preservation. However, a new-build '2900' Class, No 2999 *Lady of Legend*, was completed in 2019 by the Great Western Society using parts from the withdrawn 'Hall' Class No 4942 *Maindy Hall*.

Specification

Builders	Swindon Works (77 + 22 rebuilds)
	Didcot Railway Centre (1 new build)
Wheel arrangement	4-6-0
Build dates	1902–1913, 2019
BR power classification	4P
Cylinders	2 outside
Driving wheels	6 ft 8½ in
Tractive effort	20,530–24,395 lbs
Boiler pressure	225 psi
Number built	77 + 22 rebuilds
	+ 1 new build
GWR/BR numbering	2900–2998, 2999

Completed in 2019, new-build GWR 'Saint' Class 4-6-0 No 2999 Lady of Legend is seen here at its birthplace, Didcot, on 13 September 2020.

George Jackson Churchward

Great Western Railway (1902–1922)

Born in 1857 in Stoke Gabriel, South Devon, George Jackson Churchward not only excelled at mathematics at school but he developed a love for the countryside which he retained for the rest of his life. At the age of 16 he was apprenticed at the South Devon Railway's (SDR's) locomotive works at Newton Abbot where he trained as an engineer under the railway's Locomotive Superintendent, John Wright. The SDR was absorbed by the Great Western Railway in 1876 and Churchward was transferred to the company's drawing office at Swindon Works. Within a year, William Dean (see page 53) had taken over from Joseph Armstrong (see page 32) as the GWR's Locomotive Superintendent and in 1881 Churchward was promoted as Assistant Manager in the Carriage & Wagon Works, before becoming Manager in 1885.

Churchward continued his meteoric rise when he was promoted to Locomotive Works Manager in 1895 and Principal Assistant to Dean in 1897, the same year that he was also elected as Mayor of Swindon. By this date, Dean's health was failing and Churchward increasingly took over his responsibilities until 1902, when Dean retired and Churchward was promoted to the exalted position of Locomotive, Carriage & Wagon Superintendent. During his tenure at Swindon, Churchward made great strides in reducing both construction and maintenance costs and introduced standardisation of parts on a hitherto undreamed-of scale. Using proven French and American practices, such as tapered boilers, he designed nine standard locomotive classes in the years between 1903 and 1911. In 1908 Churchward's driving force led to the building of the famous 'A' shop at Swindon Works – covering 5 acres, it could produce 70 new locomotives and overhaul 600 each year.

Churchward's locomotive designs included the inside-cylinder 'City' Class 4-4-0s (see page 102), of which, in 1903, No 3440 *City of Truro* became the first steam locomotive to (allegedly) achieve 100 mph. His legacy at Swindon was enormous, with his powerful four-cylinder 'Star' Class 4-6-0s (see page 106), introduced in 1907, being the forerunner of the later 'Castle' Class (see page 106) locomotives designed by his successor Charles Collett (see page 138). Churchward's one failure was his unique No 111 *The Great Bear* which, when built in 1908, was the first locomotive in Britain with the 4-6-2 'Pacific' wheel arrangement. It was not a great success as its weight limited it to operating only between London and Bristol. Succeeded by Charles Collett, Churchward retired in 1922 but was sadly killed in 1933 by one of Collett's 'Castle' Class locomotives while inspecting track near his home in Swindon.

1903 GWR '2800' Class / 1938 '2884' Class 2-8-0

Designed by G. J. Churchward (see page 99), the '2800' Class 2-8-0s were a two-cylinder heavy freight locomotive introduced by the GWR in 1903. Although primarily built to haul coal trains from South Wales, they were also the principal heavy freight locomotives on main lines all over the GWR network. They fulfilled their purpose with great success, with the majority remaining in service until the 1960s.

Before mass production of the '2800' Class commenced in 1905, Churchward built a prototype, originally numbered 97, which was extensively trialled after it emerged from Swindon Works in 1903. Following modifications to the boiler (and later superheating), an increase in boiler pressure and consequently increased tractive effort, the construction of the remaining 83 locomotives started in 1905 and was completed by 1919. No 97 was renumbered 2800, the first of its class.

Fast forward to 1938 and Churchward's successor at Swindon, Charles Collett (see page 138), ordered a further 83 of these locos. Known as the '2884' Class,

they differed from the original class in that they had cab side windows and external steam pipes. Due to a severe coal shortage at the end of World War II, examples of both classes were converted to oil-burning. However, this experiment was considered a failure due to the high cost of oil, and ended in 1947.

Specification

Builder	Swindon Works
Wheel arrangement	2-8-0
Build dates	1903, 1905–1919 ('2800' Class) / 1938–1942 ('2884' Class)
BR power classification	8F
Cylinders	2 outside
Driving wheels	4 ft 7½ in
Tractive effort	35,380 lbs
Boiler pressure	225 psi
Number built	84 ('2880' Class) / 83 ('2884' Class)
GWR/BR numbering	2800–2883 ('2800' Class) / 2884–2899, 3800–3866 ('2884' Class)

Withdrawals of the '2800' Class started in 1958 and continued until 1965 when the last member, No 2876, was retired. Six of this class have been since been preserved.

Withdrawal of the '2884' Class started in 1962, when No 3827 was retired, and continued until 1965 when the last 34 members were sent for scrap. Miraculously, nine examples of this class were sold to Dai Woodham's scrapyard in Barry, where they spent many years rusting in the sea air before being bought for preservation. Six have since been preserved.

Both classes were a common sight in my hometown of Gloucester in the early 1960s, hauling heavy goods and mineral trains between South Wales and the Midlands through the central roads of Gloucester Central Station. My last sighting of a '2800' Class in action was on 5 September 1964 when I spotted No 2822 in steam at Taunton shed (83B). My last ever sighting of the '2884' Class in action was on 7 July 1965 when No 3808 passed through Gloucester Central hauling three withdrawn '2251' Class locos bound for Birds scrapyard in Bynea.

Pioneer ex-GWR '2884' Class 2-8-0 No 2884 in ex-works condition outside Swindon Works in 1961. Built at Swindon Works in 1938, this locomotive was withdrawn from Pontypool Road shed (86G) in April 1964.

1903 GWR '3700' ('City') Class 4-4-0

Before the '3700' Class or 'City' Class 4-4-0s went into production at Swindon Works, G. J. Churchward (see page 99) rebuilt an existing 'Atbara' Class 4-4-0 (No 3405 *Mauritius*, built 1901) with a Belpaire firebox and a new tapered boiler – this prototype subsequently became the GWR's Standard No 4 boiler. Based on this prototype, the production run of ten new 'City' Class 4-4-0s was completed in 1903. Originally numbered 3433–3442, they were built to haul passenger expresses on the GWR main line and were named after cities served by the company. Between 1907 and 1908 a further nine of the 'Atbara' Class, numbered 3400–3404 and 3406–3409, were rebuilt as 'Cities' with tapered boilers. All of the enlarged class were fitted with superheaters by 1912. By this time the class had been renumbered 3700–3719.

By the 1920s the 'City' Class had been superseded by more powerful 4-6-0s, such as the 'Saints' and 'Stars'. Withdrawals started in 1927, with the last, No 3712 *City of Bristol*, being taken out of service in 1931.

However, there is one star of the 'City' show! No 3440 (later 3717) *City of Truro* was not only the 2,000th locomotive to be built at Swindon Works but it was also, allegedly, the first steam locomotive to travel in excess of 100 mph when it was descending Wellington Bank in Somerset while hauling the 'Ocean Mail' train from Plymouth to Paddington on 9 May 1904. A speed of 102.3 mph was recorded but the accuracy of this has been in question ever since.

Because of its historical importance, *City of Truro* was preserved for the nation when withdrawn in 1931, and exhibited at the LNER's Railway Museum in York. It was brought out of retirement and returned to service in 1957, hauling enthusiasts' specials and normal passenger services, especially on the Didcot, Newbury and Southampton line, until being withdrawn again in 1962. It is now a static exhibit at STEAM – Museum of the Great Western Railway in Swindon.

Specification

Builder	Swindon Works
Wheel arrangement	4-4-0
Build dates	1902–1909
Cylinders	2 inside
Driving wheels	6 ft 8½ in
Tractive effort	17,790 lbs
Boiler pressure	200 psi
Number built	10 (+ 10 rebuilds)
GWR/BR numbering	3700–3719

Preserved ex-GWR '3700' Class 4-4-0 City of Truro has been restored to working order several times. It is seen here at Falsgrave on the outskirts of Scarborough with the 'Scarborough Spa Express' to York.

Swindon Works

The decision to build at Swindon in the fork between the Swindon to Gloucester and Swindon to Bristol main lines was made in 1840 by 24-year-old Daniel Gooch, the first Superintendent for Locomotive Engines of the GWR. Opened in 1843, Swindon Works transformed what was then just a rural village to a large railway town – within 60 years it had grown into a company-built town of 50,000 inhabitants, a quarter of whom were directly employed by the GWR. Under the GWR's famous locomotive superintendents – Daniel Gooch, Joseph Armstrong, William Dean, G. J. Churchward, C. B. Collett and F. W. Hawksworth – the Works turned out firstly such broad-gauge giants as the single-wheeler 2-2-2 and 4-2-2 express locos followed by the famous standard-gauge 'City' and 'County' Class 4-4-0s, 'Star', 'Castle' and 'King' Class 4-6-0s. At its peak in the 1930s, it employed around 14,000 people.

Following nationalisation in 1948, Swindon turned its hand to building many of the BR Standard Class locos including 45 Class '3' 2-6-2 tanks, 80 Class '4' 4-6-0s, twenty Class '3' 2-6-0s and 53 Class '9F' 2-10-0s, including the last steam loco to be built for BR, No 92220 *Evening Star*, which emerged in Brunswick Green livery in March 1960. The ill-thought-out 'Modernisation Plan' of 1955 brought more work for Swindon including the building of 'Warship' Class, 'Western' Class and the short-lived Type 1/Class 14 diesel-hydraulics. The more successful Class '03' 0-6-0 diesel shunters and diesel multiple units – including some of the Intercity, Cross-Country and Trans-Pennine units – followed. Although building of diesel locomotives ended in 1965, they continued to be repaired along with carriage and wagon work until March 1986 when the Works closed.

Today, STEAM – Museum of the Great Western Railway is housed in one of the listed buildings in the former Works, and English Heritage have their headquarters in another. A large retail outfit is located in other buildings.

Built at Swindon Works in 1903, GWR '3700' Class 4-4-0 No 3715 City of Hereford *is seen here just before withdrawal in October 1929.*

SE&CR 'H' Class 0-4-4T

The highly successful Class 'H' 0-4-4Ts were built to haul suburban passenger trains in southeast London on the South Eastern & Chatham Railway (SE&CR). This class was Harry Wainwright's more powerful development of the 'R1' Class 0-4-4T, which in itself was a development of William Kirtley's 'R' Class 0-4-4Ts introduced in 1891.

Seven locomotives of the 'H' Class were built at Ashford Works in 1904 and proved so successful that a further 57 had been built there by 1909. When Richard Maunsell (see page 148) took over as Chief Mechanical Engineer of the SE&CR in 1913 he discovered that the separate components for a further two locomotives of this class had been made but not put together – these two were built at Ashford in 1915. The impressive 'H' Class boiler design was later used as a replacement for seven other types of locomotive.

The 'H' Class continued with their suburban passenger duties in southeast London until these lines were electrified in the mid-1920s. They were then equipped for push-pull working and transferred to Kent and Sussex where they worked on branch line and stopping train services. Although two examples were withdrawn during World War II, the remaining 64 locomotives all passed to British Railways on nationalisation in 1948. Withdrawals began in 1951 and continued through to 1964 when the last three, Nos 31263, 31518 and 31551, were retired. One example, No 31263, has been preserved and can be seen on the Bluebell Railway in East Sussex.

Specification

Builder	Ashford Works
Wheel arrangement	0-4-4T
Build dates	1904–1909 (64), 1915 (2)
BR power classification	1P
Cylinders	2 inside
Driving wheels	5 ft 6 in
Tractive effort	17,360 lbs
Boiler pressure	160 psi
Number built	66
BR numbering	randomly with prefix 31XXX

Built at Ashford Works in 1905, ex-SE&CR 'H' Class 0-4-4T No 31263 is seen here in May 1963. It was withdrawn from Three Bridges shed (75E) in January 1964 and has since been preserved at the Bluebell Railway.

Harry Smith Wainwright

South Eastern & Chatham Railway (1899–1913)

Harry Wainwright was born in Worcester in 1864 and followed in his father's footsteps when he was appointed Carriage & Wagon Superintendent at the Ashford Works of the South Eastern Railway (SER) in 1896. Three years later the SER joined the London, Chatham & Dover Railway to become the South Eastern & Chatham Railway and Wainwright was appointed Locomotive, Carriage & Wagon Superintendent of the new company. Initially he had to oversee existing locomotive orders placed by his predecessors but his first designs, built by outside contractors and at Ashford, started to appear in 1900. Many of these elegant Edwardian locos, such as Wainwright's 'C' Class 0-6-0, 'E' Class 4-4-0 (rebuilt by Richard Maunsell as Class 'E1'), 'H' Class 0-4-4T, 'L' Class 4-4-0 and 'P' Class 0-6-0T, saw service through to the BR era in the early 1960s. Wainwright retired in 1913 and died in 1925.

Ex-SE&CR 'H' Class 0-4-4T No 31306 with a local train at East Grinstead on 19 September 1961. Built at Ashford Works in 1906, this locomotive was withdrawn from Three Bridges shed (75E) at the end of 1961.

GWR '4000' ('Star') Class 4-6-0

Designed by G. J. Churchward (see page 99), the four-cylinder '4000' or 'Star' Class 4-6-0s were built to haul heavy passenger expresses on the GWR main line. After the successful trials of his prototype two-cylinder 'Saint' Class 4-6-0s (see page 98), Churchward went one step further by developing a more powerful four-cylinder class to haul the long-distance passenger expresses. To further this aim, the GWR imported three French four-cylinder 4-4-2 compound locomotives for comparison with Churchward's prototype four-cylinder locomotive, No 40 *North Star*. Built as a 4-4-2, it was completed at Swindon Works in 1906 before being converted to 4-6-0 three years later. In trials with the French locomotives, Churchward's prototype performed very well and an order for ten 4-6-0 production locos – Nos 4001–4010, the 'Star' series – was placed in 1907. Over the next sixteen years a further 62 locos, with various modifications, were ordered in six further lots:

- Nos 4011–4020 named after knights
- Nos 4021–4030 named after kings
- Nos 4031–4040 named after queens
- Nos 4041–4045 named after princes
- Nos 4046–4060 named after princesses
- Nos 4061–4072 named after abbeys.

The 'Star' Class were well received by footplate crew and maintenance staff alike. The locomotives admirably performed their duties, hauling long-distance express passenger trains until they were gradually displaced by newer and more powerful 'Castle' (see page 98) and 'King' (see page 156) Class 4-6-0s in the mid-1920s and '30s respectively.

Between 1925 and 1940 Charles Collett (see page 138), Churchward's successor, rebuilt fifteen 'Star' Class as 'Castle' Class locos. These included the prototype 'Star', No 4000 *North Star*. Apart from these, withdrawals of the remaining 'Star' Class began in 1932 and continued until 1957 when the last example, No 4058 *Princess Margaret*, was withdrawn. One member of this class has been preserved: No 4003 *Lode Star* (built 1907, withdrawn 1951) is a static exhibit currently at the National Railway Museum in York.

Built at Swindon Works in 1907, preserved ex-GWR 'Star' Class 4-6-0 No 4003 Lode Star arrives at York in 1992 prior to being placed on display at the National Railway Museum.

Specification

Builder	Swindon Works
Wheel arrangement	4-6-0
Build dates	1906–1923
BR power classification	5P
Cylinders	4 (2 outside, 2 inside)
Driving wheels	6 ft 8½ in
Tractive effort	25,909–27,800 lbs
Boiler pressure	225 psi
Number built	73
GWR/BR numbering	4000–4072

Built at Swindon Works in 1909, GWR 'Star' Class 4-6-0 No 4026 King Richard heads through Teignmouth in 1930 with a Paddington to Plymouth express. Originally named The Japanese Monarch, this locomotive was withdrawn in February 1950.

William Paton Reid

North British Railway (1903–1919)

William Reid was born in Glasgow in 1854 and started his long career with the North British Railway as an apprentice at Cowlairs Works in the city. He slowly rose through the ranks and was appointed Chief Mechanical Engineer on the retirement of Matthew Holmes (see page 61) in 1903, a position he held until 1919. He died in 1932.

During his seventeen years at Cowlairs, Reid rebuilt many of Holmes' designs, introducing superheating for the first time on the NBR, as well as designing twelve new classes of locomotive. Although Reid favoured the 4-4-0 wheel arrangement for most of his express passenger locomotives, he also designed one class of the 4-4-2 'Atlantic' type, which saw service on the East Coast Main Line north of Edinburgh and on the Waverley route to Carlisle. Most famous of his 4-4-0s are the Class 'D29'/'Scott' Class and the 'D34'/'Glen' Class (see page 120), some members of which survived on the West Highland Line until 1961. On the freight side, his most successful 0-6-0 was without doubt the Class 'J37' (see page 125), introduced in 1914, which saw service through to the end of steam haulage in Scotland in 1967.

Built at Cowlairs Works in 1914, ex-NBR 'D30' Class 4-4-0 No 62418 The Pirate at Thornton Junction shed (62A) in 1959, just prior to withdrawal in August of that year.

1909 NBR 'J' ('Scott') Class (LNER 'D29'/'D30' Class) 4-4-0

William Reid's 'J' or 'Scott' Class (LNER Class 'D29') mixed-traffic 4-4-0s were a development of his Class 'K' 4-4-0s, which were successfully employed on fish trains from Aberdeen and Mallaig. The 'Scott' Class was virtually identical except for being fitted with larger driving wheels and a larger tender for working non-stop on the Northern British Railway's service between Edinburgh and Carlisle. Six were built in 1909 by the North British Locomotive Company and a further ten at Cowlairs Works. At the same time, two additional locomotives received superheaters and were known as 'Superheated Scotts'. These two prototypes were followed by a further 25 that were built at Cowlairs between 1914 and 1920 – they were later classified by the LNER as 'D30'. By 1936 all of the 'D29s' had also received superheaters.

Both the 'D29' and 'D30' locos were given names of characters associated with Sir Walter Scott's novels. Initially they were employed hauling express passenger trains on the NBR main lines radiating out from Edinburgh Waverley: to Carlisle via the Waverley Route, Glasgow Queen Street, Dundee, Perth and Aberdeen. By the 1930s they had been replaced by new Gresley Class 'D49' 4-4-0s and were relegated to hauling stopping passenger trains until displaced by the new Thompson Class 'B1' 4-6-0s that started appearing in the 1940s.

Withdrawals of the 'D29s' started in 1946, with the last examples, Nos 62410 *Ivanhoe* and 62411 *Lady of Avenel*, being taken out of service in 1952. Most of the 'D30s' lasted longer, with the last examples – Nos 62421 *Laird o' Monkbarns* and 62426 *Cuddie Headrigg* – being withdrawn in 1960. None of the two classes survived into preservation.

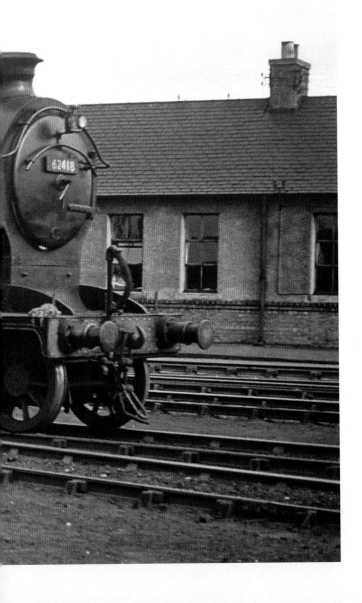

Specification

Builders	North British Locomotive Company (6 Class 'D29') / Cowlairs Works (10 Class 'D29', 27 Class 'D30')
Wheel arrangement	4-4-0
Build dates	1909–1911 (Class 'D29') / 1914–1920 (Class 'D30')
BR power classification	3P
Cylinders	2 inside
Driving wheels	6 ft 6 in
Tractive effort	19,434 lbs (Class 'D29') / 18,700 lbs (Class 'D30')
Boiler pressure	190 psi (Class 'D29') / 165 psi (Class 'D30')
Number built	43
BR numbering	62400-62442

LB&SCR Marsh Class 'H2' 4-4-2

On being appointed Locomotive Superintendent for the London, Brighton & South Coast Railway at Brighton Works in 1905, Douglas Marsh very quickly realised that there was an urgent need for more powerful passenger express locomotives. With experience previously gained under H. A. Ivatt (see page 81) at Doncaster Works, where the Great Northern Railway 'Klondyke' Class 4-4-2 'Atlantics' (see page 83) had proved to be very successful, Marsh set about designing a similar class of locomotive for the LB&SCR.

Five of the LB&SCR Class 'H1' 4-4-2s were built by Kitson & Company of Leeds between 1905 and 1906 and they proved to be very successful when hauling the London Victoria to Brighton Pullman expresses – the 'Brighton Limited' and 'The Southern Belle'.

A further six 4-4-2s were built at Brighton Works between 1911 and 1912. Designated Class 'H2', these locomotives were superheated and had a lower boiler pressure than the 'H1'. Sharing the London to Brighton expresses with the Class 'H1', they were also an immediate success. Both classes received names of south coast headlands and other geographical features – for example, *North Foreland, Beachy Head* – in the mid-1920s. At the same time, they were slowly displaced on the London–Brighton expresses by Class 'N15' 'King Arthur' 4-6-0s and 'River' Class 2-6-4 tanks. Despite this, the 'H1' and 'H2' 4-4-2s were kept busy on boat trains until the outbreak of World War II.

In 1938 the new Chief Mechanical Engineer of the Southern Railway, Oliver Bulleid (see page 191), increased the boiler pressure of the 'H2' Class from 170 psi to 200 psi, matching that of the older 'H1' Class. With boat trains suspended during the war both classes became redundant and most were moved into storage. The first withdrawals of the Class 'H1' came in 1944 and by July 1951 the class was extinct. The Class 'H2' survived longer but all had been withdrawn by April 1958 when the last survivor, No 32424 *Beachy Head*, was finally retired. While no examples were saved for preservation, a replica 'H2' is currently under construction at the Bluebell Railway in East Sussex.

Specification

Builder	Brighton Works
Wheel arrangement	4-4-2
Build dates	1911–1912
BR power classification	4P
Cylinders	2 outside
Driving wheels	6 ft 7½ in
Tractive effort	20,840 lbs (increased to 24,518 lbs in 1938)
Boiler pressure	170 psi (increased to 200 psi in 1938)
Number built	6
BR numbering	32421–32426

Ex-LB&SCR Class 'H2' 4-4-2 No 32421 South Foreland at Bournemouth Central on 30 June 1955. Built at Brighton Works in 1911, this fine locomotive was withdrawn from Brighton shed (75A) in August 1956.

Douglas Earle Marsh

London, Brighton & South Coast Railway (1905–1911)

Douglas Marsh was born in Aylsham, Norfolk, in 1862 and began his apprenticeship with the Great Western Railway at Swindon, rising to Assistant Works Manager by 1888. In 1896, he was appointed Chief Assistant Mechanical Engineer for the Great Northern Railway at Doncaster, where he worked under H. A. Ivatt (see page 81). He left in 1904 to join the London, Brighton & South Coast Railway as Locomotive Superintendent at Brighton Works.

During his period at Brighton, Marsh introduced the Class 'H1' and 'H2' 4-4-2 express locomotives, no doubt with experience gained by working under Ivatt at Doncaster. The locomotives were soon employed hauling the crack LB&SCR Pullman trains and were later rebuilt with superheaters by Richard Maunsell (see page 148). The last member of this class was withdrawn in 1958. Marsh also designed a series of 4-4-2T and 4-6-2T along with a class of 0-6-0 goods engines, and he rebuilt a whole series of Stroudley and Billinton locos of which the most famous are the diminutive 'Terrier' Class 'A1X' 0-6-0s (see page 39) which remained in service on the Hayling Island branch until 1963. Marsh retired from the LB&SCR in 1911 and died in 1933.

Ex-LB&SCR Class 'H2' 4-4-2 No 32424 Beachy Head at the head of a Pullman train at Brighton station on 5 October 1952. Built at Brighton Works in 1911, this locomotive was the last of its class to be withdrawn, in April 1958.

John George Robinson

Great Central Railway (1900–1922)

John Robinson was born in Bristol in 1856 and served an apprenticeship with the Great Western Railway at Swindon between 1872 and 1878. In that year he went to work for his father, a Locomotive Superintendent in Bristol, before joining the Waterford & Limerick Railway as Locomotive Superintendent in 1884. A prolific locomotive designer, Robinson produced twelve classes of loco for the Irish company over the next six years, some of them remaining in service on Córas Iompair Éireann (CIÉ) until 1959.

In 1900, Robinson moved back to England where he joined the Great Central Railway (GCR) as Locomotive Superintendent at Gorton Works, near Manchester. Two years later he was appointed Chief Mechanical Engineer of the GCR, a post he held until the company became part of the newly formed LNER in 1923.

Robinson was not only a prolific locomotive designer, producing 28 different classes for the GCR, but also a prolific inventor with 45 patents to his name. Most notable of his locomotive types are: his 4-4-0 'Directors' – later Class 'D10'/'D11' (see page 132) – of which 45 were built, the majority staying in service until 1960; the six massive 0-8-4T shunting engines for Wath Marshalling Yard; and the 2-8-0 heavy goods locos (LNER Class 'O4') which were chosen as the standard freight engine by the Railway Operating Department (ROD) during World War I – over 500 of these were built, many of them seeing service overseas during both world wars. Robinson retired at the end of 1922 and died in 1943.

Nearing the end of its life, ex-GCR Class 'O4' 2-8-0 No 63665 in a very work-worn condition at Retford shed (36E) on 4 May 1963. Built in 1918, this locomotive was withdrawn at the end of 1963.

1911 GCR Class '8K' (LNER Class 'O4') 2-8-0

Designed by John Robinson for the Great Central Railway, the Class '8K' 2-8-0 heavy freight locomotive was a development of the earlier Class '8A' 0-8-0. The '8K' was introduced in 1911 in anticipation of increased mineral traffic to and from the railway's enormous new docks at Immingham. The locomotives were highly successful, being of a sturdy and simple design with good steam-raising and reliability qualities. During World War I the design was chosen as the standard heavy freight locomotive for the Railway Operating Division (ROD) of the Royal Engineers. A total of 521 locomotives were built by the North British Locomotive Company, Robert Stephenson & Co, Kitson & Co, Nasmyth, Wilson & Co and by the GCR's Gorton Works. Over 300 of these locomotives were shipped to France for service during the war. Returning to Britain in 1919–1920, most of the ROD 2-8-0s were subsequently sold, to the Great Central Railway (3), Great Western Railway (100), London & North Western Railway (30), London & North Eastern Railway (273) and the London Midland & Scottish Railway (75).

Other ROD 2-8-0s eventually ended up in China, Australia, Egypt, Palestine, Syria and Iraq.

In 1922, nineteen more Class '8K' locomotives with larger boilers were built at Gorton and were subsequently classified by the GCR as Class '8M'.

Formed in 1923, the London & North Eastern Railway classified the GCR Class '8K' locos as Class 'O4'. The '8M' were classified as Class 'O5' – these were all rebuilt as 'O4' after World War II. In total, the pre-war LNER 'O4' fleet numbered 421 locomotives, although 92 of these were requisitioned in 1941 by the War Department for war service in the Middle East – none ever made it back home. Subsequently, 58 were rebuilt as Thompson Class 'O1' 2-8-0s between 1944 and 1949. On nationalisation in 1948 a total of 329 Class 'O4s' passed to the new British Railways and the vast majority were kept busy hauling heavy freight and mineral trains well into the 1960s. Although withdrawals started at the end of 1958, the last examples were kept in revenue-earning service around Doncaster and Scunthorpe until April 1966.

One example of a GCR Class '8K', No 63601, is preserved on the Great Central Railway. There are three ROD versions preserved in Australia.

Ex-GCR Class 'O4' 2-8-0 No 63848 is seen here at Gorton Works on 13 July 1957. Built in 1919, this locomotive was withdrawn in November 1962.

On 12 August 1965 I recorded No 63613 in my notebook while on a trainspotting trip at Doncaster, and later No 63586 between Scunthorpe and Grimsby. While on a trip to Colwick shed (40E) on 7 September that year I recorded Nos 63734 and 63807 – we didn't get far here as we were chased out by the shed foreman. Later on the same day I also spotted No 63646, 63590 and 63913 at Staveley GC (41H).

Specification

Builders	Gorton Works (56) North British Locomotive Company (50) Kitson & Co (20)
Wheel arrangement	2-8-0
Build dates	1911–1919
BR power classification	7F
Cylinders	2 outside
Driving wheels	4 ft 8 in
Tractive effort	31,325 lbs
Boiler pressure	180 psi
Number built	126 (+ 521 ROD 2-8-0 and 19 Class '8M')
BR numbering	63570–63920

GER Class 'S69' (LNER Class 'B12') 4-6-0

By 1911, the Great Eastern Railway's 'Claud Hamilton' 4-4-0s (see page 94) were struggling with the increasingly heavier loads of the express passenger trains on the GER main line between Liverpool Street and Norwich. Designed by Stephen Holden,

Specification

Builders	Stratford Works (51)
	William Beardmore & Co (20)
	Beyer, Peacock & Co (10)
Wheel arrangement	4-6-0
Build dates	1911–1921 (71), 1928 (10)
BR power classification	4P/3F
Cylinders	2 inside
Driving wheels	6ft 6 in
Tractive effort	21,969 lbs
Boiler pressure	180 psi
Number built	81
BR numbering	61500–61580 (due to withdrawals, 14 did not receive BR numbers)

the Class 'S69' (LNER 'B12') 4-6-0s were the answer to this motive power problem. However, due to the short turntables and restricted axle loadings on the GER at that time, the overall length of each locomotive had to be restricted. Fifty-one locomotives were built at Stratford Works in East London and a further twenty at William Beardmore & Co of Glasgow between 1911 and 1921. With their increased power, the 'B12s' were well received by footplate crew on the GER main line. After the 'Big Four Grouping' in 1923 the GER's successor, the London & North Eastern Railway, ordered a further ten locomotives from Beyer, Peacock & Co of Manchester in 1928. Later modifications made by the LNER to the Class 'B12', such as larger boilers, led to them being reclassified as Class 'B12/1', 'B12/2', 'B12/3' and 'B12/4'.

During the LNER era the 'B12s' were not just restricted to former GER routes – their low axle loading made them very suitable for other weight-restricted company lines, and between 1931 and 1942, 25 'B12s' were transferred to work on former Great North of Scotland Railway routes in northeast Scotland.

Apart from No 1506 which was withdrawn in 1913 after an accident, withdrawals started in 1945 and continued until 1961 when the last 'B12', No 61572, was retired. Since then this locomotive has been preserved and restored to its former glory on the North Norfolk Railway.

Stephen Dewar Holden

Great Eastern Railway (1908–1912)

The third son of James Holden (see page 94), Stephen Holden was born at Saltney, Cheshire, in 1870 and joined the Great Eastern Railway as an apprentice at Stratford Works in 1886, one year after his father had been appointed as Locomotive Superintendent. Here, Stephen worked his way up the GER corporate ladder, first working as a draughtsman in the drawing office followed by promotion to inspector in the motive power department. In 1892 he was promoted to Suburban District Locomotive Superintendent, in 1894 to District Locomotive Superintendent at Ipswich, in 1897 as Divisional

Locomotive Superintendent then to Assistant Locomotive Superintendent before succeeding his father as Locomotive Superintendent in 1908. In this position he continued his father's work and introduced nine further classes of steam locomotives of which by far the most notable was the Class 'S69' 4-6-0 (LNER Class 'B12') – over 80 of these fine locomotives were eventually built and gave sterling service during the LNER era, not only in East Anglia but also in the Aberdeen area where they remained in service for British Railways until 1954.

Stephen Holden retired from the GER in 1912 and predeceased his father when he died in 1918 at the young age of 48.

Ex-LNER Class 'B12' 4-6-0 No 61577 waits to depart from Kings Lynn with the Locomotive Club of Great Britain 'Eastern Counties Limited' railtour on 12 July 1959. Built by Beyer, Peacock & Co in 1928, this locomotive was withdrawn from Cambridge shed (31A) in September 1959.

Preserved ex-LNER Class 'B12' 4-6-0 No 61572 (disguised as No 61574) in steam at Barrow Hill Roundhouse in Staveley on 13 July 2001. Built by Beyer, Peacock & Co in 1928, this locomotive was withdrawn from Norwich Thorpe shed (32A) in September 1961 before being restored.

1912 LNWR Class 'G1' 0-8-0

Designed by Charles Bowen-Cooke for the London & North Western Railway, the Class 'G1' 0-8-0 heavy freight locomotives were a development of George Whale's Class 'G' 0-8-0s that were introduced in 1910. The first of the latter class was rebuilt with superheating to Class 'G1' in 1912. This prototype was followed by 170 new locomotives built between 1912 and 1918. A further 278 locomotives were rebuilt to this new specification from older Classes 'B', 'C', 'D', 'E', 'F' and 'G' locomotives between 1917 and 1934. The 'G1' Class were nicknamed 'Super Ds'.

Twenty-six of the class were acquired by the Railway Operating Division (ROD) of the Royal Engineers and shipped for war service in France during World War I – they all returned safely to Britain after the war. A total of 98 'G1' locomotives passed into the new British Railways in 1948. Withdrawals started in the 1940s and by the early 1950s all had been retired. No examples of Class 'G1' locos were saved for preservation although a very similar Class 'G2', No 49395 (the first of its class) – which I spotted in Crewe Works in August 1962 – is now part of the National Collection and currently resides at Locomotion, the railway museum in Shildon, County Durham.

Specification

Builder	Crewe Works
Wheel arrangement	0-8-0
Build dates	1912–1918
BR power classification	6F
Cylinders	2 inside
Driving wheels	4 ft 5½ in
Tractive effort	25,640 lbs
Boiler pressure	160 psi
Number built	171 (+ 278 rebuilds)
BR numbering	48892–49384 (not continuous as some are Class 'G2A' locos)

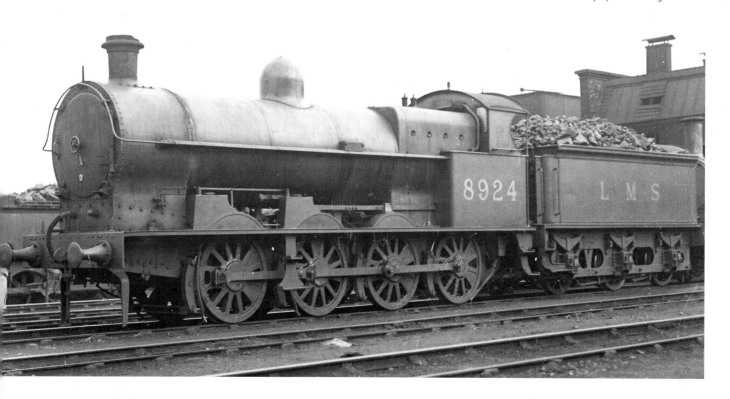

Ex-LNWR Class 'G1' 0-8-0 No 8924, circa 1946. Built at Crewe Works, this locomotive was withdrawn from Nuneaton shed (2B) at the end of 1948.

Charles John Bowen-Cooke

London & North Western Railway (1909–1920)

Charles Bowen-Cooke was born in Huntingdon in 1859 and started his apprenticeship at the London & North Western Railway's Crewe Works in 1875 under the Chief Mechanical Engineer (CME), Francis Webb (see page 46). Primarily employed in the motive power department, Bowen-Cooke worked his way up the corporate ladder at Crewe to become Chief Mechanical Engineer in 1909. While CME he developed the use of superheating and was responsible for the design and construction of several express locomotive classes including 90 of the 'George the Fifth' Class 4-4-0s, 130 of the 'Claughton' Class 4-6-0s (see page 118) and the heavy freight 'G1' Class 0-8-0s. Bowen-Cooke died in office in 1920.

Although a Class 'G2', the preserved ex-LNWR Class 0-8-0 No 49395 is very similar in appearance to a 'G1'. It is seen here emerging from Cheddleton Tunnel on the Churnet Valley Railway on 28 February 2008.

LNWR 'Claughton' Class 4-6-0

The four-cylinder 'Claughton' 4-6-0s were a class of express passenger locomotive built at Crewe Works between 1913 and 1921, designed by Charles Bowen-Cooke (see page 117) for the London & North Western Railway. Initially their numbering and naming was totally haphazard but the LNWR's successor, the London Midland & Scottish Railway, eventually renumbered the class from 5900 to 6029. The first of the class was named *Sir Gilbert Claughton*, and other names of businessmen, politicians and directors of the LNWR followed. However, not all locos were named in this way, and others were named after a seemingly random mix of holders of the Victoria Cross (for example, *Private E. Sykes*, *Private W. Wood*), Royal Navy warships (for example, *Illustrious*) and historical figures (*Lady Godiva*), while *Patriot* was named in memory of the LNWR employees who fell during World War I. Many of these names were later transferred to Fowler's new 'Patriot' Class 4-6-0s introduced in 1930 (see page 167).

From 1927, the 'Claughtons' were increasingly displaced from West Coast Main Line duties by the new and more powerful Fowler 'Royal Scot' 4-6-0s (see page 152). Many were then transferred to the Midland Division and relegated to secondary passenger work and freight trains.

In 1928, twenty 'Claughtons' were rebuilt by the LMS with larger boilers, and ten of these were also fitted with Caprotti valve gear. Withdrawals began in November 1930 when No 5902 *Sir Frank Ree* was retired, and by 1937 all but four had been taken out of service. No 6017 *Breadalbane* was withdrawn in 1940, No 5946 *Duke of Connaught* and No 6023 *Sir Charles Cust* in 1941, leaving just No 6004 (formerly *Princess Louise*) as the sole representative of the class. This loco just managed to scrape into the newly nationalised British Railways in 1948 but was withdrawn in April 1949, never to carry its new BR number of 46004. No examples have been preserved.

Specification

Builder	Crewe Works
Wheel arrangement	4-6-0
Build dates	1913–1921
Cylinders	4 (2 outside, 2 inside)
Driving wheels	6 ft 9 in
Tractive effort	27,072 lbs (LMS rebuilds: 29,570 lbs)
Boiler pressure	175 psi (LMS rebuilds: 200 psi)
Number built	130
BR numbering	46004 (withdrawn before number could be applied)

Ex-LNWR 'Claughton' Class 4-6-0 No 5964 Patriot *poses at Hasland shed (18C) in Chesterfield in August 1931. Built at Crewe Works in 1920, this locomotive was withdrawn in July 1934.*

A down express from Euston passes Camden locomotive shed, hauled by an ex-LNWR 'Claughton' Class 4-6-0, circa 1930.

NBR Class 'K' ('Glen') (LNER Class 'D34') 4-4-0

Introduced in 1913, William Reid's (see page 108) final development of the North British Railway's Class 'K' 4-4-0 was later classified by the LNER as Class 'D34'. The Class 'K' had originally been introduced by Reid's predecessor, Matthew Holmes (see page 61), in 1902. These twelve locomotives, later classified by the LNER as Class 'D26', were built with 6-ft-6-in driving wheels for express passenger work. Two more batches (1906–1907 and 1909–1910) of twelve locomotives each were built with 6-ft-0-in driving wheels for mixed traffic work – they were later classified as LNER Classes 'D32' and 'D33'. The final two batches (ten in 1913 and 22 between 1917 and 1920) of locomotives also had 6-ft driving wheels and were fitted with superheaters.

This ultimate development of the 'K' Class was classified by the LNER as Class 'D34', and all locomotives were named after Scottish glens. Despite the need for double-heading, they were successfully employed hauling passenger and fish trains on the West Highland Line between Glasgow, Fort William and Mallaig, as well as on stopping train services between Edinburgh and Dundee, and on the Waverley Route to Hawick.

The 'Glens' were replaced on the West Highland Line by Class 'K2' and 'K4' 2-6-0s and the two 'V4' 2-6-2s, and on other routes by Class 'B1' 4-6-0s. Withdrawals started in 1946, with the last-but-one examples, No 62484 *Glen Lyon* and 62496 *Glen Loy*, being retired in November 1961. No 62469 (NBR No 256) *Glen Douglas* was officially withdrawn in December 1962 but was preserved by the Scottish Railway Preservation Society and is currently on static display at the Riverside Museum in Glasgow.

I have a record in my trainspotting notebook of No 256 being inside Eastfield shed (65A) on 29 March 1964 but by 5 August it was at Dawsholm shed (65D).

Specification

Builder	Cowlairs Works
Wheel arrangement	4-4-0
Build dates	1913 (10), 1917–1920 (20)
BR power classification	3P
Cylinders	2 inside
Driving wheels	6 ft 0 in
Tractive effort	20,260 lbs
Boiler pressure	165 psi
Number built	32
BR numbering	62467–62498

Preserved ex-NBR 'Glen' Class 4-4-0 No 256 Glen Douglas double-heads ex-NBR Class 'J37' No 64632 while hauling 'The Jacobite' enthusiasts' special at Garelochead on 1 June 1963.

Cowlairs Works

Located in Springburn, Glasgow, Cowlairs Works was built in 1841 for the Edinburgh & Glasgow Railway, before going on to become the main locomotive and carriage and wagon works for the North British Railway. The first locomotives built at the Works were two powerful 0-6-0 banking engines for use on the nearby Cowlairs Incline out of Queen Street station. Under the watchful eye of Chief Mechanical Engineers such as Dugald Drummond, Matthew Holmes and William Reid, Cowlairs

Works turned out some classic steam locomotives culminating in Reid's famous 'Glen' Class (LNER Class 'D34') 4-4-0s which remained in service on the West Highland Line through to the BR era.

Like nearby St Rollox, the Works produced Horsa gliders and parts for Rolls-Royce Merlin engines during World War II. Locomotive construction had ended following the 'Big Four Grouping' of 1923 although locomotive, carriage and wagon repair work continued through the LNER era until 1948. The Works closed in 1968 and the site is now an industrial estate.

NER Class 'T2' (LNER Class 'Q6') 0-8-0

Designed by Vincent Raven for the North Eastern Railway, the Class 'T2' (LNER Class 'Q6') 0-8-0s were highly successful heavy freight locomotives that survived until the end of steam haulage in northeast England in 1967. They were a development of Wilson Worsdell's (see page 87) Class 'Q5' 0-8-0s that were introduced in 1913. Fitted with superheaters, the 'Q6' specialised in hauling coal trains from the numerous collieries that then existed in the northeast of England. Eight examples were temporarily converted to oil-burning during a period of national coal shortage in 1947.

All survived to pass into the nationalised British Railways in 1948. Withdrawals began in 1963, with the last examples being retired at the end of steam haulage on the North Eastern Region in 1967. One 'Q6' has been preserved: No 63395 was purchased by the North Eastern Locomotive Preservation Group from a scrapyard in 1968 and then restored. This group still owns the locomotive today and it has spent more time in their ownership than its collective time in revenue-earning service with NER/LNER/BR. It is currently based on the North Yorkshire Moors Railway.

Specification

Builders	Darlington Works (70)
	Armstrong Whitworth & Co (50)
Wheel arrangement	0-8-0
Build dates	1913–1921
BR power classification	6F
Cylinders	2 outside
Driving wheels	4 ft 7½ in
Tractive effort	28,800 lbs
Boiler pressure	180 psi
Number built	120
BR numbering	63340–63459

Preserved ex-NER Class 'Q6' 0-8-0 No 63395 at Grosmont shed on the North Yorkshire Moors Railway, 2 August 2022. Built at Darlington Works in 1918, this locomotive was withdrawn from Sunderland shed (52G) in September 1967 before being bought for preservation.

Vincent Litchfield Raven

North Eastern Railway (1910–1922)

Vincent Raven was born in Great Fransham, Norfolk, in 1859. He started his railway career as an apprentice with the North Eastern Railway in 1877 and by 1893 had become Assistant Mechanical Engineer to Wilson Worsdell (see page 87). Raven was promoted to Chief Mechanical Engineer when Worsdell retired in 1910 and, despite being an early advocate of mainline electrification, went on to design nine classes of steam locomotives for the NER, many of which survived into the 1960s.

Favouring three-cylinder designs, Raven introduced his Class 'Z' 4-4-2 ('Atlantic') in 1911 and they were soon putting in fine performances on East Coast Main Line expresses between York and Newcastle. Heavy freight trains, in particular coal and iron ore, were the life-blood of the NER and Raven designed two superb 0-8-0 classes, later to be classified 'Q6' and 'Q7', numbering 135 locos. Some members of the 'Q6' class remained in service until the end of steam haulage in the northeast in 1967. Similarly successful were his Class 'S3' 4-6-0s (later Class 'B16') and Class 'E1' 0-6-0TS (later Class 'J72' – see page 86). Although the latter were introduced in 1914, British Railways later went on to build 29 more between 1949 and 1951. Raven's final design was the '2400' Class 4-6-2 (later Class 'A2'), of which five were built between 1922 and 1924. Raven was knighted for his services during World War I in 1917. He retired in 1922 and died in 1934.

Darlington Works

In northeast England the LNER inherited the former North Eastern Railway's locomotive works at Darlington, which had originally been opened by the Stockton & Darlington Railway in 1863. Under the watchful eye of the NER's Chief Mechanical Engineer, Vincent Raven, the Works built many classic and long-lived steam locomotives in the early 20th century such as 50 of the Class 'E1' (LNER Class 'J72') 0-6-0Ts, 70 of the Class 'T2' (LNER Class 'Q6') 0-8-0s and fifteen of the Class 'T3' (LNER Class 'Q7') 0-8-0s.

Under LNER management the Works continued building steam locomotives, including Gresley's unique 'Hush-Hush' Class 'W1' 4-6-4 in 1929 as well as 93 of the Class 'K3' 2-6-0s and six of the Class 'K4' 2-6-0s. Following nationalisation in 1948, when the Works employed nearly 4,000 people, Darlington went on to build a further 28 of the Class 'J72' 0-6-0Ts, 23 of the Peppercorn Class 'A1' 4-6-2s and several types of BR standard locos including 65 of the Standard Class '2' 2-6-0s and ten of the Standard Class '2' 2-6-2Ts. No 84029 of that class was the last new loco built at Darlington, emerging from the workshops on 11 June 1957. From 1953 to closure in 1966, Darlington built examples of Class '08', '11', '24' and '25' diesels for BR.

Ex-NBR Class 'J37' 0-6-0 No 64537 is seen here at Polmont shed (65K) on 16 September 1962.
Built in 1914, this locomotive was withdrawn from Grangemouth shed (65F) in June 1964.

'The Jacobite' enthusiasts' special on the West Highland Line at Corpach, Fort William,
1 June 1963. The train was double-headed by ex-NBR Class 'J37' 0-6-0s Nos 64592 and 64636.

NBR Classes 'B' and 'S' (LNER Class 'J37') 0-6-0

William Reid's (see page 108) Class 'B' and Class 'S' (LNER Class 'J37') were his final development of the North British Railway's 0-6-0 heavy freight locomotive. They were the most successful and powerful of the Scottish 0-6-0 goods locomotives. Basically, the Class 'J37' was a superheated version of his earlier Class 'J35' which, in turn, was a development of Matthew Holmes' (see page 61) numerous Class 'J36'. Twenty locomotives were built at Cowlairs in 1914–1915 followed by 34 at the North British Locomotive Works. A further 50 were built by both builders between 1918 and 1921, bringing the total to 104. Initially the boiler pressure was 165 psi but this was increased to 175 psi in 1919 and to 180 psi in 1923.

The long-lived Class 'J37s' were used to good effect hauling heavy long-distance goods and mineral trains across the North British Railway's network. Half were allocated to Edinburgh St Margaret's and Glasgow Eastfield engine sheds. They all survived into the newly nationalised British Railways in 1948 and were a common sight hauling coal trains in Fife. During the summer months they could be seen hauling local passenger trains. On two trainspotting trips to Scotland in 1964 I recorded seeing many working examples at Eastfield,

Bathgate, Dunfermline, Thornton and St Margarets sheds. Again, in August 1966, I spotted seven survivors at Thornton shed just before they were withdrawn.

While withdrawals started in 1959, most 'J37s' survived until the early 1960s, with the final retirements taking place in 1966. Sadly no example was saved for preservation.

Specification

Builders	Cowlairs Works (35)
	North British Locomotive
	Company (69)
Wheel arrangement	0-6-0
Build dates	1914–1921
BR power classification	5F
Cylinders	2 inside
Driving wheels	5 ft 0 in
Tractive effort	25,210 lbs
Boiler pressure	180 psi
Number built	104
BR numbering	64536–64639

Ex-NBR Class 'J37' 0-6-0 No 64632 under the coaling plant at Glasgow Eastfield shed (65A) on 29 March 1964.

SE&CR 'L' Class 4-4-0

Designed by Harry Wainwright (see page 105) for the South Eastern & Chatham Railway, the 'L' Class 4-4-0s were built to haul heavy express passenger trains on the company's main lines between London Victoria and Dover, Hastings and Ramsgate. Unfortunately, Wainwright was removed from his post and replaced by Richard Maunsell (see page 148) just before his new 'L' Class could be ordered. As the company's Ashford Works was unable to fulfill this order it was placed with Beyer, Peacock & Co of Manchester (twelve locomotives) and, unusually, with Borsig of Berlin (ten locomotives). The latter were delivered just prior to the outbreak of World War I.

The 'L' Class performed well on their duties but increasingly heavier trains saw them replaced first by Richard Maunsell's more powerful 'L1' Class

(introduced in 1926), then by Robert Urie's 'King Arthur' Class 4-6-0s (see page 130) and, in the 1930s, by Maunsell's 'Schools' Class 4-4-0s (see page 168).

The more powerful 'L1' Class 4-4-0s were Richard Maunsell's development of Wainwright's 'L' Class. Fifteen of the locos were built by the North British Locomotive Company for the newly formed Southern Railway in 1926.

By then relegated to stopping passenger services, withdrawal of the 'L' Class started in 1956 when No 31761 was retired, and continued until the end of 1961 when the last two, Nos 31768 and 31771, were taken out of service. No examples of this class were saved for preservation.

Ex-SE&CR 'L' Class 4-4-0 No 31770 on a local train at Tonbridge, early 1958. Built by Beyer, Peacock & Co in 1914, this locomotive was withdrawn from Nine Elms shed (70A) in November 1959.

Ex-SE&CR 'L' Class 4-4-0 No 31768 heads an enthusiasts' special at Four Marks near Alton on 18 September 1960. Built by Beyer, Peacock & Co in 1914, this locomotive was withdrawn from Nine Elms shed (70A) at the end of 1961.

Specification

Builders	Beyer, Peacock & Co (12)
	Borsig (Berlin) (10)
Wheel arrangement	4-4-0
Build date	1914
BR power classification	3P
Cylinders	2 inside
Driving wheels	6 ft 8 in
Tractive effort	18,575 lbs (later increased to 18,908 lbs)
Boiler pressure	160 psi (later increased to 180 psi)
Number built	22
BR numbering	31760–31781

S&DJR Class '7F' 2-8-0

Since 1875 the Somerset & Dorset Joint Railway (S&DJR) had been jointly owned by the Midland Railway and the London & South Western Railway. The MR was in charge of locomotive policy on the steeply graded line where powerful motive power was non-existent, necessitating double-heading of coal and freight trains. To overcome this vexed shortcoming the S&DJR Class '7F' 2-8-0 was thus born.

Designed by James Clayton, Assistant Chief Locomotive Draughtsman (1907–1914) at the Midland Railway's Derby Works under Henry Fowler (see page 145), the locomotives used an existing boiler design from the MR's Compounds (see page 97), Walschaerts valve gear, Belpaire firebox and sloping, high-mounted cylinders. Also fitted with single-line tablet exchanging mechanism on both sides of the cab, the first six locomotives were built at Derby Works between February and August 1914. In service they immediately proved their worth, hauling heavy goods trains over the steeply graded section between Bath Green Park and Evercreech Junction. An order for a further five locomotives with larger boilers was placed with Robert Stephenson & Co in 1925 and these were delivered between July and August of that year.

The powerful Class '7Fs' were a complete success on the S&DJR and stayed there for their long working

Preserved ex-S&DJR Class '7F' 2-8-0 No 88 steams along the Severn Valley Railway at Hay Bridge during a visit on 22 March 2008. Built by Robert Stephenson & Co at Darlington in 1925, it was withdrawn as BR No 53808 from Bath Green Park shed in 1964. It then spent 9 years at Dai Woodham's scrapyard in Barry before being saved for preservation.

lives, occasionally visiting Derby for their overhauls – where I saw No 53807 in May 1961. During the busy summer months they were also pressed into service to haul the through trains full of holidaymakers heading for Bournemouth from the north of England.

Withdrawals started in 1959 when the first of the class, No 53800, was retired after 45 years of service. The 1914-built locos had all been withdrawn by 1962, when through passenger services on the S&DJR were withdrawn. By 1964 all the remaining 1925-built locos had also been retired. Two locos, Nos 53808 and 53809, had the good fortune to be sold to Dai Woodham's scrapyard in Barry after withdrawal, where they spent many years rusting in the sea air before being bought for preservation. Currently, No 53808 is operational on the Mid-Hants Railway and No 53809 on the North Norfolk Railway.

Preserved ex-S&DJR Class '7F' 2-8-0 No 88 (BR No 53808) approaches Blue Anchor station on the West Somerset Railway with a train for Bishops Lydeard.

As a trainspotting lad I often travelled over the S&DJR for our annual summer holidays. On 19 August 1961 I spotted Nos 53803 and 53806 hauling northbound trains between Bath and Poole. On the return trip two weeks later I recorded No 53810 hauling a southbound train between Bath and Evercreech Junction. I saw this same locomotive at Templecombe shed (82G) while returning from holiday on 10 August 1963, just five months before its withdrawal. My last sighting of a '7F' in action, No 53806, was on 9 September 1963 when I was at Midford. It was withdrawn just four months later. On 31 December that year I recorded No 53809 at Bristol Barrow Road shed (82E).

Specification

Builder	Derby Works (6)
	Robert Stephenson & Co (5)
Wheel arrangement	2-8-0
Build dates	1914 (6), 1925 (5)
BR power classification	7F
Cylinders	2 outside
Driving wheels	4 ft 7½ in
Tractive effort	35,295 lbs
Boiler pressure	190 psi
Number built	11
BR numbering	53800–53810

1918 LSWR 'N15' Class ('King Arthur') 4-6-0

Designed by Robert Urie for the London & South Western Railway (LSWR), the 'N15' or 'King Arthur' Class 4-6-0s were built to haul heavy express passenger trains on that company's main lines from Waterloo to Bournemouth and Exeter. The first batch of twenty locomotives was built by the LSWR at Eastleigh Works between 1918 and 1923 and were named after Arthurian characters. Urie retired in 1923 when the Southern Railway was formed and the new Chief Mechanical Engineer, Richard Maunsell (see page 148), then modified the design of the 'N15', of which a further 24 were built at Eastleigh between 1925 and 1927. So much was the demand for these powerful locomotives that a further batch of 30, known as 'Scotch Arthurs', was simultaneously built by the North British Locomotive Company in Glasgow between May and September 1925. By then they were also being used to haul heavy boat trains between London Victoria and Dover, expresses between Victoria and Brighton, and fast freight trains from London to Southampton Docks.

The 'N15s' were highly successful and could reach a speed of 90 mph while hauling heavy express passenger trains. From 1927 all members of the class were fitted with smoke deflectors and eventually paired with 5,000-gallon bogie tenders as the Southern Railway had no water troughs on any of its routes.

All 74 members of the class passed to British Railways on nationalisation in 1948. Withdrawals of the earlier Urie-designed 'N15s' started in 1953 with this sub-class becoming extinct by 1958. Their names were then transferred to twenty BR Standard Class '5' 4-6-0s (see page 218). Withdrawals of the later Eastleigh and NBR-built 'N15s' peaked in 1959 with the completion of the Kent Coast electrification, when seventeen were taken out of service, followed by nine in 1960, fourteen in 1961 and the final twelve in 1962. One example of this once extensive class was saved for preservation: No 30777 *Sir Lamiel* is now part of the National Collection.

Specification

Builders	Eastleigh Works (44)
	North British Locomotive
	Company (30)
Wheel arrangement	4-6-0
Build dates	1918–1927
BR power classification	5P
Cylinders	2 outside
Driving wheels	6 ft 7 in
Tractive effort	23,900–26,245 lbs
Boiler pressure	180–200 psi
Number built	74
BR numbering	30448-30457,
	30736-30755,
	30763-308006

Robert Wallace Urie

London & South Western Railway (1912–1922)

Robert Urie was born in Ayrshire in 1854 and after serving apprenticeships at several Scottish locomotive manufacturers, he went on to become Chief Draughtsman and then Works Manager at the Caledonian Railway's St Rollox Works. In 1897 he was appointed by Dugald Drummond (see page 78) as Works Manager at the London & South Western Railway's Nine Elms Works (see page 67), moving to the new works at Eastleigh (see page 137) in 1909. He was appointed Chief Mechanical Engineer of the LSWR following Drummond's death in 1912. Until his retirement in 1923, Urie had introduced three classes of powerful 4-6-0s for mainline work – his 'H15', 'N15' ('King Arthur' Class) and 'S15' (see page 136) all served through to the BR era in the early 1960s, as did his powerful 'G16' Class 4-8-0T and 'H16' 4-6-2T. Urie retired to his native Scotland in 1923 and died in 1937.

Although well outside my usual trainspotting area, I often saw the Southern Region's 'N15s' in action while on my holiday – I spotted No 30773 *Sir Lavaine* at Wareham on 23 August 1961, No 30768 *Sir Balin* at Bournemouth two days later, and No 30790 *Sir Villiars*, also at Bournemouth, five days after that – they were all 'Scotch Arthurs' built by the North British Locomotive Company. Reading South shed, a sub-shed of Guildford (70C), was also a good place to spot Southern Railway locomotives from passing Western Region (WR) trains while on the way to Paddington – I have a record of seeing 'N15' No 30777 *Sir Lamiel* there in April 1961.

Ex-SR Class 'N15' 4-6-0s Nos 30787 Sir Menadeuke and 30784 Sir Nerovens look very handsome in this photo taken at Eastleigh shed (71A) in April 1957. Both built by the North British Locomotive Company in 1925, they were withdrawn in February and October 1959 respectively.

1919 GCR Class '11F' ('Improved Directors') (LNER Class 'D11') 4-4-0

The Class '11F' (LNER Class 'D11') 4-4-0 express passenger locomotives were a development of John Robinson's (see page 112) earlier Class '11E' 4-4-0. Ten of the latter locos had been built at the Great Central Railway's Gorton Works in 1913 and had proved immediately successful, hauling express passenger trains on the railway's main lines, primarily the route between Sheffield and Marylebone. They were named after directors of the GCR and were thus nicknamed 'Directors'. British Railway's numbering was 62650–62659 and all had been withdrawn by 1955.

Introduced in 1919, Robinson's Class '11F' (LNER Class 'D11') carried on the good work. They were nicknamed 'Improved Directors' and were variously named after World War I battles, royalty and characters from Sir Walter Scott's novels. Their 6-ft-9-in-diameter driving wheels made them particularly fast locomotives although they were not suited for hauling goods trains. The batch built by the LNER in 1924 was classified as Class 'D11/2' as they had a reduced loading gauge for operating in Scotland. In later years the 'D11s' found employment hauling expresses on Cheshire Lines Committee's routes between Manchester Central and Liverpool Central.

Replaced by diesel multiple units on these routes, withdrawals started in September 1958 and continued through to early 1962 when the last example, No 62685 *Malcolm Graeme*, was retired. Fortunately, No 62660 *Butler-Henderson*, withdrawn in November 1960, was preserved and is now part of the National Collection. It currently resides at Barrow Hill Roundhouse as a static exhibit.

Ex-GCR Class 'D11' 4-4-0 No 5506 Butler-Henderson *waits to depart from Marylebone station with an express for Sheffield, circa 1935. Built at Gorton Works in 1919, this locomotive was withdrawn from Sheffield Darnall shed (41A) as BR No 62660 in November 1960 and has since been preserved.*

Specification

Builders	Gorton Works (11)
	Kitson & Co (12)
	Armstrong Whitworth & Co (12)
Wheel arrangement	4-4-0
Build dates	1919–1924
BR power classification	3P2F
Cylinders	2 inside
Driving wheels	6 ft 9 in
Tractive effort	19,645 lbs
Boiler pressure	180 psi
Number built	35
BR numbering	62660–62694

Ex-LNER Class 'D11/2' 4-4-0 No 2681 Captain Craigengelt at Eastfield shed in Glasgow, circa 1947.
Built for the LNER by Kitson & Co in 1924, this locomotive was withdrawn in July 1961.

With a gradient of just less than 1-in-38, the 2-mile-long Lickey Incline between Bromsgrove and Barnt Green in Worcestershire is the steepest mainline railway incline in Britain. Ever since it was opened in 1840 by the Midland Railway's predecessor, the Birmingham & Gloucester Railway, trains ascending it have required rear end assistance.

To overcome this problem, the unique and massive 'Lickey Banker' 0-10-0 locomotive was designed by James Anderson, acting Chief Mechanical Engineer (1915–1919) at the Midland Railway's Derby Works while Henry Fowler (see page 145) was otherwise engaged on war work. Nicknamed 'Big Bertha', the locomotive emerged from Derby Works in 1919 and, apart from overhauls, spent its whole working life banking trains up the incline.

Fitted with a large headlight on the top of the smokebox door, 'Big Bertha' was an ungainly looking machine, with the two large outside cylinders set at a high, sloping angle. These cylinders also supplied the two inside cylinders via cross-over steam ports. After 37 years of service, No 58100 was withdrawn in May 1956 and scrapped at Derby Works the following year.

'Big Bertha' was replaced by a BR Standard Class '9F' and various combinations of tank locomotives until being replaced by diesels. The unique Class 'U1' 2-8-0+0-8-2 Beyer Garratt articulated locomotive, with a tractive effort of an enormous 72,940 lbs and built by the LNER in 1925, was also trialled as a Lickey Banker on two occasions during the 1950s, but without success.

Specification

Builder	Derby Works
Wheel arrangement	0-10-0
Build date	1919
BR power classification	unclassified
Cylinders	4 (2 outside, 2 inside)
Driving wheels	4 ft 7½ in
Tractive effort	43,313 lbs
Boiler pressure	180 psi
Number built	1
BR numbering	58100

Unique ex-MR 'Lickey Banker' 0-10-0 No 58100 at its home shed of Bromsgrove (85D) just before withdrawal in 1956.

Built at Derby Works in 1919, the Midland Railway's 'Lickey Banker' was fitted with a large searchlight to aid it in banking duties up the Lickey Incline.

Designed by Robert Urie (see page 131) for the London & South Western Railway, the 'S15' Class 4-6-0s were built to haul heavy freight trains on that company's main lines from Feltham and Nine Elms to Portsmouth, Southampton, Bournemouth and Weymouth, and to Salisbury and Exeter. They were also often seen hauling overnight milk trains and stopping passenger trains on the Waterloo to Exeter main line. The locomotives had many similarities with Urie's 'N15' Class (see page 130), including a tapered boiler, Walschaerts valve gear and two cylinders.

My trainspotting notebook tells me that I saw my first 'S15', No 30508, at Bournemouth Central on 30 August 1961.
They were also a common sight at Axminster station when I was on holiday in August 1963, with my notebook recording Nos 30823, 30832 and 30841 on the 5th. I spotted No 30824 at Yeovil Town shed on 31 December of that year and No 30833 on a stopping passenger train from Waterloo at Basingstoke on 22 August 1964. My last sighting of an 'S15' in BR days was of No 30837 at Basingstoke on 10 September 1965.

The first batch of twenty Urie-designed locomotives was built at Eastleigh Works between 1920 and 1921. The second and third batches had modifications made by Urie's successor, Richard Maunsell (see page 148), which included a higher boiler pressure and subsequent higher tractive effort – fifteen were built at Eastleigh in 1927 and the final ten, also at Eastleigh, in 1936. The vast majority of these locomotives were paired with 5,000-gallon bogie tenders.

The 'S15' Class were highly successful heavy freight locomotives, popular with footplate crew and maintenance staff alike. Their versatility meant that they outlived Urie's Class 'N15s' by several years. Withdrawals began in 1962 when four were retired, followed by eighteen in 1963, seventeen in 1964 and the final six in 1965. Seven members of the class have been preserved, all of which were bought for restoration after spending many years rusting in the sea air at Dai Woodham's scrapyard in Barry. Two examples, Nos 30506 and 30825, are currently operational on the Mid-Hants Railway and the North Yorkshire Moors Railway respectively.

Specification

Builder	Eastleigh Works
Wheel arrangement	4-6-0
Build dates	1920–1921 (20), 1927 (15), 1936 (10)
BR power classification	6F
Cylinders	2 outside
Driving wheels	5 ft 7 in
Tractive effort	28,200 lbs (1921) / 29,860 lbs (1927, 1936)
Boiler pressure	175 psi (1921) / 200 psi (1927, 1936)
Number built	45
BR numbering	30496–30515, 30823–30847

Ex-SR 'S15' Class 4-6-0 No 30833 pauses at Basingstoke station with a local train from Waterloo, 22 August 1964. Built at Eastleigh Works in 1927, this locomotive was withdrawn from Feltham shed (70B) in May 1965.

Eastleigh Works

The London & South Western Railway (LSWR) had opened a carriage and wagon works at Eastleigh in 1891 and in the space of fifteen years the small village had grown into a railway town of 9,000 inhabitants. At the same time the LSWR had purchased 200 acres of land adjoining the existing works, where they opened a new locomotive works in 1910, transferring about 2,000 more men and their families from the old works at Nine Elms in London (see page 67).

Under successive Chief Mechanical Engineers – the LSWR's Dugald Drummond and Robert Urie and the SR's Richard Maunsell and Oliver Bulleid – Eastleigh turned out many outstanding classes of locomotives including the 'Schools' Class 4-4-0s, the 'King Arthur' and 'Lord Nelson' 4-6-0s and the innovative 'Merchant Navy' 4-6-2s. Following nationalisation in 1948 the Works turned its hand to rebuilding over 90 of Bulleid's air-smoothed 'Pacifics', built third-rail electric multiple units, and continued to repair and overhaul steam locomotives until 1967. Following privatisation of BR in the 1990s the Works has been used by a variety of private rail operators for overhauling preserved steam and diesel locomotives and the maintenance of electric rolling stock.

Preserved ex-LSWR Class 'S15' 4-6-0 No 506 makes a fine sight on the Severn Valley Railway on 21 April 2022.
Built at Eastleigh Works in 1920, this locomotive was withdrawn from Feltham shed (70B) in January 1964 before being bought for preservation.

Charles Benjamin Collett

Great Western Railway (1922–1941)

Charles Collett was born in London in 1871 and, after studying at London University, was apprenticed at a well-known firm of marine engine builders. In 1893 he joined the Great Western Railway at Swindon where he trained to become a draughtsman and slowly worked his way up the corporate ladder, becoming Manager of Swindon Works in 1912 and Deputy Chief Mechanical Engineer under George Jackson Churchward (see page 99) in 1919. Under Churchward, locomotive design at Swindon had made great strides with standardisation of components and proven ideas borrowed from French and American engineers that culminated in his elegant four-cylinder 'Star' Class 4-6-0s. Churchward retired in 1922 and Collett became Chief Mechanical Engineer at Swindon. During his tenure at Swindon, Collett further improved Churchward's standard designs with his first, the four-cylinder

'Castle' Class 4-6-0, being a development of the two-cylinder 'Star' Class but with a larger boiler, an increase in cylinder diameter and an increased grate area. First introduced in 1923, a total of 171 were built, with the last emerging from Swindon Works as late as 1950. They were a great success, especially with later modifications, and were regular performers on GWR and later BR (Western Region) expresses until the early 1960s.

Collett's 'King' Class 4-6-0s were introduced in 1927. An enlargement of the 'Castle' Class, they were the largest and most powerful express locomotives built by the GWR and at the time of their introduction were the most powerful 4-6-0s in Britain. Usually seen at the head of the GWR's heavy premier expresses such as the 'Cornish Riviera', they remained in service until 1962. Collett's other great success was the 'Hall' Class 4-6-0 which was a development of Churchward's 'Saint' Class. Between 1928 and 1943, 259 were built and they remained as the mixed traffic workhorse on the GWR and BR (Western Region) until 1965. Collett retired in 1941 and died in 1952.

Specification

Builder	Swindon Works
Wheel arrangement	4-6-0
Build dates	1923–1950
BR power classification	7P
Cylinders	4 (2 outside, 2 outside)
Driving wheels	6 ft 8½ in
Tractive effort	31,625 lbs
Boiler pressure	225 psi superheated
Number built	171 (15 rebuilt from 'Star' Class, 1 rebuilt from 4-6-2 No 111)
BR numbering	111, 4000, 4009, 4016, 4032, 4037, 4073–4099, 5000–5099, 7000–7037

One of the stars of 'The Bristolian' haulage, BR-built 'Castle' Class 4-6-0 No 7018 Drysllwyn Castle receives last-minute attention at Bristol Bath Road shed (82A) on 19 August 1956. Built at Swindon Works in 1949, this locomotive had recently been fitted with a double chimney. It was withdrawn from Old Oak Common shed (81A) in September 1963.

Western Region 'Castles' were a common sight for me as a lad living in Gloucester. My favourite local hero was No 5017 *The Gloucestershire Regiment 28th, 61st*, which I saw on a regular basis until its withdrawal from Horton Road shed (85B) in September 1962. On my way to school each morning I would see the 'Cheltenham Spa Express' (8.19 a.m. from Gloucester Central to Paddington) – regular performers were No 5042 *Winchester Castle* and No 5071 *Spitfire*. I also regularly saw 'The Cornishman' – the 11.20 a.m. departure from Gloucester Eastgate to Penzance behind a well-groomed Wolverhampton Stafford Road 'Castle' such as No 5045 *Earl of Dudley*. I would often see them receiving overhauls at Swindon Works or speeding through Swindon Station, their four-cylinder beat at speed was a very exciting spectacle for a young teenager! My final 'Castle' that I needed to underline in my Ian Allan 'Combined Volume' was No 4081 *Warwick Castle*, which I managed to see after travelling down to Carmarthen shed on 25 February 1963.

GWR Class '4073' ('Castle') 4-6-0

The first of the 'Castle' Class 4-6-0s, No 4073 *Caerphilly Castle*, emerged from Swindon Works in 1923. An instant success, by 1924 a total of ten had been built. They were designed by Charles Collett to haul the GWR's express passenger trains, and were a development of G. J. Churchward's 'Star' Class 4-6-0s (see page 106). Major changes included an extended frame, a new larger and lighter boiler, cabside windows and increased grate area.

The locomotives were put to work hauling the GWR's crack expresses. By 1950, after the GWR had become part of the nationalised British Railways, a total of 171 had either been built or were rebuilt from 'Star' Class locomotives. The rebuilds also included the unique 4-6-2 No 111 *The Great Bear*, which was then renamed *Viscount Churchill*.

During locomotive trials between the GWR and LNER in 1925, No 4079 *Pendennis Castle* put in a spectacular performance on the East Coast Main Line between King's Cross and Doncaster, outperforming the latter company's then most powerful locomotives,

the Gresley Class 'A1' (see page 158). The pre-war pinnacle of achievement by the GWR and its 'Castles' came in 1932 when 'The Cheltenham Flyer', hauled by No 5006 *Tregenna Castle*, covered the 77¼ miles from Swindon to Paddington at an average speed of just over 81 mph, from start to stop – this was a world record for a scheduled passenger train and earned it the title 'World's Fastest Train'.

However, the GWR's half-hearted attempt to streamline one of its 'Castles', No 5005 *Manorbier Castle*, in 1935 was not a success and the ill-thought-out fins and bulbous smoke box door were soon removed.

Although the majority of the class were named after English and Welsh Castles within the GWR sphere of operation, some were subsequently renamed after Earls, British Battle of Britain aircraft types, past and present GWR directors, a British army regiment that fought in the Korean War and a classical music composer. Rebuilds from 'Star' Class locomotives quite often kept their original names, for instance Nos 5083

to 5092 were named after abbeys. The last 'Castle' to be built, No 7037, was appropriately named *Swindon*.

The 'Castles' finest hour was yet to come and in 1947 certain members of the class were fitted with four-row superheaters, followed, in 1956, by the fitting of double chimneys. These modifications further improved their sustained high-speed performance. Thirty-five years after they were first introduced, the 'Castles' swan song came in 1958 when No 7018 *Drysllwyn Castle* reached 102 mph when hauling 'The Bristolian' from Bristol to Paddington – this electrifying non-stop run covered the 117½ miles in just under 94 minutes at an average speed of 75 mph.

However, with the introduction of diesel-hydraulic locomotives on the Western Region in the late 1950s, the 'Castles' days were numbered. While a few 'Star' rebuilds had already been withdrawn, the first original 'Castle' to be withdrawn was No 4091 *Dudley Castle* in 1959. There then followed a succession of withdrawals: seven in 1960, four in 1961, 54 in 1962, 49 in 1963, 36 in 1964 and the last twelve in 1965. My final sighting of a 'Castle' in BR days was on 27 November 1965 when the last survivor, No 7029 *Clun Castle*, hauled the last Western Region steam train to travel from Paddington to Cheltenham via Gloucester. Earmarked for preservation, this fine loco remained in active service at Gloucester Horton Road shed and as station pilot at Gloucester Central through December before being withdrawn. It was certainly the end of a glorious era.

Fortunately, eight members of the 'Castle' Class were saved from the cutter's torch, with some examples, after restoration, returning to the main line on special chartered trains:

- No 4073 *Caerphilly Castle*
- No 4079 *Pendennis Castle*
- No 5029 *Nunney Castle*
- No 5043 *Earl of Mount Edgcumbe*
- No 5051 *Earl Bathurst*
- No 5080 *Defiant*
- No 7029 *Clun Castle*.

Also preserved, No 7027 *Thornbury Castle* is unlikely to be restored as its boiler is being used for the new-build replica of a GWR '4700' Class 2-8-0.

Bereft of its front number plate, BR-built 'Castle' Class 4-6-0 No 7011 Banbury Castle of Worcester shed (85A) is manually turned on the turntable at Southall shed (81C) in 1964. Built at Swindon Works in 1948, this locomotive was withdrawn from Oxley shed (84B/2B) in February 1965.

Cheltenham Spa Express

London (Paddington) to Gloucester and Cheltenham Spa

The 'Cheltenham Spa Express' was introduced in 1923 and, for a short time in the 1930s, became the fastest train in the world. Nicknamed the 'Cheltenham Flyer', this high-speed service was brought to an end on the outbreak of war in 1939, never to return. However, the 'Cheltenham Spa Express' was revived in 1956 when the Western Region of British Railways gave the name to the 8 a.m. departure from Cheltenham (St James') and the 4.55 p.m. return service from Paddington. Unusually, the eight-coach restaurant car train was hauled between Cheltenham (St James') and Gloucester (Central) by a tank engine – these were normally '5101' Class 2-6-2Ts, but on occasions even '9400' Class 0-6-0PTs could be seen grappling with the load. The up train reversed direction at Gloucester (Central), with a Horton Road (85B) 'Castle' in charge for the 8.19 a.m. departure to Paddington. The immaculately groomed 'Castle' and the eight brown and cream coaches made a stirring sight for me on my way to school each morning. The up train arrived at Paddington at 10.35 a.m. while the down train departed at 4.55 p.m. and arrived back at Cheltenham (St James') at 7.35 p.m. On both up and down trains, the train ran non-stop between Kemble and Paddington.

By 1964 'Western' Class diesel-hydraulics were in charge and the loco headboard had disappeared. A new connection was laid in at Standish Junction which allowed trains to run via the ex-Midland Railway station of Gloucester (Eastgate) and to continue to Cheltenham Spa (Lansdown) without the need for reversing direction. The name was dropped in 1973 and Gloucester (Eastgate) was closed on 1 December 1975.

Ex-GWR 'Castle' Class 4-6-0 No 5094 Tretower Castle at Twyford, speeding towards Paddington with the 'Cheltenham Spa Express' on 3 May 1958. Built at Swindon Works in 1939, this locomotive was withdrawn in September 1962.

LMS Class '3F' ('Jinty') 0-6-0T

Designed by Henry Fowler for the London Midland & Scottish Railway, the Class '3F' 0-6-0 tank locomotives, nicknamed 'Jinty', were a development of his rebuilds of Samuel Johnson's Midland Railway '2441'

Specification

Builders	Vulcan Foundry (120)
	North British Locomotive Company (75)
	Hunslet Engine Company (90)
	W. G. Bagnall (32)
	William Beardmore & Co (90)
	Horwich Works (15)
Wheel arrangement	0-6-0T
Build dates	1924-1931
BR power classification	3F
Cylinders	2 inside
Driving wheels	4 ft 7 in
Tractive effort	20,835 lbs
Boiler pressure	160 psi
Number built	422
BR numbering	47260-47681

Class 0-6-0Ts that were originally introduced in 1899. The 'Jinty' was designed for short-haul goods trains and shunting, but seven of the class were fitted for push-pull passenger working. A further seven were built for the Somerset & Dorset Joint Railway in 1929. While on a southbound journey over the S&DJR on 19 August 1961, I recorded No 47542 shunting coal wagons at Radstock – on the return journey on 1 September I noted No 47557 performing the same duty. Several were allocated to Bromsgrove shed (85D) in the early 1960s for banking duties on the Lickey Incline. Nos 47417, 47422, 47506, 47539 and 47623 were also allocated to my local shed of Gloucester Barnwood (85C) at that time and they were a common sight to me pottering about on the Midland line.

At the beginning of World War II a few examples were sent to France for war work and two were converted to 5 ft 3 in gauge for operations in Northern Ireland.

Withdrawals of the remaining 417 locos started in 1959 when 25 were retired, followed by 48 in 1960, 34 in 1961, 75 in 1962, 40 in 1963, 49 in 1964, 63 in 1965, 77 in 1966 and the final six in 1967. Since then, nine of the class have been preserved although only two are currently operational.

A collection of ex-LMS 'Jinties', including Nos 47327, 47325 and 47629, outside Derby Works on 8 October 1961.

Henry Fowler

Midland Railway (1909–1923)
London Midland & Scottish Railway (1925–1931)

Henry Fowler was born in Evesham in 1870 and after studying metallurgy in Birmingham served an apprenticeship at the Lancashire & Yorkshire Railway's Horwich Works. From 1891 to 1895 he worked in the L&YR's testing department under George Hughes (see page 150), finally becoming the Head of Department, followed by five more years as Gas Engineer for the company. Fowler joined the Midland Railway in Derby in 1900 as Gas Engineer & Chief of the Testing Department, being promoted to Assistant Works Manager in 1905, Works Manager in 1907 and Chief Mechanical Engineer in 1909.

Following his secondment as Director of Production in the Ministry of Munitions during World War I, for which he was later knighted, Fowler was appointed Deputy CME (under George Hughes, see page 150) of the newly formed London Midland & Scottish Railway in 1923. Hughes retired in 1925 and Fowler took over as CME of the LMS, a position he held until his retirement in 1931. Sir Henry Fowler died in 1938.

During his time as CME of the LMS, Fowler was responsible for the design of many types of locomotive, built in their hundreds, the majority (albeit with some rebuilding by William Stanier) remaining in service into the BR era in the mid-1960s. They include the Class '6P' 'Patriot' and '7P' 'Royal Scot' 4-6-0s, Class '3MT' 2-6-2Ts, Class '3F' 'Jinty' 0-6-0Ts, Class '2P' 4-4-0s, Class '4MT' 2-6-4Ts, Class '4F' 0-6-0s and Class '7F' 0-8-0s. He even managed to escape from the small-engine policy of Derby with his 2-6-0+0-6-2 Garratts (see page 154) and Somerset & Dorset Joint Railway '7F' 2-8-0s (see page 128).

One of Bath Green Park's (82F) ex-LMS Class '3F' 0-6-0Ts, No 47557, waits for the road back home to clear at Midsomer Norton South station, Somerset & Dorset Joint Railway, circa 1961. Built in 1928, this locomotive was withdrawn from Bath Green Park shed in February 1964.

LMS Class '4F' 0-6-0

Specification

Builders	Derby Works (185)
	North British Locomotive Company (80)
	Kerr, Stuart & Co (50)
	Crewe Works (165)
	St Rollox Works (60)
	Andrew Barclay Sons & Co (25)
	Horwich Works (10)
Wheel arrangement	0-6-0
Build dates	1924–1941
BR power classification	4F
Cylinders	2 inside
Driving wheels	4 ft 8½ in
Tractive effort	24,555 lbs
Boiler pressure	175 psi
Number built	575
BR numbering	44027–44606

Henry Fowler's (see page 145) Class '4F' 0-6-0 goods locomotives were a development of his Midland Railway Class '3835' 0-6-0s, which were introduced in 1911 – a total of 197 of the latter class were built, including five for the Somerset & Dorset Joint Railway in 1922. Very similar in appearance to Fowler's '4Fs', their BR numbering was 43835 to 44026.

Whilst primarily designed for freight work for the London Midland & Scottish Railway, the '4Fs' were also employed on passenger services, especially during the summer months, and could be seen performing this duty across the LMS network in England and as far afield as the Midland & Great Northern Joint Railway in East Anglia and the Somerset & Dorset Joint Railway.

Withdrawals of the '4Fs' began in 1959 with 44 retired, followed by 41 in 1960, 23 in 1961, 74 in 1962, 134 in 1963, 153 in 1964, 95 in 1965 and the final eleven in 1966. Only three of this once-numerous class have been preserved: Nos 44027, 44123 and 44422. None are currently operational.

Ex-LMS Class '4F' 0-6-0 No 44197 approaches Hellifield station with a mineral train, 26 August 1960. Built at St Rollox Works in 1925, this locomotive was withdrawn from Skipton shed (24G) in September 1964.

An ex-LMS Class '4F' 0-6-0 hauling a short engineers' train on the Settle–Carlisle Line in the 1950s. The train has just crossed Ribblehead Viaduct and is heading for Blea Moor Tunnel.

My trainspotting notebook for 19 August 1961 records Nos 44146, 44560 and 44417 seen on a southbound journey over the S&DJR. On the return journey on 1 September I spotted Nos 44558 and 44561 at work on the same route. I have also many memories of No 44123, as well as No 44422, struggling with the daily coal train empties past my school on the way up from the Bristol Road Gasworks to Tuffley Junction in Gloucester during the early–mid 1960s. Little did I think that these two locos would end up being preserved.

Richard Edward Lloyd Maunsell

Southern Railway (1923–1937)

Richard Maunsell was born in Ireland in 1868 and went on to start an apprenticeship under Henry Ivatt (see page 81) at the Great Southern & Western Railway's (GS&WR) Inchicore Works in Dublin in 1886. He later moved to England where he became a draughtsman for the Lancashire & Yorkshire Railway at Horwich Works, followed by a period as a locomotive foreman. In 1894, Maunsell left England to work as Assistant Locomotive Superintendent of the East India Railway, but returned to Ireland two years later to take up the position of Works Manager at Inchicore, finally becoming Locomotive Superintendent of the GS&WR in 1911.

In 1913, Maunsell was appointed as Locomotive Superintendent of the South Eastern & Chatham Railway at Ashford Works. Over the next ten years he designed six classes of steam locomotive, all built at Ashford, including his 'N' and 'N1' Class 2-6-0s which gave sterling service well into the BR era – some surviving until 1966.

In 1923 the SE&CR became part of the new Southern Railway (SR) and Maunsell was appointed Chief Mechanical Engineer of this much-enlarged company, remaining in office until his retirement in 1937. As CME of the Southern, Maunsell not only oversaw the expansion of London suburban third-rail electrification, but was also responsible for the introduction of eight classes of steam locomotive, all of which saw service into the 1960s. Of note are his 4-4-0 'Schools' Class (see page 168) and the 4-6-0 'Lord Nelson' Class which, when introduced in 1926, were the most powerful 4-6-0s in Britain. He retired in 1937 and died in 1944.

SR 'Lord Nelson' Class 4-6-0

For a short period, the 'Lord Nelson' Class express locomotives were the most powerful 4-6-0s in Britain, based on their tractive effort. Designed by Richard Maunsell for the Southern Railway, they were all named after Royal Navy admirals and were primarily built to haul Continental boat trains between Victoria and Dover. They also later saw service between Waterloo and Southampton Docks and Bournemouth, and between Waterloo and Exeter Central. As there were no water troughs on the latter switch-back route, 5,000-gallon 8-wheeled tenders were fitted. Construction was slow at Eastleigh Works, and in service they received a mixed reception from footplate crew. Smoke deflectors were added in the late 1920s. The class's poor reputation for steaming was eventually laid to rest by Maunsell's replacement, Oliver Bulleid (see page 191), when he fitted larger diameter chimneys and multiple jet blast pipes to the class in the late 1930s.

The introduction of Bulleid's new and more powerful 4-6-2s in the 1940s soon led to the 'Lord Nelsons' being demoted to secondary work. Withdrawals began in August 1961, with the last one, 862/30862 *Lord Collingwood*, being taken out of service in October 1962. One example, No 850/30850 *Lord Nelson*, is preserved and is currently based at the Mid-Hants Railway.

Built at Eastleigh Works in 1929, ex-SR 'Lord Nelson' Class 4-6-0 No 862 Lord Collingwood is at the head of a West of England express at Salisbury in the 1930s. This locomotive, as No 30862, was the last of its class to be withdrawn, in October 1962.

Preserved ex-SR 'Lord Nelson' Class 4-6-0 No 850/30850 Lord Nelson near Medstead on the Mid-Hants Railway on 13 September 2009. Built at Eastleigh Works in 1926, this powerful locomotive was withdrawn in August 1962 and purchased for preservation.

Specification

Builder	Eastleigh Works
Wheel arrangement	4-6-0
Build dates	1926–1929
BR power classification	7P
Cylinders	4 (2 outside, 2 inside)
Driving wheels	6 ft 7 in
Tractive effort	33,510 lbs
Boiler pressure	220 psi
Number built	16
BR numbering	30850–30865

LMS Class '5MT' ('Crab') 2-6-0

Designed by George Hughes for the LMS, the mixed-traffic Class '5MT' 2-6-0 is more commonly known by its nickname, 'Crab'. Although designed by Hughes, the locomotives were all built during the time of Henry Fowler (see page 145). The class featured several advanced components including a new boiler as previously fitted to Hughes' Lancashire & Yorkshire Railway powerful 4-6-4 tank locomotives. Their slightly ungainly appearance was marked by the unusually steeply angled cylinders. When built they were fitted with a standard Midland Railway tender which was slightly narrower than the locomotive.

In service they performed well and could be seen in action on LMS routes from Bristol in the south to the Ayrshire coalfields in Scotland. Although they were occasionally called on to haul passenger trains, they were primarily used on heavy unfitted goods trains on steeply graded routes. I would often see them on freight trains on the Midland line in my hometown of Gloucester and during the summer months they could occasionally be seen at the head of weekend excursion trains. Their swan song in the mid-1960s was hauling heavy coal trains on the steeply graded Dalmellington branch in Ayrshire. While on a trainspotting trip to Ayr shed (67C) on 28 July 1964 I recorded a total of sixteen 'Crabs' that were used for this

service. On the same day I also spotted seven at Hurlford shed (67B).

Amazingly, the class remained intact until 1961 when three members were withdrawn, followed by 61 in 1962, 52 in 1963, 54 in 1964, 48 in 1965, 25 in 1966 and the final two in 1967. Three 'Crabs' have been preserved: No 42700 at the National Railway Museum, York; No 42765 at the East Lancashire Railway; the third, No 42859, has been at the centre of a legal action and is not currently restored.

Built at Crewe Works in 1927, ex-LMS 'Crab' 2-6-0 at Ayr shed (67C) on 28 July 1964. Employed hauling coal trains from the Ayrshire coalfield to the coast, this hardworking locomotive was withdrawn at the end of 1966.

Specification

Builders	Horwich Works (70)
	Crewe Works (175)
Wheel arrangement	2-6-0
Build dates	1926–1932
BR power classification	5MT
Cylinders	2 outside
Driving wheels	5ft 6 in
Tractive effort	26,580 lbs
Boiler pressure	180 psi
Number built	245
BR numbering	42700–42944

George Hughes

Lancashire & Yorkshire Railway (1904–1921)
London & North Western Railway (1922)
London Midland & Scottish Railway (1923–1925)

George Hughes was born in Cambridgeshire in 1865 and became a premium apprentice at the London & North Western Railway's Crewe Works in 1882. In 1887 he went to work as a fitter and erector of steam locomotives at the Lancashire & Yorkshire Railway's new works in Horwich. Over the next eighteen years Hughes slowly worked his way up the L&YR's promotional ladder – in 1888 he was in charge of testing at Horwich; in 1894 he was running the

Built at Horwich Works in 1927, ex-LMS 'Crab' 2-6-0 No 42715 of Newton Heath shed (9D) rests between freight duties at Normanton on 22 August 1965. This locomotive was withdrawn from Stockport Edgeley shed (9B) in February 1966.

Horwich gas works; in 1895 he was promoted to Chief Assistant in the Carriage & Wagon Department at Newton Heath; in 1899 he became Works Manager at Horwich and Principal Assistant to Henry Hoy, finally succeeding him as Chief Mechanical Engineer in 1904.

While at Horwich, Hughes was particularly interested in the development of heavy goods locos and experimented with high-temperature superheating and compounding. His locomotive designs for the L&YR include the four-cylinder 4-6-0s nicknamed 'Dreadnoughts' and their subsequent development as powerful 4-6-4Ts, which were actually built under LMS ownership in 1924.

Hughes remained as CME of the L&YR until the end of 1921. At the beginning of 1922, the L&YR amalgamated with the LNWR and Hughes became the CME of the expanded company. Following the 'Big Four Grouping' of 1923 he became CME of the London Midland & Scottish Railway but he retired to Norfolk only two years later. A cheerful man to the end, he died in Stamford in 1945. Of course, Hughes' greatest contribution to steam locomotive development were the 245 distinctive 'Crab' 2-6-0s, built by the LMS at Horwich and Crewe between 1926 and 1932. A highly successful mixed-traffic loco, many of this class remained in active service for BR in England and Scotland until 1967.

The task of Henry Fowler's (see page 145) 'Royal Scot' Class 4-6-0 was to haul express passenger trains on the London Midland & Scottish Railway without the need for the then practice of double-heading of older LNWR and MR locos. As originally built, the class had parallel boilers and no smoke deflectors. They were later rebuilt by William Stanier (see page 170) with tapered boilers and angled smoke deflectors.

Successful trials with the GWR's 'Castle' Class 4-6-0 (see page 139) No 5000 *Launceston Castle* between Euston and Carlisle in 1926 persuaded Fowler that this wheel arrangement was more preferable than his planned compound 4-6-2. As the new locomotives were urgently needed by the LMS, the first 50 were built by the North British Locomotive Company in Glasgow – all in one year! Once built they were pressed into service immediately, hauling top link expresses on the West Coast Main Line without any prior testing. A further twenty locomotives were built in 1930 at Derby Works.

The 'Royal Scot' Class were first named after a mixture of British army regiments and historical locomotives of the London & North Western Railway, but by 1936 all of the class had been named after regiments. Straight-sided smoke deflectors were fitted from 1932 onwards. With the introduction of Stanier's more powerful 'Princess Royal' Class 4-6-2s in 1933, the 'Royal Scot' Class started to be relegated to less exacting passenger duties.

Built as No 6152 *The King's Dragoon Guardsman* at Derby in 1930, this 'Royal Scot' Class loco permanently swapped identities with the first engine of this class, No 6100 *Royal Scot* in 1933, when it was sent with a train of carriages to the Century of Progress Exposition in Chicago. Fitted with a large headlamp, the engine and train then covered over 11,000 miles of the railroads of Canada and the USA and was visited by over 3 million people. On its return to Britain the two locos retained their new identities.

The unique, but unsuccessful, LMS high-pressure locomotive No 6399 *Fury*, designed by Fowler and built in 1929, was rebuilt by William Stanier in 1935 with a standard tapered boiler, new frames and cylinders, and became 'Royal Scot' Class No 6170 *British Legion*. This set the standard for the rebuilding of all the 'Royal Scot' Class which started in 1943 and ended in 1955. Angled smoke deflectors were later added to the class apart from No 46106 *Gordon Highlander*, which reverted to a straight-sided version in 1952.

Withdrawals began in October 1962, by which time some members of the class had already been relegated to more mundane duties such as hauling the summer-Saturday's holiday trains from the north and midlands to the West Country as far as Bristol. Imagine my shock when I first saw No 46100 *Royal Scot* of Nottingham shed (16A) entering Gloucester Eastgate station with one of these trains. Withdrawals continued through to 1966 when the last member, No 46115 *Scots Guardsman* (star of the short 1936 documentary film *Night Mail*) was taken out of service. Two members of the class have been preserved: No 46100 *Royal Scot* (also known as No 6152 *The King's Dragoon Guardsman*) and No 46115 *Scots Guardsman*.

Fresh out of the North British Locomotive Company workshops in 1927, Henry Fowler's LMS 'Royal Scot' Class 4-6-0 No 6130 awaits pairing with its tender. When built it was named Liverpool but this was changed to The West Yorkshire Regiment in 1935. The locomotive was rebuilt in 1949 and withdrawn at the end of 1962.

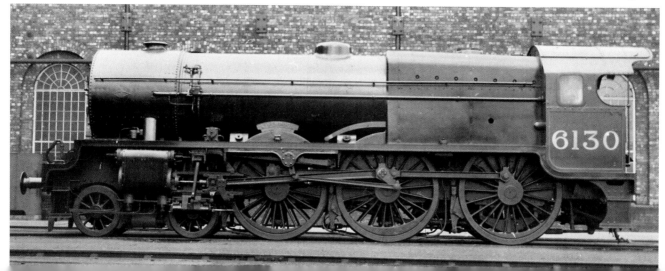

Preserved ex-LMS 'Royal Scot' Class 4-6-0 No 46100 Royal Scot heads a train along the Cumbrian Coast Line near Braystones on 16 April 2016. Built at Derby Works in 1927, this locomotive permanently swapped identities with sister loco No 6152 in 1933. It was withdrawn in October 1962 and purchased for preservation.

On 14 August 1961 I was en route from Gloucester to Swanage via the Somerset & Dorset Joint Railway for our family holiday. At Bath Green Park shed (82F) I spotted No 46140 *The King's Royal Rifle Corps* which had arrived earlier with a through train for Bournemouth – for a few years in the very early 1960s 'Royal Scots' were regular visitors to Green Park, having arrived there from the north via Gloucester and the Mangotsfield avoiding line.

At this time, there were regular appearances of this class on summer-Saturdays – as an example, on a Saturday in August 1961 I had spotted Nos 46117, 46151, 46161 and 46164 while trainspotting in Gloucester. I also recorded three at Corkerhill shed (67A) on 29 March 1964, three at Carlisle Kingmoor (12A) and two at Upperby (12B) sheds on 29 July that year, and one at Perth shed (63A) the next day.

On 19 May 1962 I was trainspotting on the West Coast Main Line north of Nuneaton when I spotted three members of this class – Nos 46111, 46152 and 46169 – in action. A couple of months later I recorded six of this class when I visited Crewe Works and seven at Willesden shed (1A).

Specification

Builders	North British Locomotive Co (50) Derby Works (20)
Wheel arrangement	4-6-0
Build dates	1927, 1930
Stanier rebuilds	1943–1955
BR power classification	7P
Cylinders	3 (2 outside, 1 inside)
Driving wheels	6 ft 9 in
Tractive effort	33,150 lbs
Boiler pressure	250 psi
Number built	70 (+ 1 rebuilt from No 6399 *Fury*)
BR numbering	46100–46170

LMS 'Garratt' Class articulated 2-6-0+0-6-2

As successor to the Midland Railway in 1923, the London Midland & Scottish Railway was faced with continuing the former company's small engine policy. In short this meant the double-heading of all heavy trains including coal trains southwards from the Nottinghamshire coalfields to London. To overcome this expensive operation, Henry Fowler (see page 145) designed an articulated 2-6-0+0-6-2 class of locomotives which was built by Beyer, Peacock & Co of Manchester in two batches.

Delivery of the first three 'Garratt' locomotives from Beyer, Peacock & Co came in 1927. A further 30 locos were built in 1930, which provided the LMS with a large fleet of powerful goods locos for the first time – although slightly longer than the unique LNER 'U1' 2-8-0+0-8-2, they were significantly less powerful. The majority of the class, subsequently fitted with revolving coal bunkers, were allocated to Toton shed in Nottinghamshire where they were employed on heavy coal trains down the Midland main line to

Ex-LMS 'Garratt' Class 2-6-0+0-6-2 No 47994 heads a coal train at Wellingborough on 3 October 1957. Built by Beyer, Peacock & Co in 1930, this powerful freight loco was withdrawn in March 1958.

North London. However, some were occasionally seen further afield as witnessed by myself as a young lad in Gloucester in the 1950s when I spotted a 'Garratt' slowly approaching Eastgate station from the Bristol direction.

Renumbered 47967–47999 in 1948, the class was gradually withdrawn between 1955 and 1958 when the locos were replaced by BR Standard Class '9F' 2-10-0s. None survived into preservation.

Specification

Builders	Beyer, Peacock & Co
Wheel arrangement	2-6-0+0-6-2
Build dates	1927 (3), 1930 (30)
BR power classification	not classified
Cylinders	4 outside
Driving wheels	5 ft 3 in
Tractive effort	45,620 lbs
Boiler pressure	190 psi
Number built	33
BR numbering	47967–47999

LMS 'Garratt' Class 2-6-0+0-6-2 No 4970 at Toton shed in 1946. Built by Beyer, Peacock & Co in 1930, this loco was withdrawn in July 1955.

Ex-LMS 'Garratt' Class 2-6-0+0-6-2 No 47998 at Toton shed on 23 June 1956. Built by Beyer, Peacock & Co in 1927, this loco was withdrawn in September 1956.

1927 GWR '6000' ('King') Class 4-6-0

Designed by Charles Collett (see page 138), the Great Western Railway's 'King' Class 4-6-0s were the company's most powerful express locomotives. Frederick W. Hawksworth (see page 198) – from 1941 the CME of the GWR – as Chief Draughtsman was also heavily involved in many parts of the design. With an increased boiler pressure, longer cylinder stroke, smaller diameter wheels and larger cylinders than Collett's 'Castle' Class 4-6-0s (see page 139), the 'Kings' had an increased tractive effort of 40,300 lbs. The leading bogie unusually had outside bearings on the front pair of wheels.

The first twenty locomotives were ordered in 1927 and the first, No 6000 *King George V*, rolled out of Swindon's workshops in June of that year. The 'King' Class were put to work hauling the heaviest of the GWR's expresses such as the 'Cornish Riviera Limited', but their weight restricted them to the Paddington to Plymouth (via both Westbury and Bristol), Paddington to Birmingham Snow Hill/Wolverhampton Low Level, and Paddington to Cardiff routes. A second batch of ten locomotives was ordered in 1930.

Soon after being built, No 6000 was shipped to the USA to represent the GWR at the Baltimore & Ohio Railroad's Centenary celebrations. For this occasion it was fitted with a large brass bell on the front buffer beam and a cabside plaque, both of which it carried until it was withdrawn and later preserved.

In early 1936, No 6007 *King William III* was involved in an accident near Shrivenham and was subsequently written off. A replacement was delivered in March of that year. No 6014 *King Henry VII* was temporarily fitted with streamlined fins, a V-shaped cab and a bulbous smoke box door in 1935 but this dismal failure of the GWR's attempt to join the streamlined railway revolution was soon forgotten. No 6028 *King George VI* was originally named *King Henry II* and No 6029 *King Edward VIII* was originally named *King Stephen*.

Withdrawals began in February 1962 and by the end of that year the whole class had been withdrawn. Three members of the 'King' Class have since been preserved: No 6000 *King George V*, No 6023 *King Edward II* and No 6024 *King Edward I*.

The latter two spent twelve years rusting in the sea air at Dai Woodham's scrapyard in Barry before rising from the dead and being sold for preservation. I have a record of seeing them when I visited Barry on 7 April 1963.

Built at Swindon Works in 1930, ex-GWR 'King' Class 4-6-0 No 6020 King Henry IV heads a Paddington to Wolverhampton Low Level express through Beaconsfield on 20 September 1958. This powerful loco was withdrawn from Wolverhampton Stafford Road shed (84A) in July 1962.

Built at Swindon Works in 1927, ex-GWR 'King' Class 4-6-0 No 6005 King George II heads a West of England express near Reading West on 27 October 1962. This magnificent locomotive was withdrawn just one month later from Old Oak Common shed (81A).

Preserved blue-liveried ex-GWR 'King' Class 4-6-0 No 6023 King Edward II, with a Plymouth Laira (83D) shedplate, photographed at Didcot Railway Centre on 8 April 2015.

Specification

Builder	Swindon Works
Wheel arrangement	4-6-0
Build dates	1927–1930, 1936
BR power classification	8P
Cylinders	4 (2 inside, 2 outside)
Driving wheels	6ft 6 in
Tractive effort	40,300 lbs
Boiler pressure	250 psi
Number built	31 (replacement built for No 6007)
BR numbering	6000–6029

As the class were barred from reaching my hometown of Gloucester I did not see 'Kings' too often and then it was only a few months before they were all withdrawn. My first sight of these magnificent machines in action was at Birmingham Snow Hill on 8 January 1962 when I recorded Nos 6002, 6017 and 6020 on Paddington expresses. The last record I have of them (apart from the scrap lines at Swindon and Barry) was on 14 April 1962 when I recorded Nos 6012, 6016, 6021, 6025 and 6026 at Paddington station in the late afternoon – the latter, King John, was at the head of the 'Cambrian Coast Express'.

1928 LNER 'A3' Class 4-6-2

The London & North Eastern Railway's 'A3' Class 4-6-2s were the company's most powerful express locomotives when they were introduced in 1928. Designed by Nigel Gresley, they were a development of his 'A1' Class 4-6-2 locomotives of which 52 had been built, including two that were built for the Great Northern Railway in 1922. Twenty of the 'A1' locomotives were built by the North British Locomotive Company, the rest were built at Doncaster Works.

While working for the GNR Gresley was inspired by the American Pennsylvania Railroad's 4-6-2s that had been introduced in 1914. This led him to design the three-cylinder Class 'A1' 4-6-2, which were designed to replace the GNR's less powerful Ivatt 'Atlantics' (see page 83).

The outcome of Gresley's many experiments with the original Class 'A1s' in the 1920s was the new Class 'A3' of which No 2743 *Felstead* was the first example, built in 1928. The last, No 2508 *Brown Jack*, was built in 1935. All the Class 'A1s', apart from the first to be built, were rebuilt as Class 'A3' between 1927 and 1948. However, the first 'A1' built for the GNR in 1922, No 4470 *Great Northern*, was rebuilt as a Thompson Class 'A1/1' in 1945 and numbered 113/60113.

Specification

Builder	Doncaster Works
Wheel arrangement	4-6-2
Build and rebuild dates	1928–1948
BR power classification	7P6F
Cylinders	3 (2 outside, 1 inside)
Driving wheels	6 ft 8 in
Tractive effort	30,362–36,465 lbs
Boiler pressure	220 psi
Number built	78 (27 new, 51 rebuilt from 'A1')
BR numbering	60035–60112

World-famous preserved ex-LNER 'A3' Class 4-6-2 No 60103 Flying Scotsman heads a train along the Settle–Carlisle Line at Ais Gill on 13 August 2017. Built as an LNER Class 'A1' at Doncaster Works in 1923 and rebuilt as an 'A3' in 1947, this superb loco was withdrawn from King's Cross shed (34A) in January 1963 before being sold for preservation to Alan Pegler.

The names of the Class 'A1' and 'A3' locomotives were a mixture of famous racehorses and senior LNER officials. However, the first was named after its parent company, *Great Northern*, and one was named after the LNER's most famous long-distance train, the *Flying Scotsman*.

The 'A1' and 'A3' locomotives both gave sterling service on the East Coast Main Line, especially with the 'Flying Scotsman' train between London and Edinburgh which had become a non-stop service in 1928. To enable this, corridor tenders had been fitted to some of the locomotives allowing footplate crews to changeover without stopping the train. In 1933, modified Class 'A1' No 4472 *Flying Scotsman* attained 100 mph near Little Bytham on the East Coast Main Line – this was the first time a steam locomotive had officially recorded this speed. Then, in 1935, Class 'A3' No 2750 *Papyrus* was recorded as attaining 108 mph at the same location.

During the post-war years several modifications were made to the Class 'A3s', including the fitting of double Kylchap chimneys and German-type smoke deflectors.

The introduction of diesel haulage on the East Coast Main Line in the late 1950s soon led to the withdrawal of the 'A3s' with the first, No 60104 *Solario*, being retired in 1959. Six more followed in 1961, twelve in 1962, 33 in 1963, 23 in 1964 and two in 1965. The last remaining 'A3', No 60052 *Prince Palatine*, survived until 1966. Only one example of this class has been preserved, the justifiably world famous No 4472/60103 *Flying Scotsman*.

Nigel Gresley

London & North Eastern Railway (1923–1941)

Nigel Gresley was born in Edinburgh in 1876 and was brought up in Derbyshire. Educated at Marlborough School he was apprenticed at the London & North Western Railway's Crewe Works before moving to continue his training under John Aspinall (see page 57) at the Lancashire & Yorkshire Railway's Horwich Works. After three years as Assistant Superintendent in the L&YR Carriage & Wagon Department at Newton Heath, he was appointed Superintendent of the Carriage & Wagon Department of the Great Northern Railway in 1905. Six years later, he succeeded H. A. Ivatt (see page 81) as Chief Mechanical Engineer of the GNR.

In 1923 the GNR became part of the newly formed London & North Eastern Railway and Gresley was appointed Chief Mechanical Engineer, a position he held at the LNER's Doncaster Works until his death in 1941.

During his time at both the GNR and LNER, Gresley was responsible for designing 26 different locomotive types including the 'A1' 4-6-2 in 1922, the 'A3' 4-6-2 in 1928 and the 'V2' 2-6-2 in 1936 (see page 184). His most famous locomotive must be the beautifully streamlined 'A4' 4-6-2 (see page 180), which first appeared in 1935. A locomotive of this class, No 4468 *Mallard*, still holds the world speed record for steam locomotives, achieved in 1938 with a top speed of 126 mph.

Then owned by Alan Pegler, 'A3' Class 4-6-2 No 4472 Flying Scotsman halts at Gloucester Central station to take on water while hauling the Ffestiniog Railway enthusiasts' special from Doncaster to Cardiff on 18 March 1964.

Living in the West Country I did not see this class too often! However, on a trainspotting trip to London on 14 April 1962 I recorded Nos 60047, 60061, 60062, 60065 and 60106 in a short space of time at King's Cross station. While on a trip to Scotland on 29 March 1964 I recorded seeing Nos 60094 at St Rollox (65B), Nos 60037, 60041, 60057, 60087, 60099 and 60101 stored at Bathgate shed (64F), Nos 60042, 60080, 60083, 60100 at St Margarets (64A) and No 60083 at the head of a sleeper train at Edinburgh Waverley. While travelling on 'The Waverley' express from Carlisle to Edinburgh on 29 July 1964 I recorded No 60052 passing southbound just south of Hawick. I spotted Nos 60042 and 60077 at St Margarets shed on the same trip and on 2 August I recorded Nos 60041, 60042, 60051, 60077, 60084, 60085 and 60112 at the same shed.

Yorkshire Pullman

London (King's Cross) to Hull, Leeds, Bradford and Harrogate

Introduced by the London & North Eastern Railway in 1935, the 'Yorkshire Pullman' was suspended during World War II and reinstated in 1946. From 1948 it was operated by the Eastern and North Eastern regions of the newly formed British Railways. The heavy eleven-coach Pullman express – with portions for Hull (detached at Doncaster) and Bradford (detached at Leeds) – was usually hauled between King's Cross and Leeds by an 'A3' Pacific until the new Peppercorn 'A1' Class Pacifics entered service in 1948–49. By the winter of 1960/61, less than twelve months before the arrival of 'Deltic' diesels, the steam-hauled up train was leaving Harrogate at 10.07 a.m. and, after collecting the Bradford portion at Leeds and the Hull portion at Doncaster, arrived at King's Cross at 2.45 p.m. The down train left King's Cross at 5.20 p.m. and arrived at Harrogate at 10.02 p.m.

The arrival of the 'Deltics' and new Metropolitan-Cammell Pullman cars in the autumn of 1961 brought a rapid acceleration to the down train, with 38 minutes being slashed off the King's Cross–Leeds schedule. The up train saw a similar acceleration a year later. The Hull portion became the separate 'The Hull Pullman' in 1967 and, consequently, the stop at Doncaster was omitted and the schedule further speeded up with the down train taking only 181 minutes between King's Cross and Leeds. The train was withdrawn in 1978.

Ex-LNER Class 'A3' 4-6-2 No 60039 Sandwich leaving Welwyn South Tunnel on the East Coast Main Line with the down 'Yorkshire Pullman', circa 1957. Built at Doncaster Works in 1934, this locomotive was withdrawn from King's Cross shed (34A) in March 1963.

Designed by Charles Collett (see page 138), the Great Western Railway's 'Hall' Class 4-6-0s were the company's most successful and prolific mixed-traffic locomotives. The prototype of this class was rebuilt from 'Saint' Class 4-6-0 (see page 98) No 2925 *Saint Martin*, but with smaller diameter wheels, realigned cylinders and a modern cab with side windows. There followed three years of trials before the 'Hall' production line at Swindon swung into action. *Saint Martin* was numbered 4900 at the end of 1928 and the first fourteen new examples were sent to the demanding switchback Cornish main line between Plymouth and Penzance. Their performance there was highly successful and further orders followed in quick succession during the 1930s and into World War II. They were soon to be seen in action on all the GWR main lines, equally at home hauling long goods trains or semi-fast passenger trains until the 1960s.

Apart from the prototype, all of these locomotives were named after English and Welsh country houses that fell within the GWR's sphere of operations. The last 'Hall', No 6958 *Oxburgh Hall*, was built in April 1943. There then followed Frederick W. Hawksworth's 'Modified Hall' Class (see page 199).

One example, No 4911 *Bowden Hall*, was destroyed in a Luftwaffe air raid in Keyham, Plymouth in April 1941. Apart from that, withdrawals started slowly in 1959, reaching a peak of 73 in 1962, followed by 67 in 1963, 56 in 1964 and the final 49 in 1965 when steam haulage ended on the Western Region.

Eleven examples were sold to Dai Woodham's scrapyard in Barry and spent many years rusting in the sea air before being bought for preservation:

- No 4920 *Dumbleton Hall* (now on display in Japan as *Hogwarts Castle*)
- No 4930 *Hagley Hall*
- No 4936 *Kinlet Hall*
- No 4942 *Maindy Hall* (rebuilt as 'Saint' Class No 2990 *Lady of Legend*)
- No 4953 *Pitchford Hall*
- No 4965 *Rood Ashton Hall*
- No 4979 *Wootton Hall*
- No 5900 *Hinderton Hall*
- No 5952 *Cogan Hall* (parts used in new-build replica No 6880 *Betton Grange*)
- No 5967 *Bickmarsh Hall*
- No 5972 *Olton Hall* (renamed *Hogwarts Castle* for the Harry Potter films).

Ex-GWR 'Hall' Class 4-6-0 No 6913 Levens Hall passes through Swindon station with a westbound goods train in 1962. Built at Swindon Works in 1941, this loco was withdrawn from Gloucester Horton Road shed (85B) in June 1964.

Specification

Builder	Swindon Works
Wheel arrangement	4-6-0
Build dates	1928–1943
BR power classification	5MT
Cylinders	2 outside
Driving wheels	6 ft
Tractive effort	27,275 lb
Boiler pressure	225 psi
Number built	258 (+ 1 rebuilt 'Saint' Class)
BR numbering	4900–4990, 5900–5999, 6900–6958

The 'Halls' were a common sight in my childhood hometown of Gloucester during the late 1950s and early '60s. I used to record them having overhauls in Swindon Works and regularly travelled behind them on my trainspotting trips to South Wales – for example, on 25 February 1963, No 4929 *Goytrey Hall* took me down to Cardiff. My last trip behind a 'Hall' was on 9 September 1965 when No 4920 *Dumbleton Hall* took me from Banbury to Oxford while hauling the York to Bournemouth inter-regional train. It's strange to think that this loco is now in Japan.

The rerouted 'Pines Express' from Bournemouth passes through Eastleigh behind ex-GWR 'Hall' Class 4-6-0 No 4920 Dumbleton Hall *in September 1965.* Built at Swindon in 1929 and withdrawn at the end of 1965, this loco has found a new home in Japan as Hogwarts Castle.

In glorious ex-works condition, ex-GWR 'Hall' Class 4-6-0 No 4917 Crosswood Hall *stands outside its birthplace on 15 March 1958. Built at Swindon Works in 1929, this loco was withdrawn from Westbury shed (82D) in September 1962.*

The '5700' Class 0-6-0 pannier tanks became one of the most numerous classes of steam locomotives in Britain. Designed by Charles Collett (see page 138) for the Great Western Railway, they were developed from the GWR '2021' Class 0-6-0 saddle tanks. A total of 863 locomotives of this standardised class were built at Swindon Works and by various manufacturers between 1929 and 1950. They were widely distributed across the GWR network and were employed on shunting, light goods, suburban passenger and branch line duties.

There were many variations within the '5700' Class, including:

- Locos with steam brake and no automatic train control for shunting only (introduced in 1930)
- Locos with modified cab and increased weight (1933)
- Locos with condensing apparatus working over London Transport's Metropolitan Line (1933)
- Locos with steam brake and increased weight (1948).

Some were also fitted with spark-arresting chimneys for working on military and industrial sites where the risk of fire was high.

In their later years, withdrawn examples were sold to the National Coal Board for use at pits, with the last example remaining in use until 1975 (I recall seeing one of these in operation at a colliery in Maerdy, South Wales, on 12 April 1966). London Transport also took some for hauling ballast and engineering trains, with the last examples not being withdrawn until 1971.

With the introduction of diesel shunters, withdrawals from British Railways Western Region started in 1956 and continued until the end of 1965. However, the last examples were retired from Croes Newydd shed (6C – then in the London Midland Region) towards the end of 1966.

A total of sixteen Class '5700' locomotives have been saved for preservation and can be seen in various conditions at heritage railways in England and Wales.

Specification

Builders	Swindon Works (613)
	North British Locomotive Co (100)
	W. G. Bagnall & Co (50)
	Armstrong Whitworth & Co (25)
	Beyer, Peacock & Co (25)
	Kerr, Stuart & Co (25)
	Yorkshire Engine Company (25)
Wheel arrangement	0-6-0PT
Build dates	1929–1950
BR power classification	3F
Cylinders	2 inside
Driving wheels	4 ft 7½ in
Tractive effort	22,515 lbs
Boiler pressure	200 psi
Number built	863
BR numbering	3600–3799, 4600–4699, 5700–5799, 6700–6779, 7700–7799, 8700–8799, 9600–9682, 9700–9799

Ex-GWR '5700' Class 0-6-0PTs Nos 4610 and 4694 give rear end assistance to a bulk cement train travelling from Exeter St Davids to Exeter Central on 1 September 1964.

I remember a mega shed bash to South Wales on 7 April 1963 when we visited a total of 21 engine sheds and sub-sheds in one day – it was a Sunday, so most locos were tucked inside for the day. In my trainspotting notebook for this exhausting trip I recorded an amazing 145 examples of the '5700' Class. By this date the writing was well and truly on the wall for them as they were soon to be consigned to the scrapyard. One interesting record that I have in my notebook is that I spotted No 4698 at Cinderford on a goods train on 5 July 1965. The last time that I saw a '5700' Class in action was on 16 December 1965 when I recorded No 3675 on a local freight train at Gloucester Central station.

Built at Swindon Works in 1949, preserved BR-built '5700' Class 0-6-0PT No 9681 heads an engineers' train at Upper Forge on the Dean Forest Railway, 28 December 2012. This loco was withdrawn from Cardiff East Dock shed (88L) in August 1965 before being purchased for preservation.

Fitted with a spark-arresting chimney, ex-GWR '5700' Class 0-6-0PT No 5744 stands outside Swindon Works in ex-works condition, October 1955. This locomotive was built by the North British Locomotive Company in 1929 and withdrawn from Westbury shed (82D) in April 1962.

Ex-LMS rebuilt 'Patriot' Class 4-6-0 No 45512 Bunsen is seen here at Crewe in 1963. Built at Crewe Works in 1932, it was rebuilt in 1948 and withdrawn from Carlisle Kingmoor shed (12A) in March 1965.

First of its class, unrebuilt ex-LMS 'Patriot' Class 4-6-0 No 45500 Patriot at Carlisle Citadel station on 3 August 1957. This loco was rebuilt from an LNWR 'Claughton' Class (see page 118) at Derby Works in 1930 and withdrawn from Carnforth shed (24L) in March 1961.

LMS 'Patriot' Class 4-6-0

Designed by Henry Fowler (see page 145) for the London Midland & Scottish Railway, the 'Patriot' Class locomotives were a development of the LNWR's 'Claughton' Class 4-6-0 (see page 118) express locomotives designed by Charles Bowen-Cooke and introduced in 1913. Twenty of these locomotives had been rebuilt with larger boilers by the LMS in 1928 and it was this boiler that was used for the first two 'Patriots'. The class visually resembled Fowler's new 'Royal Scot' Class (see page 152). Nicknamed 'Baby Scots', they used the same chassis but had straight smoke deflectors. By 1934 a total of 50 new locomotives (plus the two 'Claughton' rebuilds) had been built although their naming was somewhat confusing, with names of North Wales and Lancashire coastal resorts and LMS dignitaries mixed up with holders of the Victoria Cross, a public school, army regimental names and Lady Godiva. There were also nine that were unnamed.

From 1946 to 1949, eighteen members were rebuilt with tapered boilers, new cab and tender and angled smoke deflectors, being very similar to the rebuilt 'Royal Scot' Class (see page 152). Withdrawals of the unrebuilt examples started in 1960, with all 24 being taken out of service by 1962. The rebuilt examples lasted until 1965 when the last, No 45530 *Sir Frank Ree*, was withdrawn from Carlisle Kingmoor shed (12A). No example of this class, either unrebuilt or rebuilt, has been preserved although a new build of unrebuilt No 5551 *The Unknown Warrior* is being constructed at Crewe Heritage Centre.

While both unrebuilt and rebuilt examples were normally employed on express passenger duties along the West Coast Main Line and its offshoots such as the North Wales Coast Line, some could often be seen much further afield. For example, in Gloucester in the very early 1960s I regularly saw unrebuilt locos No 45504 *Royal Signals*, No 45506 *Royal Pioneer Corps* and No 45519 *Lady Godiva*, of Bristol Barrow Road shed (82E), on the Midland route to Bristol. On a trainspotting trip to London on 4 September 1962 I spotted five rebuilt examples at Willesden shed (1A), and at Carlisle Upperby shed (12B) on 29 July 1964 I noted four of the rebuilt examples.

Specification

Builders	Crewe Works (42) Derby Works (10)
Wheel arrangement	4-6-0
Build dates	1930–1934
George Ivatt rebuild dates	1946–1949
BR power classification	6P5F (rebuilds: 7P)
Cylinders	3 (2 outside, 1 inside)
Driving wheels	6 ft 9 in
Tractive effort	26,520 lbs (rebuilds: 29,570 lbs)
Boiler pressure	200 psi (rebuilds: 250 psi)
Number built	52 (including 18 rebuilds)
BR numbering	45500–45551

SR 'V' ('Schools') Class 4-4-0

The 'V' or 'Schools' Class 4-4-0 express locomotives were a much-improved version of Wainwright's 'L' Class 4-4-0s (see page 126) that were originally built for the South Eastern & Chatham Railway. They were designed by Richard Maunsell (see page 148) to be used on main lines across the Southern Railway system, especially those that had shorter turntables at their engine sheds. Once the permanent way had been strengthened, they could even operate on the Hastings to Tonbridge line with its restricted loading gauge. The 'Schools' Class were well received by footplate crews and were also the most powerful 4-4-0s in Britain by tractive effort.

Ex-SR 'Schools' Class 4-4-0 No 30925 Cheltenham *at Ashford shed (73F) on 25 April 1962. Built at Eastleigh Works in 1934 and withdrawn at the end of 1962, this loco has since been preserved by the National Railway Museum.*

The class were all named after public schools although many of these, for example *Shrewsbury* and *Malvern*, did not fall into the Southern Railway's sphere of operation. The class was a big success when introduced and were employed hauling expresses on the South Eastern Main Line and to Eastbourne, Ramsgate, Hastings and Portsmouth. The dieselisation of the Hastings route in 1957 and the completion of electrification of the South Eastern Main Line in 1961 led to their downfall, although some spent their last years working on the Bournemouth to Weymouth route.

Withdrawals began in January 1961 and by the end of 1962 all of the class had been retired. Three examples have been preserved: No 925/30925 *Cheltenham*, No 926/30926 *Repton* and No 928/30928 *Stowe*.

Ex-SR 'Schools' Class 4-4-0 No 30905 Tonbridge at London Victoria station on 19 October 1958. Built at Eastleigh Works in 1930, it was withdrawn from Basingstoke shed (70D) at the end of 1962.

Although well outside my usual trainspotting area, I did occasionally see members of this class just before they were withdrawn, either when I was on holiday or passing Reading South shed on the way to Paddington. My first record of one was No 30906 *Sherborne* at Reading in 1960, then No 30918 *Hurstpierpoint* at Wareham on 23 August 1961, No 30911 *Dover* at Bournemouth two days later and, at Basingstoke in April 1962, No 30902 *Wellington* and No 30903 *Charterhouse*.

Specification

Builder	Eastleigh Works
Wheel arrangement	4-4-0
Build dates	1930–1935
BR power classification	5P
Cylinders	3 (2 outside, 1 inside)
Driving wheels	6 ft 7 in
Tractive effort	25,130 lbs
Boiler pressure	220 psi
Number built	40
BR numbering	30900–30939

William Stanier

London Midland & Scottish Railway (1932–1944)

William Stanier was born in Swindon in 1876. His father was Chief Clerk to William Dean (see page 53) at Swindon Works and, in 1892, the young Stanier joined the company as an apprentice draughtsman. He then worked his way up the GWR promotional ladder, being appointed Assistant Works Manager by G. J. Churchward (see page 99) in 1912 before becoming Principal Assistant to Charles Collett (see page 138) in 1922 – his time under both Churchward and Collett had a great influence on Stanier's later work for the LMS.

Stanier was finally head-hunted by the London Midland & Scottish Railway in 1932 following the retirement of Sir Henry Fowler (see page 145) as Chief Mechanical Engineer. He quickly set about reorganising and standardising the company's mixed bag of locomotive designs, swiftly introducing some very successful locomotive classes that were to form the backbone of motive power for the LMS and BR until the end of steam in 1968. In addition to rebuilding Fowler's 'Royal Scot' Class with tapered boilers, Stanier's prolific output included 842 'Black Five' 4-6-0s (see page 174), 191 'Jubilee' 4-6-0s (see page 172) and 852 '8F' 2-8-0s (see page 179). However, his most famous locomotive designs were the powerful 'Princess' and 'Coronation' Pacifics (see page 186) that were the mainstay of West Coast Main Line passenger express services for 30 years.

William Stanier was knighted in 1943 and retired in 1944. He died in 1965.

LMS 'Princess Royal' Class 4-6-2 No 6201 Princess Elizabeth at Crewe Works in August 1938. This powerful express loco was built at Crewe Works in 1933 and withdrawn from Carlisle Upperby shed (12B) in October 1962. It has since been preserved and is awaiting overhaul at the Midland Railway Centre at Butterley.

Designed by William Stanier, the London Midland & Scottish Railway's 'Princess Royal' Class 4-6-2s were the most powerful class of express passenger locomotives then built for that company. They were designed to haul heavy express passenger trains on the West Coast Main Line between Euston and Glasgow Central.

Stanier was heavily influenced by the time he had spent working for the GWR at Swindon Works, and his new 'Princess Royal' Class had many similarities with the latter company's 'King' Class 4-6-0s (see page 156).

Initially, three locomotives of this class were built at Crewe in 1933. The third was built as an experimental 'Turbomotive' using a steam turbine. A second batch of ten locomotives was built in 1935. Each locomotive was named after a British royal princess, with the 'Turbomotive' being renamed *Princesss Anne* in 1952 when it was rebuilt as a conventional locomotive.

Following its introduction, the 'Princess Royal' Class was employed hauling the LMS's heaviest express on the West Coast Main Line. These included the company's premier train, the 'Royal Scot', which travelled between Euston and Glasgow Central and, for the first time, the powerful 'Princess Royals' could ascend the two steep inclines – Shap and Beattock – along this route unaided. However, although very powerful, the class weren't known for their high speed, though Stanier's later streamlined 'Coronation' Class (see page 186) certainly were.

Shortly after being rebuilt as a conventional locomotive, the 'Turbomotive', then named No 46202 *Princess Anne*, was involved in the notorious Harrow & Wealdstone crash in 1952 and written off. Withdrawals of the other locomotives had started in October 1961, with the last, 46200 *The Princess Royal*, being withdrawn in November 1962. Two members of this class have been preserved: No 6201/46201 *Princess Elizabeth* and No 6203/46203 *Princess Margaret Rose*.

I only saw one member of this class in action and that was on 19 May 1962 when I was trainspotting alongside the West Coast Main Line north of Nuneaton. By then the electrification masts were going up and English Electric Type 4s were aplenty. However there was still a lot of steam action, with No 46209 *Princess Beatrice* of Crewe North making an appearance. While on a trainspotting trip to London in the summer of 1962 I visited Camden shed (1B) where No 46206 *Princess Marie Louis* was among the many, soon to be retired, celebrity residents. My last sighting of a 'Princess Royal' was of withdrawn No 46200 *The Princess Royal* in storage at Carlisle Upperby shed (12B) on 29 July 1964.

Specification

Builder	Crewe Works
Wheel arrangement	4-6-2
Build dates	1933 (3), 1935 (10)
BR power classification	8P
Cylinders	4 (2 outside, 2 inside)
Driving wheels	6 ft 6 in
Tractive effort	40,286 lbs
Boiler pressure	250 psi
Number built	12 (+ 1 'Turbomotive')
BR numbering	46200–46212 (1 destroyed in Harrow & Wealdstone crash, 1952)

Ex-LMS 'Princess Royal' Class 4-6-2 No 46200 The Princess Royal at Carlisle Upperby shed (12B) on 7 September 1963. Built at Crewe Works in 1933, this loco was withdrawn in November 1962 and remained stored at Upperby for two years before being scrapped.

1934 LMS 'Jubilee' Class 4-6-0

When the London Midland & Scottish Railway's 'Jubilee' Class 4-6-0s were first introduced in 1934, they had a mixed reception from footplate crews. However, inadequacies such as poor steaming capability were later resolved and for 30 years this class, designed by William Stanier (see page 170), proved to be a successful express locomotive that saw action all over the extensive LMS network.

The first 'Jubilees' were actually the last five of what were intended to be Henry Fowler's 'Patriot' Class (see page 167) which were built instead with Stanier's taper boiler. The first of the class, LMS No 5552, was named *Silver Jubilee* in 1935 to commemorate the Silver Jubilee of King George V. The class was named after countries and states of the British Empire, British admirals, Royal Navy ships and famous British sea battles.

Over time, several examples were fitted with double chimneys, including No 45596 *Bahamas* which has since been preserved in this state. Two members, No 45735 *Comet* and No 45736 *Phoenix*, were rebuilt in 1942 with larger boilers, higher boiler pressure (250 psi) and double chimneys, and were reclassified as 7P.

'Jubilees' were a common sight on the Midland Main Line out of St Pancras until ousted by 'Royal Scot' 4-6-0s in the late 1950s. They were also a familiar sight until the mid-1960s on the Midland route to Bristol, the West Coast Main Line and the Settle–Carlisle Line. It was not uncommon to see them as far north as Aberdeen, hauling the West Coast Postal TPO to London Euston.

No 45637 *Windward Islands* was involved in the notorious Harrow & Wealdstone crash in 1952 and written off. Apart from that, withdrawals began slowly in 1960–61 and rose to 41 in 1962, followed by 31 in 1963, 64 in 1964, 33 in 1965, seven in 1966 and the final eight in 1967. Four examples have been preserved: No 5593/45593 *Kolhapur*, No 5596/45596 *Bahamas*, No 5690/45690 *Leander* and No 5699/45699 *Galatea*.

Specification

Builders	Crewe Works (131)
	Derby Works (10)
	North British Locomotive Co (50)
Wheel arrangement	4-6-0
Build dates	1934–1936
BR power classification	6P5F (rebuilds: 7P)
Cylinders	3 (2 outside, 1 inside)
Driving wheels	6 ft 9 in
Tractive effort	26,610 lbs (rebuilds 29,570 lbs)
Boiler pressure	225 psi (rebuilds: 250 psi)
Number built	191 (including 2 rebuilds)
BR numbering	45552–45742

My local regulars were No 45682 *Trafalgar*, No 45685 *Barfleur* and No 45690 *Leander*, all of Bristol Barrow Road shed (82E), which I used to see on a daily basis in the early 1960s. 'Jubilees' of Leeds Holbeck shed (55A) were also a common sight on trains, such as 'The Devonian', to and from the north. While on a visit to Crewe Works in August 1962 I recorded 24 examples of this class. In 1964 I spotted four at Carlisle Kingmoor and four at Upperby sheds on 29 July, and on the next day recorded No 45629 *Straits Settlements* on the West Coast Postal at Perth. At Carlisle station on 1 August I spotted nine of this class in action. Several of this class were allocated to Shrewsbury shed and could be seen hauling trains on the Central Wales Line to Swansea – I have a record of spotting No 45577 *Bengal* at Shrewsbury station with one of these trains on 18 April 1964. The last 'Jubilee' that I saw in action on BR was No 45565 *Victoria* leaving Gloucester Eastgate with a train for Bristol on 1 January 1965.

Ex-LMS 'Jubilee' Class 4-6-0 No 45577 Bengal at Shrewsbury station on 18 April 1964 with the 2.40 p.m. train to Swansea Victoria. Built by the North British Locomotive Company in 1934, this loco was withdrawn from Shrewsbury shed (89A/6D) in September 1964.

Ex-LMS 'Jubilee' Class 4-6-0 No 45596 Bahamas makes a fine sight on the Settle–Carlisle Line at Outhgill on 22 February 2020. Built by the North British Locomotive Company in 1935 and fitted with a double chimney in 1961, this loco was withdrawn from Stockport Edgeley shed (9B) in July 1966 and has since been preserved on the Keighley & Worth Valley Railway.

1934 LMS Class '5MT' ('Black Five') 4-6-0

Designed by William Stanier, the highly successful and numerous mixed-traffic Class '5MT' ('Black Five') 4-6-0 was introduced in 1934 and survived until the last days of steam on British Railways. Stanier's previous experience at Swindon led him to develop an LMS version of Collett's 'Hall' Class 4-6-0 (see page 162), with both sharing a two-cylinder specification, similar boiler dimensions and design, and 6-ft driving wheels. So successful were Stanier's locomotives that they continued to be constructed by British Railways until 1951, by which time 842 had been built.

The 'Black Fives' were not only built at Crewe Works (241) but also at Derby Works (54), Horwich Works (120), Vulcan Foundry (100) and by Armstrong Whitworth (327). Many were fitted with domeless boilers. The success of the versatile 'Black Fives' lay in their easy maintenance, good steaming qualities and their ability to haul passenger expresses or heavy goods trains more-or-less anywhere in Britain.

In the years after World War II, numerous experimental versions of the 'Black Five' were introduced by Stanier's successor, George Ivatt (see page 204), incorporating the following:

- 1947 – Stephenson link motion (outside), Timken roller bearings
- 1947 – Timken roller bearings
- 1947 – Timken roller bearings, double chimney
- 1948 – Caprotti valve gear
- 1948 – Caprotti valve gear, Timken roller bearings
- 1948 – Caprotti valve gear, Timken roller bearings, double chimney
- 1949 – Fitted with steel firebox
- 1950 – Skefko roller bearings
- 1950 – Timken roller bearings on driving coupled axle only
- 1951 – Caprotti valve gear, Skefko roller bearings.

Only five 'Black Fives' were named, all after Scottish regiments: No 5154/45154 *Lanarkshire Yeomanry*, No 5155/45155 *The Queen's Edinburgh*, No 5156/45156 *Ayrshire Yeomanry*, No 5157/45157 *The Glasgow Highlander* and No 5158/45158 *Glasgow Yeomanry*.

The first withdrawal was in 1961, although this locomotive, No 45401, had been written off after a collision. Twenty-one were withdrawn in 1962, followed by 29 in 1963, 67 in 1964, 97 in 1965, 171 in 1966, 305 in 1967 and the remaining 151 in 1968. A total of eighteen 'Black Fives' have been preserved, including Nos 44871 and 45110, which were two of the four locomotives to haul the last mainline passenger train on British Rail (the 'Fifteen Guinea Special') on 11 August 1968.

Specification

Builders	Crewe Works (241)
	Derby Works (54)
	Horwich Works (120)
	Vulcan Foundry (100)
	Armstrong Whitworth & Co (327)
Wheel arrangement	4-6-0
Build dates	1934–1951
BR power classification	5MT
Cylinders	2 outside
Driving wheels	6 ft 0 in
Tractive effort	25,455 lbs
Boiler pressure	225 psi
Number built	842
BR numbering	44658–45499

One of my favourite journeys behind a 'Black Five' was on 28 July 1964 when I travelled on the 'Port Road' from Dumfries to Stranraer Harbour behind No 45463. What an amazing journey across the wilds of Galloway that was! I was lucky to experience it, as the line from Dumfries to Challoch Junction closed eleven months later. The 'Black Fives' were a common sight in my hometown of Gloucester and were to be seen in action on passenger and freight trains right up until the official end of steam haulage on the Western Region at the end of 1965 (and a bit beyond) – the very last two that I saw were Nos 44840 and 44945 travelling northwards towards Cheltenham on 2 January 1966. As an impoverished art student I also visited Manchester Victoria in July 1968 to witness the dying days of steam on BR – 'Black Fives' Nos 44735, 44809, 45096, 45268 and 45269 were the last five BR steam locomotives that I ever saw in action.

BR built and fitted with Caprotti valve gear, ex-LMS 'Black Five' 4-6-0 No 44738 at Crewe on 20 June 1957.
Built at Crewe Works in 1948, this loco was withdrawn from Speke Junction shed (8C) in June 1964.

Preserved ex-LMS 'Black Five' 4-6-0 No 44871 crossing Rannoch Moor on its way from Fort William following
'The Jacobite' duties on 16 October 2010. Built at Crewe Works in 1945, this loco was withdrawn in August 1968.

Brand new LNER 'P2' Class 2-8-2 No 2001 Cock o' the North at Doncaster Works on 11 July 1934. It was rebuilt in 1944 by Edward Thompson as Class 'A2/2' 4-6-2 No 60501 and withdrawn from York shed (50A) in February 1960.

The London & North Eastern Railway's powerful 'P2' Class 2-8-2s were built for working heavy expresses over the demanding Edinburgh to Aberdeen main line. Designed by Nigel Gresley (see page 159), the first locomotive, No 2001 *Cock o' the North*, was built at Doncaster Works in 1934 and was fitted with Lentz-type poppet valve gear (later replaced by Walschaerts valve gear) and a Kylchap double chimney. The boiler was the same design as that used on Gresley's 4-6-2s but with a larger firebox. The front-end was the same as his wind-tunnel-designed and unique Class 'W1' 'Hush Hush' 4-6-4 locomotive. The second locomotive, No 2002 *Earl Marischal*, was fitted with Walschaerts valve gear and additional smoke deflectors. The remaining four locomotives were all fitted new with streamlining similar to the Class 'A4' (see page 180).

Test runs were made with heavy loads and soon the locomotives were in service hauling heavily loaded trains such as the 'Aberdonian' on the Edinburgh to Aberdeen route that they were designed for. Not built for speed, the 'P2s' could attain 60 mph while hauling a nineteen-carriage train of 650 tons. Problems with maintenance during World War II, coupled with criticism of the long wheelbase, led to the class being rebuilt by Edward Thompson as Class 'A2/2' 4-6-2s in 1943–44.

Two new builds of the iconic Class 'P2' locomotives are currently being constructed in northern England. One is a replica of No 2001 *Cock o' the North* and the other is new-build No 2007 *Prince of Wales*.

Costing £6 million, the new-build 'P2' Class 2-8-2 No 2007 Prince of Wales, *seen here in June 2019, is taking shape at the new Darlington Locomotive Works. Completion is scheduled for 2025.*

Specification

Builder	Doncaster Works
Wheel arrangement	2-8-2
Build dates	1934–1936
Cylinders	3 (2 outside, 1 inside)
Driving wheels	6 ft 2 in
Tractive effort	43,462 lbs
Boiler pressure	220 psi
Number built	6
LNER numbering	2001–2006

LNER 'P2' Class 2-8-2 No 2001 Cock o' the North *at Haymarket shed in Edinburgh, from where it performed its duties hauling heavy expresses on the demanding route to Aberdeen.*

In ex-works condition, ex-LMS Class '8F' 2-8-0 No 48755 of Stafford shed (5C) passes through Lancaster station with a fitted freight train in 1962. Built in 1945, this loco is unusually paired with a Fowler tender. It was withdrawn in September 1966.

Preserved ex-LMS Class '8F' 2-8-0 No 48151 at work on the Settle–Carlisle Line at Lazonby on 25 July 2012.

1935 LMS Class '8F' 2-8-0

The Class '8F' 2-8-0 heavy freight locomotive was the freight equivalent of William Stanier's (see page 170) highly successful 'Black Five' 4-6-0 (see page 174). It was built in large numbers not only for the London Midland & Scottish Railway but also, during World War II, for the LNER and the War Department. During the war it was chosen to be Britain's standard freight locomotive until the cheaper War Department Austerity 2-8-0 (see page 196) was introduced in 1943. The '8F' also saw action in several theatres of war including Italy, Iran, Egypt and Palestine. Some were lost at sea. After the war ended, many '8Fs' were not only sold to the railways of these countries but also to Iraq and Turkey. Three locomotives that were operated by the Longmoor Military Railway became BR Nos 48773 to 48775 and were the only '8Fs' to be based in the Scottish Region.

Following the end of the war, the '8Fs' that remained in Britain continued to perform their heavy freight task diligently for the newly nationalised London Midland Region of British Railways. Withdrawals began in earnest in 1964, with 26 being retired, followed by 95 in 1965, 162 in 1966, 231 in 1967 and 150 in 1968.

Six of the LMS/British Railways' '8Fs' are preserved in Britain, five of them having been bought from Dai Woodham's scrapyard in Barry. Two of the War Department versions have been repatriated from Turkey, while others have been preserved there as well as one in Iraq.

I visited Kirkby-in-Ashfield shed (16E) on 7 September 1965 and recorded nineteen '8Fs' in the shed. The following day I was travelling over the Somerset & Dorset Joint Railway for the last time and recorded No 48760 at Norton Hill Colliery. On the return journey from Templecombe to Bath I noted No 48706 at Evercreech Junction and the following at Bath Green Park shed (82F): Nos 48309, 48444, 48525, 48732 and 48760.

The '8Fs' were also a common sight in my hometown of Gloucester, even beyond the official end of steam haulage on the Western Region on 31 December 1965. These are the last sightings I had of them in Gloucester: No 48296 on a goods train and No 48375 light engine at Barnwood on 16 January 1966; Nos 48177 and 48669 in steam at Horton Road shed on 26 February 1966; No 48435 light engine at Barnwood going towards Gloucester on 16 March 1966. My final ever sightings of '8Fs' in action came on 8 September 1967 when I travelled on the electrified route from Sheffield Victoria to Manchester Piccadilly via Woodhead Tunnel. On this leg of the journey I recorded Nos 48381 and 48763. On the return journey from Liverpool to Manchester Exchange I saw Nos 48046, 48327, 48348 and 48549. And that was it!

Specification

Builders	Crewe Works (137)
	Horwich Works (75)
	Darlington Works (53)
	Doncaster Works (50)
	Swindon Works (80)
	Brighton Works (93)
	Eastleigh Works (23)
	Ashford Works (14)
	North British Locomotive Co (208)
	Vulcan Foundry (69)
	Beyer, Peacock & Co (50)
Wheel arrangement	2-8-0
Build dates	1935–1946
BR power classification	8F
Cylinders	2 outside
Driving wheels	4 ft 8½ in
Tractive effort	32,440 lbs
Boiler pressure	225 psi
Number built	852
BR numbering	48000–48775

Ex-LMS Class '8F' 2-8-0 No 48010 of Woodford Halse shed (2F) at Gloucester Horton Road shed (85B) in 1962. Built in 1935, this loco was withdrawn in January 1968.

Arguably the most successful express steam locomotive of all time, the streamlined Class 'A4' 4-6-2 was designed by Nigel Gresley (see page 159) for the London & North Eastern Railway. Prior to their being designed and built, Gresley had seriously considered building a streamlined diesel, similar to the German 'Flying Hamburger', for a high-speed service between King's Cross and Newcastle. However, diesels at that time had a limited passenger capacity, and so the 'A4' was born. The class was a development of Gresley's Class 'A3' (see page 158) but with a higher boiler pressure and extended firebox. The fitting of Kylchap double chimneys from 1938 further improved performance. However, the most distinctive feature of the class was the streamlining that not only increased speed but also deflected smoke. Streamlined valances were also fitted to the sides of the locomotives but these were removed for easier maintenance access during World War II.

The first four members of the class debuted on the LNER's new 'Silver Jubilee' express service between King's Cross and Newcastle in 1935. It was an instant success with the public. In a press run, the first 'A4' to be built, No 2509 *Silver Link*, achieved a speed of 112½ mph, breaking the British rail speed record in the process. The success of the 'Silver Jubilee' led to the introduction of two more LNER high-speed trains in 1937: 'The Coronation' from King's Cross to Edinburgh, and the 'West Riding Limited' from King's Cross to Leeds.

However, the star of the show was 'A4' No 4468 *Mallard*, which achieved a world speed record of 126 mph while hauling a test train down Stoke Bank on the East Coast Main Line in 1938. This record has never been broken. In service the 'A4s' were totally reliable and consistently operated at 100 mph while hauling service passenger trains.

While the first four 'A4s' were named to compliment the 'Silver Jubilee' (*Silver Link, Quicksilver, Silver King, Silver Fox*) the remainder of the class were initially given the names of birds. However, over the succeeding years many were renamed and given the names of LNER dignitaries, countries of the British Empire and even an American president.

After World War II the 'A4s' continued their dominance of hauling non-stop express trains on the East Coast Main Line. The high point of the post-war years was the introduction of the 'Capitals Limited' (renamed 'The Elizabethan' in 1953) non-stop express between King's Cross and Edinburgh. With their corridor tenders to allow crew changeovers, the 'A4s' continued to cut the journey time. This climaxed in

Specification

Builder	Doncaster Works
Wheel arrangement	4-6-2
Build dates	1935–1938
BR power classification	8P6F
Cylinders	3 (2 outside, 1 inside)
Driving wheels	6 ft 8 in
Tractive effort	35,455 lbs
Boiler pressure	250 psi
Number built	35
BR numbering	60001–60034 (1 destroyed in World War II)

Nearly at the end of its life, ex-LNER Class 'A4' 4-6-2 No 60024 Kingfisher at Glasgow Buchanan Street on 23 August 1966 after hauling a 3-hour express from Aberdeen. This superb loco was withdrawn two weeks later and scrapped.

1954 when it came down to 6½ hours for the 393-mile journey – at that time it was the longest scheduled non-stop railway journey in the world.

Sadly, nothing lasts forever and the introduction of 'Deltic' diesels in 1961 eventually led to the downfall of the 'A4s'. Some were transferred to Scotland to operate the Glasgow to Aberdeen 3-hour expresses but this swansong ended in September 1966, after which the final members of the class were withdrawn.

One 'A4', No 4469 *Sir Ralph Wedgwood*, was destroyed in a Luftwaffe air raid in York in 1942 and never replaced. The first withdrawals of the remaining 'A4s' began in 1962 when five were retired, followed by ten in 1963, seven in 1964, six in 1965 and the final six in 1966. Fortunately, six of this class have been preserved:
- No 4464/60019 *Bittern*
- No 4468/60022 *Mallard*
- No 4488/60009 *Union of South Africa*
- No 4489/60010 *Dominion of Canada* (in Canadian Railway Museum)
- No 4496/60008 *Dwight D. Eisenhower* (in National Railroad Museum, USA)
- No 4498/60007 *Sir Nigel Gresley*.

My first 'A4' sightings came on a trainspotting trip to London on 14 April, 1962 when I recorded Nos 60003, 60015, 60021, 60025 and 60028 while on a visit to King's Cross station. The next sighting was of Nos 60011, 60016 and 60031 at St Rollox shed (65B) in Glasgow on 29 March 1964. On the same day I spotted Nos 60023, 60026 and 60034 stored at Bathgate shed (64F) and Nos 60006 and 60007 at Dalry Road shed (64C). My next trip to Scotland was in July/August 1964 and I managed to see Nos 60027 and 60034 en route from Buchanan Street to Perth on 27 July. Two days later I spotted No 60026 at St Margarets shed (64A) and on the 30 July I recorded 60012 at Dundee Tay Bridge shed (62B). Returning to Glasgow later that day I recorded seeing Nos 60006, 60019, 60027 and 60031 between Perth and Buchanan Street. On 31 July I travelled from Glasgow to Aberdeen on a 3-hour express which was unfortunately diesel hauled. However, en route I spotted Nos 60027 and 60009, while at Kittybrewster shed (61A) there was No 60007 in storage. Ferryhill shed (61B) was a different matter with Nos 60004, 60006, 60010, 60012, 60016, 60023 and 60026 in residence. The best was yet to come as the trip back to Glasgow was behind No 60019 *Bittern* and en route I spotted No 60009 again. Eleven 'Streaks' in a day!

My final trip behind an 'A4' was on 23 August 1966 when I travelled behind No 60024 *Kingfisher* from Stirling to Glasgow Buchanan Street on one of the 3-hour expresses from Aberdeen. Looking magnificent until the end, this locomotive was withdrawn along with the other five remaining members of its class on 5 September. It was the end of a glorious era.

Looking in fine fettle, ex-LNER Class 'A4' 4-6-2 No 60027 Merlin at Haymarket shed (64B) in 1954. Built at Doncaster Works in 1937, this loco was withdrawn from St Margarets shed (64A) in September 1965.

The Elizabethan

London (King's Cross) to Edinburgh (Waverley) and Aberdeen

The outbreak of World War II stopped the golden age of high-speed travel on the East Coast Main Line. It was only resumed in 1949, when the new 'Capitals Limited' was inaugurated by the Eastern, North Eastern and Scottish Regions of British Railways as the new non-stop express between King's Cross and Edinburgh. From here it went on to serve Aberdeen at a more leisurely pace. By 1952 the train had been speeded up to nearly match the pre-war schedules, and in 1953 it was renamed as 'The Elizabethan' in honour of Queen Elizabeth II's coronation. Running only during the summer months, the heavily loaded train – weighing in at around 420 tons – was probably the most demanding ever seen in Britain, but Gresley's 'A4' Pacifics were certainly up to the job. Locomotives used on this run were fitted with corridor tenders allowing crews to change over without a stop, making this the longest scheduled non-stop railway journey in the world.

The last steam-hauled 'The Elizabethan' ran on 8 September 1961, to be replaced by the new English Electric 3,300 hp 'Deltic' diesels. The train ran for the 1962 and 1963 summer seasons behind these new machines, but as they did not have a corridor connection, a stop was made at Newcastle for a crew change. The train ceased to run in September 1963.

Ex-LNER world speed record holder 'A4' Class 4-6-2 No 60022 Mallard departs from Edinburgh Waverley with the up non-stop 'The Elizabethan' to King's Cross in September 1961. Built at Doncaster Works in 1938, this locomotive was withdrawn in April 1963 and has since been preserved at the National Railway Museum in York.

LNER 'V2' Class 2-6-2

Designed by Nigel Gresley (see page 159), the London & North Eastern Railway's Class 'V2' 2-6-2s were a highly successful mixed traffic locomotive equally at home hauling passenger expresses or fast-fitted freight trains. Despite being barred from the Great Eastern Main Line because of their 22-ton axle load, they were versatile maids of all work. They could be seen in action on the East Coast Main Line from King's Cross to Aberdeen, the former Great Central route between Sheffield and Marylebone, and the Waverley Route between Carlisle and Edinburgh. In service they could haul up to twenty carriages and could attain 90 mph while hauling an express.

With good free steaming qualities, the 'V2s' excelled at heavy haulage during World War II. Many modifications were also made to the class during their lifetime including to the suspension, the cylinder castings and external steam pipes, and a few were fitted with Kylchap chimneys.

Eight 'V2s' were named. The first of the class was named after an LNER express freight train, 'Green Arrow'. Two were named after northeastern public schools and five after northeastern army regiments.

Withdrawals began in 1962, with 69 consigned to the scrapheap, 43 in 1963, 32 in 1964, 26 in 1965 and the final fourteen in 1966. No 60800 *Green Arrow* is the only member of the class to have been preserved.

Ex-LNER 'V2' Class 2-6-2 No 60880 speeds along the East Coast Main Line at Eaton Wood near Retford with a fitted freight train, circa 1961. Built at Doncaster Works in 1940, this highly successful mixed traffic loco was withdrawn from Doncaster shed (36A) in September 1963.

A fine study of the front end of ex-LNER 'V2' Class 2-6-2 No 60916 at Newcastle Central station in early 1964.
Built at Darlington Works in 1940, this loco was withdrawn from Darlington shed (51A) in June 1964.

My first sightings of the 'V2' Class came on 14 April 1962 when I was on a trainspotting trip to London – at King's Cross station on that day I spotted Nos 60814 and 60871. The next time I saw a 'V2' was on 29 March 1964 when I was visiting Motherwell shed (66B) and found No 60957 in residence. This was followed on the same day by No 60816 at St Rollox (65B), No 60969 at Bathgate (64F) and Nos 60814, 60846, 60882, 60895, 60910, 60931, 60976 and 60922 at St Margarets (64A). Nos 60835 and 60970 were at Carlisle Kingmoor shed (12A) on 29 July 1964 and Nos 60816, 60818, 60822, 60919 and 60973 were at Dundee Tay Bridge shed (62B) the following day. I saw No 60931 at Carlisle station on 1 August. My next port of call on this trip was to St Margarets shed (64A) where I spotted Nos 60813, 60882, 60955, 60957 and 60970. My last sighting of a 'V2' on this trip was on 2 August 1964 at Eastfield shed (65A) where No 60846 was in residence. My final ever sighting of this class in action was of No 60813 light engine at Thornton Junction on 23 August 1966 – having previously been stored at Bathgate shed, it was withdrawn the following month.

Specification

Builder	Doncaster Works
Wheel arrangement	2-6-2
Build dates	1936–1944
BR power classification	6MT
Cylinders	3 (2 outside, 1 inside)
Driving wheels	6 ft 2 in
Tractive effort	33,730 lbs
Boiler pressure	220 psi
Number built	184
BR numbering	60800–60983

LMS 'Coronation' Class 4-6-2

When built, the 'Coronation' Class 4-6-2 was the most powerful express steam locomotive in Britain. Designed by William Stanier (see page 170), it was an improved version of his 'Princess Royal' Class 4-6-2 (see page 171). The class was designed to haul express passenger services on the West Coast Main Line between Euston and Glasgow Central. The first ten were built with streamlined casing. Half of these were specifically used to haul the new non-stop 'Coronation Scot' express between London and Glasgow, although a stop was made at Carlisle for a crew changeover. On a press run on 29 June 1937 to promote this new train, the No 6220 *Coronation* broke the British speed record when it achieved 114 mph just south of Crewe station.

Five batches of the 'Coronation' Class were built under the tenure of Stanier: Batch 3 and Batch 5 locomotives were built without streamlined casing. After the first, which was named *Coronation*, the next five locomotives were named after female royalty and the following ten after duchesses. The next 21 were named after cities served by the LMS although No 6244 was renamed *King George VI* in 1941. Smoke deflectors were added in 1945 and, between 1946 and 1949, all of the streamlined versions had their casing removed to ease maintenance. In 1947 a further two new modified locomotives were built at Crewe during the tenure of George Ivatt (see page 204): LMS No 6256 was named *Sir William A. Stanier F.R.S.* and No 46257, completed in 1948, was named *City of Salford*.

The loco that was sent to represent Britain at the 1939–40 New York World's Fair was built by the London Midland & Scottish Railway as No 6229 *Duchess of Hamilton*, at Crewe in 1938. Her number and nameplate was swapped with the first engine of the class, No 6220 *Coronation*, for the duration of what turned out to be a much longer-than-planned visit. Fitted with a streamlined casing and accompanied

by eight matching crimson lake-and-gold striped carriages, the loco was also fitted with a headlight, brass bell and special couplings for the duration of her stay in North America. After completing a tour of over 3,000 miles around the continent, the loco and her train were exhibited at the World's Fair but became stranded in the US following the outbreak of World War II. The loco was finally shipped back to Britain in 1942 where she reverted back to No 6229 *Duchess of Hamilton*. Used as officers' messes, the carriages only returned in 1946.

The 'Coronation' Class locos were painted in a bewildering variety of liveries. During LMS days the first five were initially finished in lined Caledonian blue for hauling the 'Coronation Scot' express, then two versions of lined crimson lake followed for the remainder up to No 6244. In wartime, the class all received plain black then lined black, with a unique blue-grey for No 6234. In British Railways' days, firstly all members except No 6234/46234 (see above) were finished in differing versions of lined black followed by experimental blue, standard blue, lined green, BR lined maroon and LMS lined maroon.

Carrying the iconic tartan 'Royal Scot' headboard, preserved Stanier ex-LMS 'Coronation' Class 4-6-2 No 46233 Duchess of Sutherland on the climb to Shap summit at High Scales with a 'Cumbrian Mountain Express' charter train from Euston to Carlisle on 31 January 2015. Built at Crewe Works in 1938, this fine locomotive was withdrawn from Edge Hill shed (8A) in February 1964. It was then acquired by the Princess Royal Class Locomotive Trust, and is usually based at the West Coast Railway Company's Carnforth shed.

With the diesel invasion of the West Coast Main Line then in full swing, withdrawals began in December 1962, with the last batch being taken out of service in October 1964. Three members have since been preserved: No 6229/46229 *Duchess of Hamilton* (with streamlined casing fitted), No 6233/46233 *Duchess of Sutherland* and No 6235/46235 *City of Birmingham*.

In the very short time that I saw them in action I have many fond memories of these powerful express passenger locomotives. I first saw them on a trainspotting trip to the West Coast Main Line north of Nuneaton on 19 May 1962 – on that day I spotted Nos 46225, 46234, 46241, 46249 and 46257 in action hauling passenger trains. My trip to Crewe Works later that summer revealed Nos 46222, 46234, 46237, 46239, 46241, 46246, 46251, 46252 and 46255. Also that summer I visited Camden shed (1B) in London and recorded Nos 46227, 46229, 46236, 46239 and 46240 in residence.

On 28 March 1964 I joined several hundred of my fellow trainspotters and embarked on a mega shed bash in Glasgow and Edinburgh. We travelled overnight from Birmingham New Street to Glasgow Central behind No 46256 *Sir William A. Stanier F.R.S.* On the 29th we were conveyed in a fleet of coaches to ten engine sheds beginning with Polmadie (66A), where No 46257 was in residence. Later that night and totally exhausted we returned from Edinburgh Waverley to Crewe behind *Sir William*. Later that year I revisited Scotland and also Carlisle and recorded the following 'Coronation' Class locos shortly before their withdrawal: on 29 July, Nos 46244, 46255 and 46257 at Carlisle Kingmoor (12A), Nos 46226, 46228, 46238 and 46241 at Upperby shed (12B), and No 46225 on a parcels train at Carlisle station; on 1 August, Nos 46226, 46237, 46244, 46250 at Upperby shed, No 46255 at Carlisle station and later at Polmadie shed, and No 46235 near Glasgow Central. Those were the last of this class that I saw in action just before its withdrawal.

Specification

Builder	Crewe Works
Wheel arrangement	4-6-2
Build dates	1937–1948
BR power classification	8P
Cylinders	4 (2 outside, 2 inside)
Driving wheels	6 ft 9 in
Tractive effort	40,000 lbs
Boiler pressure	250 psi
Number built	38
BR numbering	46220–46257

Royal Scot

London (Euston) to Glasgow (Central)

Introduced by the London & North Western Railway and the Caledonian Railway in 1862, the 'Royal Scot' continued to be operated by the London Midland & Scottish Railway from 1923 to 1947, and by the London Midland and Scottish regions of British Railways from 1948. From 1950 the two prototype diesel-electric locomotives – Nos 10000 and 10001 – were a regular feature hauling this famous Anglo-Scottish train, and in 1952 a new set of BR coaches replaced the pre-war coaching stock. At the same time, journey times improved so that both up and down journeys between Euston and Glasgow (Central) were completed in 8 hours – despite an unscheduled stop at Carlisle for crew changing. Further improvements came in the autumn of 1959 when the Carlisle stop was advertised in the new timetable and the journey times reduced to 7 hrs 15 min – this was made possible by reducing the number of coaches used.

By 1962, with electrification of the West Coast Main Line (WCML) now underway, the train was usually hauled by an English Electric Type 4 diesel, but the departure from Euston had been retimed to 9.30 a.m., and with a stop at Carlisle the train reached Glasgow at 4.50 p.m. (Mon–Fri). The Saturday working took 40 minutes longer and on Sundays the train was virtually reduced to stopping-train status, with stops at Rugby, Crewe, Carlisle, Beattock and Motherwell, arriving at Glasgow at 7.20 p.m.

Following electrification of the WCML to Glasgow in 1974, the 'Royal Scot' continued to run until 2003, when the name was dropped.

A mid-1950s scene at Carlisle (Citadel) station. Ex-LMS 'Coronation' Class 4-6-2 No 46244 King George VI has just arrived with the down 'Royal Scot' from Euston. Sister locomotive No 46231 Duchess of Atholl waits in the centre road to take over the train for the rest of its journey to Glasgow (Central).

1941 SR 'Merchant Navy' Class 4-6-2

Designed by Oliver Bulleid for the Southern Railway and built at Eastleigh Works during World War II, the air-smoothed 'Merchant Navy' Class 4-6-2s were a complete break with tradition. They incorporated many new developments in steam technology which allowed simpler manufacture during a period of wartime austerity. This included the use of welding during construction, a novel chain-driven valve gear and the use of thermic lances in their boilers. The driving wheels were also a unique design – the Firth Brown single disc wheels were in complete contrast to the usual spoked wheels. Other features included a one-piece steel rear trailing truck and a welded firebox. The boiler was surrounded by an air-smoothed steel casing which helped to deflect smoke. Electric lighting was supplied to the locomotive and cab by a steam-powered generator.

The class were all named after merchant navy shipping lines. The first of its class, No 21C1 *Channel Packet*, emerged from Eastleigh Works in early 1941 and by 1945 a total of twenty had been constructed. A final batch of ten more were built during the early years of the nationalised British Railways, and completed in 1949. Due to their length and heavy axle loading the class, famed for their power, speed and ride quality, were restricted to operating express trains from Victoria to Dover, Waterloo to Weymouth, and Waterloo to Exeter. However, they suffered from many design faults including maintenance of the chain-driven valve gear, wheel slippage when starting a heavy train, high coal consumption and restricted visibility. Because of this

Specification

Builder	Eastleigh Works
Wheel arrangement	4-6-2
Build dates	1941–1949 (rebuilt 1956–1960)
BR power classification	8P
Cylinders	3 (2 outside, 1 inside)
Driving wheels	6 ft 2 in
Tractive effort	37,515 lbs (rebuilds: 33,495 lbs)
Boiler pressure	280 psi (rebuilds: 250 psi)
Number built	30
BR numbering	35001–35030

BR-built unrebuilt 'Merchant Navy' Class 4-6-2 No 35027 Port Line passes through Brixton with the 'Golden Arrow' in August 1954. Built at Eastleigh Works in 1948, it was rebuilt in 1957, and withdrawn in September 1966, before being bought for preservation.

the decision was taken to rebuild the entire class to a more conventional design. The air-smoothed casing was removed and the chain-drive was replaced by Walschaerts valve gear. A new smokebox, a wider diameter chimney and smoke deflectors completed the rebuilds.

The modified 'Merchant Navy' Class emerged from Eastleigh Works between 1956 and 1960 and were universally well received by footplate crew and maintenance staff alike. They continued to dominate the mainline route from Waterloo to Exeter via Salisbury until September 1964, when WR 'Warship' diesels took over, and from Waterloo to Bournemouth until July 1967 when steam haulage ended on the Southern Region.

Withdrawals started in 1964, with seven being retired, followed by seven in 1965, six in 1966 and the final ten in 1967. Eleven of the class have been saved for preservation – of these, ten were sold to Dai Woodham's scrapyard in Barry and thus escaped the cutter's torch. Many of these are stored awaiting restoration, three are currently operational, while No 35029 *Ellerman Lines* has been sectioned to show the internal workings by the National Railway Museum in York.

The first documented record of my seeing a 'Merchant Navy' ('MN') was on 23 August 1961 when I was trainspotting at Wareham while on holiday in Swanage. In a few hours I recorded Nos 35020, 35021 and 35024. At Bournemouth Central two days later I saw Nos 35011, 35016 and 35021 and on 30 August, also at Bournemouth, recorded Nos 35001, 35016, 35021 and 35024.

Fast forward to 7 April 1962 when I was trainspotting for the first time at Basingstoke, where I spotted the following 'Merchant Navys': Nos 35002, 35009, 35019, 35023, 35024 and 35028. Next stop was Salisbury on the 6 September that year where I spotted the following: Nos 35003 (on up 'Atlantic Coast Express' or 'ACE'), 35006, 35014 (on down 'ACE'), 35025 and 35030. Our summer holiday in 1963 was in Lyme Regis, reached from my hometown of Gloucester via the Somerset & Dorset Joint Railway. Most of my holiday was spent trainspotting, with the following 'Merchant Navy' results: 3 August travelled behind No 35016 between Templecombe and Axminster with a recorded maximum speed of 87 mph; 5 August at Axminster station, Nos 35001 (on up 'ACE'), 35006, 35009 and 35013; 8 August at Exeter, Nos 35001, 35006, 35009, 35022, 35026 and 35030, and I returned to Axminster behind No 35004. On our return home on 10 August I spotted Nos 35009 and 35016 speeding through Templecombe station.

I next visited Basingstoke on 31 August and spotted eleven 'MNs' in a just a few hours. In 1964 I visited Basingstoke once again on 22 August (I was hooked on this station by now!) and spotted thirteen 'MNs'. Later that year while on holiday at Woolacombe (reached by train from Gloucester) I visited Exeter once again on 1 September. Although there was still a plethora of Bulleid 'Light Pacifics', the 'Merchant Navys' were thin on the ground and I only spotted Nos 35007 and 35029, the latter arriving on the down 'ACE' only a few days before this famous train's withdrawal. Back to Basingstoke on 9 January 1965 where I spotted seven 'MNs'.

My final trip there was on 10 September 1965 when I recorded only two: Nos 35012 and 35029, the latter at the head of the down 'Bournemouth Belle'. The next 'Merchant Navys' that I saw were Nos 35003 and 35004 at Eastleigh on 2 October 1965, the latter shortly before withdrawal at the end of that month. The last sights I had of these magnificent machines was on 31 January 1967 when I visited Waterloo station and spotted Nos 35013 and 35019.

Oliver Vaughan Snell Bulleid

Southern Railway (1937–1949)

Oliver Bulleid was born in Invercargill, New Zealand, in 1882 but came to Britain with his mother after the death of his father in 1889. In 1900 he began his apprenticeship with the Great Northern Railway at Doncaster Works and, in 1904, became Locomotive Running Superintendent and then, in 1905, manager of the Works. Bulleid moved to Paris in 1908 where he worked for the Westinghouse Electric Corporation in its brake and signal division. Returning to England in 1910, he worked for the Board of Trade until 1912 when he was appointed assistant to the GNR's Chief Mechanical Engineer, Nigel Gresley (see page 159), a post he also held in the newly formed London & North Eastern Railway from 1923. In this post he was involved in the development of the Class 'U1' 2-8-0+0-8-2 Garratt and the Class 'P1' and 'P2' 2-8-2 locomotives (see page 177).

Bulleid's big break came in 1937 when he was appointed CME of the Southern Railway following the retirement of Richard Maunsell (see page 148). During his tenure as CME of the Southern, Bulleid designed and produced many ground-breaking steam locomotive types such as the innovative 'Merchant Navy' and 'West Country'/'Battle of Britain' Pacific locos (see page 202), the utilitarian Class 'Q1' 0-6-0 freight loco (see page 192) and the less successful 'Leader' Class with its steam-powered bogies. In 1949 Bulleid was appointed CME of Coras Iompair Eireann (Irish Railways) where he designed and built his infamous turf-burning locomotive. He retired in 1958 and died, in Malta, in 1970.

SR 'Q1' Class 0-6-0

The unique 'Q1' Class 0-6-0 goods locomotives were a wartime utilitarian design with all but the basic essentials removed. Designed by Oliver Bulleid (see page 191) for the Southern Railway and built in equal numbers at Brighton and Ashford Works, they were also the most powerful 0-6-0 steam locomotive to operate in Britain. Unlike other Bulleid locomotives, the firebox was made of copper and the boiler was similar to that used on Maunsell's 'Lord Nelson' Class 4-6-0s (see page 148), but the wheels were of the Firth Brown disc design as first used on Bulleid's 'Merchant Navy'

Class 4-6-2s (see page 190). All in all a very strange-looking class but extremely powerful. Although primarily a goods locomotive, they were occasionally pressed into service hauling passenger trains.

Although intended to be a short-lived austerity class, the 'Q1s' remained in service until the 1960s. First withdrawals began in 1963 when thirteen were retired, then twenty in 1964, four in 1965 and the final three in 1966. One locomotive, No 33001 (C1), has been preserved and currently can be seen at the National Railway Museum in York.

Seen here at Reading South shed on 28 April 1963, ex-SR 'Q1' Class 0-6-0 No 33019 was built in 1942 and withdrawn in December 1963.

Ex-SR 'Q1' Class 0-6-0 No 33006 at Eastleigh shed (71A/70D) in June 1965. This wartime utilitarian loco was built in 1942 and withdrawn in January 1966.

I have very few records of seeing a 'Q1' apart from the following: on 7 April 1962 No 33036 was seen somewhere near Reading when on a trip to Basingstoke; No 33009 was seen at Reading South shed on 14 April 1962; No 33012 again at Reading South shed on 4 September 1962. On 26 June 1964 I spotted Nos 33032, 33029 and 33034 in Over Sidings, Gloucester, while on their very last journey to Cohens scrapyard in Morriston, Swansea.

Specification

Builders	Brighton Works (20)
	Ashford Works (20)
Wheel arrangement	0-6-0
Build date	1942
BR power classification	5F
Cylinders	2 inside
Driving wheels	5 ft 1 in
Tractive effort	30,080 lbs
Boiler pressure	230 psi
Number built	40
BR numbering	33001–33040

LNER 'B1' Class 4-6-0

Designed by Edward Thompson for the LNER, the mixed-traffic 'B1' Class 4-6-0s were a highly successful class introduced during the austerity years of World War II. After the war they continued to be built by the nationalised British Railways and were to be seen hauling freight and passenger trains on former LNER routes in the Scottish, North Eastern and Eastern Regions until the 1960s. They even travelled regularly over the Midland route to Bristol hauling summer-Saturday holiday trains destined for the West Country during the early 1960s.

The 'B1' was the replacement for the 'B17' Class 4-6-0 and was the LNER's answer to the very successful LMS 'Black Five' (see page 174) and GWR 'Hall' (see page 162) two-cylinder mixed-traffic locomotives. They were cheap to build during a time of wartime austerity and powerful, although not liked by footplate crew for their poor ride quality. The first 'B1' emerged from Darlington Works at the end of 1942 and was named *Springbok* in honour of the visit to Britain by the South African prime minister. A total of 41 locomotives were subsequently named after species of antelope (Nos 61000–61040) and a further eighteen in a random order after directors of the LNER.

While one 'B1' was withdrawn after an accident in 1950, the main withdrawals from service began in 1961 when one loco was retired, followed by 120 in 1962, 62 in 1963, 54 in 1964, 81 in 1965, 64 in 1966 and the final 27 in 1967. Some examples were taken into BR departmental stock following withdrawal, where their boilers were used for carriage heating, The last examples of these were finally withdrawn in 1968. Only two examples have been preserved: No 61264 (rescued from Dai Woodham's scrapyard in Barry where it was the only LNER locomotive) and No 61306 (subsequently named *Mayflower*).

Specification

Builders	Darlington Works (60)
	Gorton Works (10)
	Vulcan Foundry (50)
	North British Locomotive Company (290)
Wheel arrangement	4-6-0
Build dates	1942–1952
BR power classification	5MT
Cylinders	2 outside
Driving wheels	6 ft 2 in
Tractive effort	26,878 lbs
Boiler pressure	225 psi
Number built	410
BR numbering	61000–61409

I first saw 'B1s' when on a trainspotting trip to Stratford Works and shed (30A) on 4 September 1962 – they were Nos 61045, 61048, 61156, 61301, 61355, 61362 and 61375.

My hometown of Gloucester was not exactly awash with 'B1s' but on summer-Saturdays in the early 1960s they often appeared at the head of holiday trains from the north to the West Country as far as Bristol. Churchdown station, midway between Gloucester and Cheltenham, was a favourite spot of mine for trainspotting on summer Saturdays. On 27 July 1963 I spotted 'B1' 4-6-0 No 61138 of Colwick shed (40E) hauling a Bristol to Sheffield train through the station on the former London Midland Region line. On that day I also saw two more passing through Churchdown: No 61090 on a Paignton to Bradford train and No 61075 on a Weston-super-Mare to Sheffield train. On 29 August 1964 I spotted Nos 61153 and 61327 at Bristol Barrow Road shed (82E).

In my trainspotting travels to Scotland in 1964 I often saw 'B1s' at ex-LNER sheds such as St Margarets (64A) in Edinburgh, Eastfield (65A) in Glasgow, Bathgate (64F), Dunfermline (62C), Thornton (62A), Dundee Tay Bridge (62B) and Aberdeen Ferryhill (61B). I also had sightings of them at Corkerhill (67A) and Ayr (67C). Also on 12 June 1965 I recorded No 61013 *Topi* passing through Gloucester Eastgate light engine. Fast forward to 13 August 1965 when I was on a roundabout rail trip in the Eastern Region: at Doncaster I recorded No 61196 light engine and between Doncaster and Scunthorpe I spotted Nos 61055, 61208 and 61394 in action.

My last sightings of 'B1s' came on my trip to Scotland in August 1966: Nos 61072, 61340, 61350 and 61407 at Dunfermline shed (62C) and Nos 61099, 61103, 61132, 61148, 61308, 61344 at Thornton shed (62A) on 23 August. On the same day while travelling from Dunfermline to Stirling via Alloa by train I saw my last 'B1' in action: No 61101 was seen hauling a coal train near Oakley.

Edward Thompson

London & North Eastern Railway (1941–1946)

Edward Thompson was born in Marlborough, where his father was a master at the college, in 1881. Like Nigel Gresley (see page 159), Thompson was also educated at Marlborough School but then went on to study mechanical science at Cambridge, gaining a BA Honours in the subject in 1902. Following this he was apprenticed at the Lancashire & Yorkshire Railway's Horwich Works before being appointed Assistant Divisional Locomotive Superintendent on the North Eastern Railway. During World War I he served in the Royal Engineers and was mentioned in dispatches, subsequently joining the Great Northern Railway in 1919 to become Carriage & Wagon Superintendent at Doncaster. He held this post until 1930 when he was promoted to Workshop Manager at Stratford Works.

Nigel Gresley's death in 1941 was unexpected, and catapulted Thompson into the top job at the LNER where he was Chief Mechanical Engineer until his retirement to Westgate-on-Sea in 1946. He died in 1954.

The high point of Thompson's six years at Doncaster must surely be his two-cylinder Class 'B1' 4-6-0s, of which 410 were built between 1942 and 1952. They were highly successful performers although their life was cut short following the introduction of diesels in the early 1960s – the last examples were withdrawn in 1967 and two have been preserved. Many other Thompson locos were rebuilds of Gresley's engines: the 'A1/1' 4-6-2 (a rebuild of Gresley's first 'A1' Pacific), 'A2/1' 4-6-2 (enlarged Gresley 'V2' 2-6-2), and 'A2/2' (rebuilds of Gresley's 'P2' 2-8-2). Thompson's fifteen 'A2/3' Class 4-6-2s were built from new, with the last examples being withdrawn in 1965. Other Thompson locos included the Class 'O1' 2-8-0 and the 70-strong class 'K1' 2-6-0 (see page 213), the latter class built by the North British Locomotive Works between 1949 and 1950.

Nearly new LNER 'B1' Class 4-6-0 No 1018 at York station in 1947. It was named Gnu, which is the shortest locomotive name in Britain. Built at Darlington Works in early 1947, it was withdrawn from York shed (50A) in November 1965.

WD Standard Class '8F' 2-8-0

Intended for wartime action both at home and abroad, the WD Class '8F' 2-8-0s were the most numerous of any British locomotive class. Designed by Robert Riddles (see page 215) for the War Department (WD), they were a utilitarian, low-cost version of the LMS Stanier Class '8F' 2-8-0 (see page 179). The differences in design were that the WD version had a parallel boiler whereas the Stanier '8F' had a tapered version, the firebox was round-topped rather than a Belpaire type and it was constructed of steel rather than copper. The last one to be built (BR No 90732) was named *Vulcan*.

Many WD 2-8-0s saw action in mainland Europe after D-Day in 1944. After the war the War Department sold 930 locomotives. Two hundred went to the LNER (Class 'O7') and 533 went to the new British Transport Commission. These two batches were then renumbered 90000–90732 by British Railways. Of the remainder, twelve were exported to Hong Kong, 184 to the Netherlands and one to the USA. Two locomotives were retained by the WD for use on the Longmoor Military railway in Hampshire and three were scrapped.

The BR WD Class '8F' 2-8-0s were widely employed hauling heavy freight trains across both the London Midland, Eastern and North Eastern Regions of BR. The 'WDs' were also found in the Scottish Region hauling coal trains in Fife. They also ventured onto Western Region metals and I often saw them in the early 1960s making their familiar 'clanking' noise when hauling iron ore trains through Gloucester Central bound for South Wales.

Although withdrawals began in 1959, the majority survived until 1962 when mass extinction started, with the last five being withdrawn in 1967. Only one of these ungainly locomotives has been preserved and even this one, built in 1945, had to be imported by the Keighley & Worth Valley Railway from Sweden, years after being sold to Swedish State Railways by the Dutch Railways. It has since been restored to its original condition and carries the BR number 90733.

Specification

Builders	North British Locomotive Company (545)
	Vulcan Foundry (360)
Wheel arrangement	2-8-0
Build dates	1943–1945
BR power classification	8F
Cylinders	2 outside
Driving wheels	4 ft 8½ in
Tractive effort	34,215 lbs
Boiler pressure	225 psi
Number built	935
BR numbering	90000–90732

I recall seeing Nos 90018, 90024, 90053, 90063, 90068, 90073, 90156, 90390, 90395, 90448, 90498, 90675 and 90687 in action in the Doncaster area on 13 August 1965. My last memories of this class are recorded in my trainspotting notebook for 23 August 1966 on my final trip to Scotland: No 90560 seen hauling a freight train near Falkirk; Nos 90039, 90199, 90386, 90489, 90534 and 90547 at Dunfermline shed (62C); No 90444 on a freight train at Randolph Sidings near Thornton Junction; Nos 90071, 90350, 90441, 90547, 90600, 90628 and 90640 at Thornton shed (62A); Nos 90020 and 90386 seen on freight trains between Thornton and Dunfermline; No 90041 at Alloa shed (sub-shed of Dunfermline) – this was my last sighting of a 'WD'.

Ex-WD Class '8F' 2-8-0 No 90031 passes through Lincoln with a freight train on 20 June 1960. Built in 1943, it was withdrawn from New England shed (34E) in May 1963.

Ex-WD Class '8F' 2-8-0 No 90009 at Sunderland shed (52G) in 1958. This freight workhorse was built in 1943 and withdrawn in September 1967.

Frederick W. Hawksworth

Great Western Railway/British Railways (1941–1949)

Frederick Hawksworth was born in Swindon in 1884 and joined the GWR as an apprentice at the age of 14. A company man through and through, he slowly worked his way up the GWR hierarchy and was appointed Chief Locomotive Draughtsman at the time of the introduction of Charles Collett's 'King' Class 4-6-0s (see page 156) in 1927. Hawksworth was appointed as Chief Mechanical Engineer of the GWR following Collett's retirement in 1941. Despite wartime shortages he assembled a team of 100% GWR men and by 1944 had introduced the 'Modified Hall' Class 4-6-0s which were a highly successful development of Collett's 'Hall' Class. Plans for a

powerful 'Pacific' loco never got off the drawing board but the period between 1945 and 1947 was busy at Swindon, with the introduction of Hawksworth's 'County' Class 4-6-0s (see page 200) and improved 'Castles' (see page 139) with four-row superheaters. Despite being a two-cylinder engine, the 'County' class was certainly a break away from GWR tradition with their high-pressure Stanier '8F' boilers and 6-ft-3-in driving wheels.

Other loco types introduced under Hawksworth were the '1600' Class and '9400' Class 0-6-0PTs, the latter with a taper boiler, and the '1500' Class 0-6-0PT which were the only GWR locos fitted with external Walschaerts valve gear. Following nationalisation in 1948 Hawksworth remained in control at Swindon but was now responsible to the new Railway Executive. He retired in 1949 and died at the age of 92 in 1976.

Preserved BR-built 'Modified Hall' Class 4-6-0 No 7903 Foremarke Hall emerges from Greet Tunnel on the Gloucestershire Warwickshire Railway with a recreated 'Cheltenham Spa Express' on 29 March 2019. Built at Swindon Works in 1949, this loco was withdrawn from Cardiff East Dock shed (88L) in June 1964.

1944 GWR '6959' ('Modified Hall') Class 4-6-0

Designed by F. W. Hawksworth, the Great Western Railway's 'Modified Hall' Class mixed traffic 4-6-0s were a development of Charles Collett's 'Hall' Class locomotives (see page 162) that were introduced in 1928 – these in turn were a development of Churchward's 'Saint' Class introduced by the GWR in 1902. This new class continued the 'Hall' Class tradition of naming the locomotives after Welsh and English country houses. Although very similar in appearance to the 'Halls' and using the same GWR standard No 1 boiler, the 'Modified Halls' were a big departure from traditional GWR practice, with radical changes in the construction of the frames, cylinders, smokebox, superheater and front bogie. Improved draughting and hopper ashpans also helped to counteract the varying quality of coal which had been a problem towards the end of World War II. Many were also fitted with the new high-sided tenders also designed by Hawksworth. The locomotives were built at Swindon Works in four batches between 1944 and 1950, by which time the GWR had become part of the nationalised British Railways.

The 'Modified Halls' were a great success, steamed well, ran freely, were capable of sustained high-speed running, easy to maintain and liked by footplate crew. They could be seen performing on main lines all over the GWR/Western Region system hauling both fitted freight and passenger trains. They could also be seen hauling inter-regional passenger trains on the Great Central main line between Banbury, Woodford Halse and Leicester, and also between Oxford, Reading West, Basingstoke and over the Southern Region to the south coast.

Ex-GWR 'Modified Hall' 4-6-0 No 6980 Llanrumney Hall *after completing an overhaul inside its Swindon Works birthplace on 24 November 1963. Built in 1947, this loco was withdrawn from Tyseley shed (2A) in October 1965.*

The first 'Modified Hall' to be withdrawn, in January 1963, was No 6962 *Soughton Hall* with many surviving, albeit after a short working life, until the end of steam traction on the Western Region in December 1965. Six examples have since been preserved:

- 6960 *Raveningham Hall*
- 6984 *Owsden Hall*
- 6989 *Wightwick Hall*
- 6990 *Witherslack Hall*
- 6998 *Burton Agnes Hall*
- 7903 *Foremarke Hall.*

No 7927 *Willington Hall* was also saved from the scrapheap but is being cannibalised to provide parts for GWR 'County' and 'Grange' Class new-build locomotives.

On my last visit to Swindon Works on 8 April 1964 I spotted No 7915 receiving an overhaul and No 6967 outside in ex-works condition. Members of this class that I spotted at the end of 1965, only a few months before the end of steam on the Western Region, were as follows: No 7912 on a Bournemouth to York train at Banbury on 7 September; No 6991 on a down goods train at Basingstoke on 10 September; the latter loco was also seen in steam at Horton Road shed (85B) in Gloucester on 30 October and 27 November; No 7914 at Gloucester hauling a goods train to South Wales on the same day; No 7917 on an engineers' train at Barnwood, Gloucester, on 30 November: Nos 6999 and 7919 in steam at Horton Road shed on 6 December – these were the last two 'Modified Halls' that I saw on BR.

Specification

Builder	Swindon Works
Wheel arrangement	4-6-0
Build dates	1944-1950
BR power classification	5MT
Cylinders	2 outside
Driving wheels	6 ft
Tractive effort	27,275 lbs
Boiler pressure	225 psi superheated
Number built	71
BR numbering	6959-6999, 7900-7929

The Great Western Railway's mixed traffic 'County' Class 4-6-0s were the ultimate development of the two-cylinder 'Saint' Class locomotives (see page 98) that the GWR had introduced in 1902. Designed by F. W. Hawksworth (see page 198), they also included features used on his recent 'Modified Hall' Class (see page 199). This new class was named after English and Welsh counties served by the GWR, and in a change to tradition the brass nameplates were straight and fitted to the continuous wheel splashers. Although this was cosmetic treatment, in other ways the 'Counties' were certainly a big break with GWR tradition. Double chimneys were fitted to some examples, the boiler was a development of Stanier's Class '8F' 2-8-0 boiler with a high pressure of 280 psi (lowered to 250 psi from 1956). The 'Counties' also had a tractive effort of 32,580 lbs (greater than a 'Castle' Class loco) but this was later reduced to 29,090 lbs when the boiler pressure was reduced. Modified double chimneys were fitted to all members of the class from 1956. The class were also all fitted with Hawksworth's new high-sided tenders. The locomotives were built at Swindon Works in two batches between 1945 and 1947.

The 'Counties' were not totally welcomed by footplate crew or maintenance staff. They were a break with GWR tradition being of non-standard design, expensive to build and suffered from steaming problems, especially on the Cornish main line and the Paddington to Bristol route. However, they were at home on both express passenger and fast-fitted freight duties and were particularly well suited to the Wolverhampton Low Level to Shrewsbury route where they put up cracking performances.

Sadly, no examples were bought for preservation, probably because none ended up rising from the dead in Dai Woodham's memorable scrapyard in Barry. However, a replica new build of No 1014 *County of Glamorgan* is now under construction at the Didcot Railway Centre using parts from many withdrawn GWR locomotives and the boiler from withdrawn LMS '8F' 2-8-0 No 48518.

Specification

Builder	Swindon Works
Wheel arrangement	4-6-0
Build dates	1945–1947
BR power classification	6MT
Cylinders	2 outside
Driving wheels	6 ft 3 in
Tractive effort	32,580 lbs (reduced to 29,090 lbs from 1956)
Boiler pressure	280 psi (reduced to 250 psi from 1956)
Number built	30
BR numbering	1000–1029

My first memory of a 'County' was when I travelled by train from Gloucester to Perranporth in the summer of 1958 – No 1006 *County of Cornwall* hauled our train from Plymouth North Road for the next part of the journey to Truro. In the early 1960s Swindon shed (82C) was the final allocation for many of this class and I often used to see them on stopping passenger trains to and from Gloucester Central. I have a record of spotting Nos 1000 and 1028 at Cardiff East Dock shed (88L) on 7 April 1963. After a very short working life, the first 'Counties' to be withdrawn, in September 1962, were No 1004 *County of Somerset*, No 1018 *County of Leicester* and No 1026 *County of Salop*. The last one to be withdrawn was No 1011 *County of Chester*. My final sighting of a 'County' was No 1011 at Gloucester hauling a Railway Correspondence & Travel Society special train just before the loco's withdrawal at the end of November 1964 – it had its front number painted in yellow on the buffer beam. It was still outside Swindon Works when I passed by on 9 January 1965, shortly before its final journey to Cashmore's scrapyard in Newport.

Ex-GWR 'County' Class 4-6-0 No 1012 County of Denbigh *at Swindon station with a stopping service to Bristol in 1962. Built at Swindon Works in 1946, this loco was withdrawn from Swindon shed (82C) in April 1964.*

Ex-GWR 'County' Class 4-6-0 No 1028 County of Warwick *at St Erth with 'The Cornishman' in September 1960. Built at Swindon Works in 1947, this loco was withdrawn from Swindon shed (82C) at the end of 1963.*

SR 'West Country' and 'Battle of Britain' Classes ('Light Pacifics') 4-6-2

Designed by Oliver Bulleid (see page 191) for the Southern Railway and mostly built at Brighton Works (with six at Eastleigh Works), the air-smoothed 'West Country'/'Battle of Britain' Class mixed-traffic 4-6-2s were a lighter version of his innovative 'Merchant Navy' Class (see page 190). Because of their lighter axle-loading weight, smaller boiler and shorter length they could travel over much of the Southern Railway's network, and were equally at home on the 'Withered Arm' in North Cornwall hauling a one-coach train as powering an express on the Victoria to Dover main line.

Although the first batch of twenty locomotives was ordered in 1941, due to wartime constraints the first 'Light Pacific' only emerged from Brighton Works in May 1945. This was No 21C101 (34001) *Exeter*. Construction continued until the last of the 110 locos, No 34110 *66 Squadron*, emerged from Eastleigh Works in January 1951. The locos were named after West Country destinations served by the Southern Railway, RAF Battle of Britain squadrons, RAF fighter airfields, RAF fighter aircraft types and wartime dignitaries.

The class also suffered from the same problems as the 'Merchant Navies', such as the chain-driven valve gear, and 60 locomotives were subsequently rebuilt at Eastleigh between 1957 and 1961. The air-smoothed casing was removed, boiler pressure reduced, the chain-driven valve gear replaced by Walschaerts valve gear, and smoke deflectors were added. However, their added weight meant that they could not travel on the SR routes west of Exeter.

Electrification from Victoria to Dover and Ramsgate in 1959, the dieselisation of routes west of Salisbury in 1964 and electrification of the Waterloo to Bournemouth route in 1967 all conspired to bring about the eventual downfall of the 'Light Pacifics'. Withdrawals began in 1963 with ten retired, followed by 29 in 1964, sixteen in 1965, eighteen in 1966 and the final 37 in 1967. Fortunately, an astonishing eighteen examples were bought by Dai Woodham's scrapyard in Barry, thus escaping the death sentence. Along with two others bought directly from BR, there are now twenty 'Light Pacifics' (ten unrebuilt, ten rebuilt) in different stages of preservation ranging from rusting hulks to gleaming operational machines.

Specification

Builders	Brighton Works (104)
	Eastleigh Works (6)
Wheel arrangement	4-6-2
Build dates	1945–1951
BR power classification	7P5F
Cylinders	3 (2 outside, 1 inside)
Driving wheels	6 ft 2 in
Tractive effort	31,000 lbs
Boiler pressure	280 psi (250 psi in rebuilt locos)
Number built	110 (including 60 rebuilds)
BR numbering	34001–34110

BR-built unrebuilt 'Battle of Britain' Class 4-6-2 No 34072 257 Squadron at Holme Lane on the Swanage Railway on 4 March 2019. Built at Brighton Works in 1948, this loco was withdrawn from Eastleigh shed (71A/70D) in October 1964 before being purchased for preservation on the Swanage Railway.

Built at Brighton Works in 1946, ex-SR 'West Country' Class 4-6-2 No 34044 Woolacombe at Basingstoke station with a Waterloo to Bournemouth train on 22 August 1964. This loco was rebuilt in 1957 and withdrawn from Bournemouth shed (71B/70F) in May 1967.

I saw many 'Light Pacifics' during my years as a trainspotter in the 1960s, either on my trips over the Somerset & Dorset Joint Railway, on holiday trips to North Devon, Exeter and Bournemouth, and at one of my favourite haunts, Basingstoke. Here are some of my observations, with numbers seen on each occasion: 23 August 1961, Wareham – 7; 25 August 1961, Bournemouth Central – 12; 30 August 1961, Bournemouth Central – 19; 1 September 1961, S&DJR – 2: 7 April 1962, Basingstoke – 12; 5 August 1963, Axminster – 14; 8 August 1963, Axminster/Exeter – 30 (including No 34080 *74 Squadron* from Axminster to Exeter Central); 10 August 1963, No 34054 *Lord Beaverbrook* from Axminster to Templecombe; 31 August 1963, Basingstoke – 34; 6 September 1963, Salisbury – 16; 31 December 1963, Yeovil shed (72C) – 3; No 34079 *141 Squadron* came through Gloucester on an enthusiasts' special on 14 June 1964; 29 August 1964, No 34079 *141 Squadron* from Barnstaple Junction to Woolacombe; 1 September 1964, Exeter – 27; 9 January 1965, Basingstoke – 15; 9 September 1965, Basingstoke – 15; and my final sightings of 'Light Pacifics' came on 31 January 1967 when I popped into Waterloo and recorded Nos 34095 *Brentor* and 34044 *Woolacombe* in action.

Henry George Ivatt

London Midland & Scottish Railway/British Railways (1945–1951)

The son of H. A. Ivatt (see page 81), Henry George Ivatt was born in Dublin in 1886 when his father was the Locomotive Engineer of the Great Southern & Western Railway of Ireland. Following a private education, he was apprenticed at the London & North Western Railway's Crewe Works in 1904 and by 1910 had had experience as a draughtsman, assistant shed foreman and assistant superintendent of outdoor machinery. Following war service in France, Ivatt was appointed Assistant Locomotive Superintendent of the North Staffordshire Railway, the company becoming part of the London Midland & Scottish Railway in 1923.

Moving to the LMS's Derby Works in 1928, Ivatt was subsequently appointed as Locomotive Works Superintendent there three years later. From 1932 to 1937 he was Divisional Mechanical Engineer for the LMS in Scotland before returning to Derby where he became the chief assistant to the CME, William Stanier (see page 170). Stanier retired in 1944 and was replaced by Charles Fairburn, but his sudden death a year later catapulted Ivatt into the top position of Chief Mechanical Engineer of the LMS.

Following nationalisation in 1948, Ivatt stayed on as CME of the London Midland Region before retiring from BR in 1951. There then followed a spell as director of Brush Traction in Loughborough before finally severing his links with the railway industry in 1964. He died in 1976 at the age of 90.

Ivatt's output as a locomotive designer at the LMS and BR is fairly impressive and under his watch the last two 'Coronation' 4-6-2s (Nos 46256 and 46257) were built along with the first two mainline diesel-electric prototypes (Nos 10000 and 10001). The three new classes of loco designed by Ivatt were the 130 Class '2MT' 2-6-2T, 128 Class '2MT' 2-6-0 (known as 'Mickey Mouse') and 162 Class '4MT' 2-6-0 (known as 'Doodlebugs' – see page 206).

BR-built Ivatt Class '2MT' 2-6-2T No 41287 at Guildford station, June 1965. Built at Crewe Works in 1950, this loco was withdrawn from Eastleigh shed (71A/70D) in July 1966.

LMS Ivatt Class '2MT' 2-6-2T

The Class '2MT' 2-6-2T was designed to replace many different classes of veteran tank locomotives then employed on light branch line work by the London Midland & Scottish Railway. Designed by H. G. Ivatt, production continued through to the British Railways era and the locomotives were not only employed on the LMS network in England but, by the 1950s, could be seen at work on Southern Region branch lines. A few of the class were allocated to Bristol for hauling trains on the Midland route from Temple Meads to Bath Green Park.

The Class '2MT' was a development of the LMS Fowler 2-6-2Ts of which 70 had been built between 1930 and 1932. The new locos had several new features including rocking grates and self-emptying ashpans. Fifty locos were fitted for push-pull operations. A tender version of these locos was also built between 1946 and 1953 (BR Nos 46400–46527), with three batches being built at Darlington and delivered to the North Eastern Region, and the last two batches being built at Swindon Works for secondary route operations in Mid-Wales. A slightly modified version of the tank engines appeared as the BR Standard Class '2' 2-6-2T (Nos 84000–84029) built from 1953 to 1957.

Withdrawals of the class started in 1962 when 21 were retired, followed by eighteen in 1963, 26 in 1964, 26 in 1965, 31 in 1966 and the final eight in 1967. Four members have been preserved and all are currently operational: Nos 41241, 41298, 41312 and 41313.

Preserved BR-built Ivatt Class '2MT' 2-6-2T No 41312 hauling a recreated 'Pines Express' at Midsomer Norton South station, Somerset & Dorset Railway Trust, on 17 September 2022. Built at Crewe Works in 1952, this loco was withdrawn in July 1967.

I have many fond memories of being hauled by these locos in the early 1960s on the Axminster to Lyme Regis branch and the Evercreech Junction to Highbridge branch of the Somerset & Dorset Joint Railway. My trainspotting notebook for 3 August 1963 records that No 41249 headed my train from Mangotsfield to Bath Green Park and, later on, No 41307 hauled me from Axminster to Lyme Regis. The same loco headed my train to Axminster on the 10 August and, later on, No 41208 hauled me from Bath Green Park to Mangotsfield.

When on holiday in North Devon in 1964 I spotted Nos 41208 (again), 41216, 41223, 41249 and 41283 at Barnstaple Junction on 29 August. On a visit to Exeter on 1 September my notebook tells me that I spotted No 41308 piloting 'Battle of Britain' Class No 34082 615 Squadron into Central station with a Waterloo to Plymouth express running 50 minutes late. While on a train journey from Rugby to Peterborough on 9 August 1965 I recorded No 41212 at Seaton with a push-pull train for Stamford.

On my last visit to the S&DJR on 6 September 1965 I was hauled by No 41249 from Evercreech Junction to Highbridge and No 41216 in the opposite direction. No 41206 was also outside the near-derelict shed at Highbridge. Nos 41223, 41249, 41283, 41290, 41296 and 41307 were all at Templecombe shed (82G) while Nos 41208, 41214 and 41243 were stored out of use at Bath Green Park shed (82F) on that day.

Specification

Builders	Crewe Works (120)
	Derby Works (10)
Wheel arrangement	2-6-2T
Build dates	1946–1952
BR power classification	2MT
Cylinders	2 outside
Driving wheels	5ft 0 in
Tractive effort	17,400 lbs
Boiler pressure	200 psi
Number built	130
BR numbering	41200–41329

LMS Ivatt Class '4MT' 2-6-0

With their high running plate, the Class '4MT' 2-6-0s were considered to be rather ungainly and were nicknamed 'Doodlebugs'. Designed by H. G. Ivatt (see page 204) for the London Midland & Scottish Railway, the class was produced to perform freight and secondary passenger duties. Although construction started in 1947, 159 were built for British Railways until 1952. The first 50 were built with double chimneys. Initially they suffered from poor steaming qualities but performance improved when the double chimney was replaced by a single chimney. Also with high running plates, the BR Standard Class '4' 2-6-0s

Nos 76000–76114, built between 1952 and 1957, were a development of this design.

Widely seen in action on the London Midland Region, they also dominated the former Midland & Great Northern Joint Railway's route in East Anglia from the early 1950s until its closure in 1959. Withdrawals started in 1963 when six were retired, followed by fifteen in 1964, 42 in 1965, 34 in 1966, 59 in 1967 and the final six in 1968. Only one example is preserved: No 43106 was built at Darlington in 1951 and withdrawn from Lostock Hall shed in June 1968. Its last journey on BR tracks was on 1 August 1968 when it travelled to its new home on the Severn Valley Railway, only three days before the official end of steam traction on BR.

I didn't see 'Doodlebugs' too often but on going through my later trainspotting notebooks I recorded the following sightings. On my last visit to Swindon Works on 4 April 1964 I recorded seeing Nos 43002, 43015, 43044, 43047, 43056, 43090, 43109 and 43132 – they were all from 'up north' and I can only assume they were in for overhaul. I spotted No 43047 at Gloucester on 20 July 1964, Nos 43004, 43023 and 43040 at Carlisle Kingmoor shed (12A) on 29 July 1964, No 43025 at Upperby shed (12B) and No 43027 at Carlisle station on the same day, No 43023 at Carlisle station on 1 August 1964 and Nos 43025 and 43045 at Upperby shed on the same day. No 43115 was seen in Gloucester on 10 October 1964. No 43106 was in ex-works condition at Eastleigh on 2 October 1965 and my final sighting was of No 43036 stored at Motherwell shed (66B) on 25 August 1966.

BR-built Ivatt Class '4MT' 2-6-0 No 43033 hauling a local train at Stockport Tiviot Dale in 1964. Built at Horwich Works in 1949, this loco was withdrawn from Lostock Hall shed (24C/10D) in March 1968.

Specification

Builders	Horwich Works (75)
	Doncaster Works (50)
	Darlington Works (37)
Wheel arrangement	2-6-0
Build dates	1947–1952
BR power classification	4MT
Cylinders	2 outside
Driving wheels	5ft 3 in
Tractive effort	24,170 lbs
Boiler pressure	225 psi
Number built	162
BR numbering	43000–43161

BR-built Ivatt Class '4MT' 2-6-0 No 43145 at Melton Constable on the Midland & Great Northern Joint Railway on 30 May 1953. Built at Doncaster Works in 1951 this 'Doodlebug' was withdrawn from Colwick shed (40E) in January 1965.

Peppercorn Class 'A1' 4-6-2

Although designed by Arthur Peppercorn for the London & North Eastern Railway, the 'A1' Class 4-6-2s were built during the first two years of the nationalised British Railways. Prior to that, the first of the class, No 60113 *Great Northern*, was a 1945 rebuild of Gresley Class 'A1' 4-6-2 No 4470, with the same name and originally built for the Great Northern Railway in 1922. As a rebuild it was later designated as a Class 'A1/1'.

Numbered 60114–60162, the 49 new 'A1s' were built at Doncaster Works and Darlington Works in 1948 and 1949. All were fitted with a double Kylchap chimney and Nos 60153–60157 were also fitted with Timken roller bearings on all axles, which had a very positive effect on the mileages achieved between heavy overhauls. The locomotives were put to work hauling heavy expresses on the East Coast Main Line and were popular with footplate crew.

The names later fitted to the 'A1s' came from a diverse range of sources including famous racehorses, names of LNER/NER/GNR railway dignitaries, names associated with Sir Walter Scott novels, pre-Grouping railway companies, place names and birds.

Sadly, the new 'A1s' had a short life. No 60113, the only Class 'A1/1', was withdrawn in 1962 along with six of the 'A1s'. A further six were withdrawn in 1963 followed by eleven in 1964, 24 in 1965 and the last two in 1966. A preservation attempt on the last to be withdrawn, No 60145 *Saint Mungo*, sadly failed.

Fast forward to 2008 when a brand new Peppercorn Class 'A1', No 60163, emerged from Darlington Locomotive Works on 1 August. Taking fourteen years to build at a cost of £1.6 million, the locomotive was named *Tornado* in honour of RAF Tornado aircrews then flying in the Gulf War. Since then it has attracted huge crowds of onlookers wherever it has travelled, either when working charter trains on the main line or as a visitor to heritage railways.

Specification

Builders	Doncaster Works (1 rebuild of Gresley Class 'A1' + 26) Darlington Works (23 + 1 new build)
Wheel arrangement	4-6-2
Build dates	1945 (rebuild of Gresley Class 'A1'), 1948–1949, 2008
BR power classification	8P6F
Cylinders	3 (2 outside, 1 inside)
Driving wheels	6 ft 8 in
Tractive effort	37,400 lbs
Boiler pressure	250 psi
Number built	1 rebuild + 49 + 1 new build
BR numbering	60113 (1945 rebuild of Gresley Class 'A1'), 60114–60162, 60163 (new build)

Class 'A1' 4-6-2 No 60124 Kenilworth at Darlington shed (51A) on 14 August 1965. Built at Doncaster Works in 1949, this locomotive was withdrawn in March 1966.

I didn't see 'A1s' too often as I lived in Gloucester but my trainspotting notebooks reveal the following sightings: Nos 60119, 60138 and 60149 at King's Cross station on 14 April 1962; No 60148 at King's Cross station on 4 September 1962; No 60152 and 60160 at St Margarets shed (64A) on 29 March 1964; No 60131 spotted from a Gourock to Glasgow Central train on 27 July 1964 and at Carlisle on 1 August where it had arrived with a train from Leeds; No 60118 at Glasgow Polmadie shed (66A) and Nos 60127, 60129, 60147 and 60152 at St Margarets shed (64A) on 2 August 1964. My final sighting of a BR Class 'A1' was on 7 September 1965 when I was on a train from Birmingham New Street to Derby – imagine my surprise when I saw No 60145 *St Mungo* in a siding on the approach to Derby. Although scheduled for preservation, this loco was withdrawn from York North shed (50A) in June 1966 and scrapped at Drapers of Hull.

Arthur Henry Peppercorn

London & North Eastern Railway (1946–1947)
British Railways/Eastern & North Eastern Region (1948–1949)

Arthur Peppercorn was born in Leominster, Herefordshire, in 1889 and started his railway career as an apprentice at the Great Northern Railway at Doncaster in 1905. He gained further experience as an assistant locomotive superintendent at several GNR engine sheds before serving with the Royal Engineers during World War I. On returning to Doncaster he became Carriage & Wagon Works Manager for the newly formed LNER in 1923, and over the succeeding years held important posts at York, Stratford, Darlington and Doncaster before becoming Assistant Chief Mechanical Engineer under Edward Thompson (see page 195) in 1945. Thompson retired in 1946 and Peppercorn was promoted to Chief Mechanical Engineer, a position he held through nationalisation in 1948 when he was made CME of the Eastern & North Eastern Regions of BR. He retired in 1949 and died in 1951.

During Peppercorn's short tenure as CME at Doncaster he introduced two outstanding classes of Pacific locomotive which sadly had short working lives due to the introduction of diesels in the 1950s and 1960s. Fifteen of his 'A2' 4-6-2s were built at Doncaster between 1947 and 1948 – the last survivor, No 60532 *Blue Peter*, survived until 1966 and was then saved for preservation. The 49 members of his 'A1' Class 4-6-2s were built at Doncaster and Darlington between 1948 and 1949 – known for their reliability and high mileages between overhaul, they had all been withdrawn by 1966. Although none were preserved, a new-build 'A1', No 60163 *Tornado*, was rolled out of Darlington Works in 2008 and has since been in service hauling charter trains around Britain.

Completed at Darlington in 2008, new-build Peppercorn Class 'A1' 4-6-2 No 60163 Tornado *at Waitby on the Settle–Carlisle Line, 22 May 2021.*

The Flying Scotsman

London (King's Cross) to Edinburgh (Waverley)

The successor to the 'Special Scotch Express', 'The Flying Scotsman' restaurant car express between London (King's Cross) and Edinburgh (Waverley) was introduced by the London & North Eastern Railway in 1924. With the help of corridor tenders it became a non-stop service between King's Cross and Edinburgh in 1928. It remained in operation during World War II and continued to be run by the Eastern, North Eastern and Scottish regions of British Railways from 1948.

In the summer of 1949, the new 'Capitals Limited' express took over the non-stop service and 'The Flying Scotsman' consequently lost this honour, with stops en route at Grantham and Newcastle (Central). In 1955 the train was once again accelerated, running non-stop between King's Cross and Newcastle (Central), and cutting the London to Edinburgh journey time to 7 hours. Gresley's 'A4' Pacifics were replaced in 1962 by new 3,300 hp 'Deltic' diesels – these powerful locomotives, assisted by newly introduced long stretches of 100 mph running along the East Coast Main Line, soon cut the 393-mile journey time, including the Newcastle stop, to a record-breaking 6 hours.

In turn, the 'Deltics' were replaced by HST 125 sets between 1976 and 1981, and the opening of the Selby diversion reduced the journey time further. Electrification of the East Coast Main Line was completed in 1990 and, since then, InterCity 225 sets with a maximum permissible speed of 125 mph have provided an even faster service. Since privatisation, the train has continued to run with a speeded-up service, complete with special 'Flying Scotsman' livery being introduced in 2011. Strangely, the 10 a.m. down working from King's Cross does not carry the name in the timetable.

Peppercorn Class 'A1' 4-6-2 No 60139 Sea Eagle heads non-stop through York station on the middle road with 'The Flying Scotsman' in 1959. Built by British Railways at Darlington Works in 1948, this locomotive was withdrawn in June 1964.

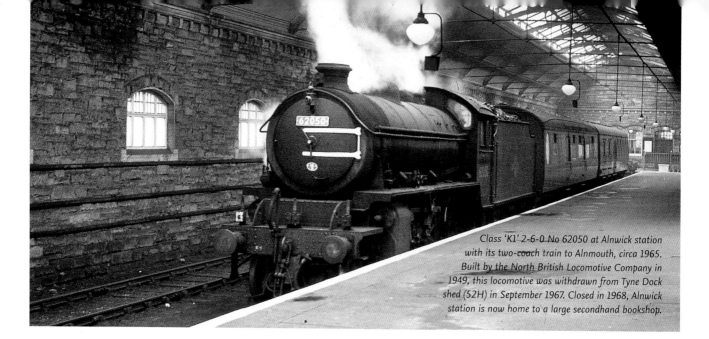

Class 'K1' 2-6-0 No 62050 at Alnwick station with its two-coach train to Alnmouth, circa 1965. Built by the North British Locomotive Company in 1949, this locomotive was withdrawn from Tyne Dock shed (52H) in September 1967. Closed in 1968, Alnwick station is now home to a large secondhand bookshop.

BR (NER/ER) Class 'K1' 2-6-0

The Class 'K1' mixed-traffic 2-6-0s were a development, by Arthur Peppercorn (see page 209), of Nigel Gresley's (see page 159) six Class 'K4' 2-6-0s which had been built for the London & North Eastern Railway between 1937 and 1939. In 1945, Gresley's successor at the LNER, Edward Thompson, rebuilt Class 'K4' No 3445 (61997) *MacCailin Mor* into the first (and only) Class 'K1/1'. When Arthur Peppercorn replaced Thompson in 1947 he set about using the rebuilt loco as a basis for a whole new class of two-cylinder 2-6-0s which became Class 'K1'. Modifications to the Class 'K1/1' included increased length, larger tenders and easier access to cylinder steam chests. A total of 70 of these new locomotives were built in the early years of the nationalised British Railways by the North British Locomotive Company between 1949 and 1950.

The new 'K1s' were universally well received by footplate crew and maintenance staff and could be seen in action on freight and passenger duties primarily in the northeast of England, on the West Highland Line and Mallaig Extension in Scotland, and also in March on the Eastern Region. Sadly they had a very short working life as they soon had to make way for new diesels. Withdrawals started in 1962, when the 'K1/1' rebuild No 61997 was retired, and the last but one was taken out of service in 1967. No 62005 was the last to be withdrawn but was saved for preservation. It is based on the North Yorkshire Moors Railway but it occasionally spends the summer months at Fort William, where it takes turns hauling 'The Jacobite' service to Mallaig.

Built in 1949, Class 'K1' 2-6-0 No 62011 is seen here at Eastfield shed (65A) in Glasgow shortly after delivery from the North British Locomotive Company.

To my regret I have only seen Class 'K1s' in action once, when I was on a roundabout rail trip from Peterborough to Doncaster, Scunthorpe, Grimsby, Louth, Spalding and back to Peterborough on 13 August 1965. Between Scunthorpe and Grimsby I recorded seeing Nos 62035 and 62067, presumably hauling freight trains. This was my first and last sighting!

Specification

Builder	North British Locomotive Company
Wheel arrangement	2-6-0
Build dates	1949–1950
BR power classification	5P6F
Cylinders	2 outside
Driving wheels	5 ft 2 in
Tractive effort	32,080 lbs
Boiler pressure	225 psi
Number built	70
BR numbering	62001–62070

1951 BR Standard Class '7' ('Britannia') 4-6-2

The Standard Class '7' or 'Britannia' mixed-traffic 4-6-2 was Robert Riddles' first locomotive design for the newly nationalised British Railways. In 1948 the pre-nationalisation locomotive designs of the GWR, LMS, LNER and SR underwent exchanges to determine the best qualities of their ageing steam locomotives. The results of these exchanges were then used to formulate the new standard classes of locomotives to be built for British Railways. The new classes were actually designed by Ernest Cox under the watchful eye of Robert Riddles, who had been appointed Chief Mechanical & Electrical Engineer of the new Railway Executive.

Using features from Bulleid's 'Merchant Navy' and 'Light Pacifics' (see pages 190 and 202), the 'Britannias' also had a compromised driving wheel diameter, enabling them to fulfill their mixed-traffic role, and only two outside cylinders and valve gear for ease of maintenance. Raised running plates allowed easier access between the frames. They also had a self-cleaning smokebox and an ergonomically designed footplate and cab interior.

Built at Crewe Works in 1951, the first batch of 25 locomotives were pressed into service, mainly on the Eastern Region, without proper testing. They all had to be temporarily withdrawn later that year due to wheel slippage on their axles, and vibration. The second batch of twenty locos was delivered in 1952/53 and the final batch of ten locos in 1954.

The 'Britannias' were named after well-known, historical Britons (for example, *Oliver Cromwell*), with the exception of locos that operated on the Scottish Region, which were named after Scottish firths (for example, *Firth of Forth*) and those that operated on the Western Region that were named after former 'Star' Class locos (such as *Morning Star*). No 70048 was later named *The Territorial Army 1908–1958* and No 70047 never received a name.

The first batch of 'Britannias' went to work on the former Great Eastern main line between Liverpool Street and Norwich, transforming the passenger service. On dieselisation of this route in the late 1950s they were transferred to the London Midland Region (LMR). A further batch went to the Western Region where there were mixed results, although the Cardiff Canton locos did perform well on expresses to and from Paddington. These were also later transferred to the LMR. The Southern Region received two examples, No 70004 *William Shakespeare* and No 70014 *Iron Duke*, which were allocated to Stewarts Lane shed specifically for hauling the 'Golden Arrow' boat train to and from Dover. They were transferred to Longsight, Manchester in 1958. By the 1960s the class were concentrated either in the LMR, with the majority located at Crewe and Carlisle, or in the Scottish Region at Glasgow Polmadie.

Withdrawals began in 1965 with two taken out of service, then twelve in 1966, 40 in 1967 and the final one, 70013 *Oliver Cromwell*, in 1968. Both this locomotive and No 70000 *Britannia* have since been preserved.

Preserved BR Standard Class '7' 4-6-2 No 70000 Britannia has just crossed Arten Gill Viaduct on the Settle–Carlisle Line, 3 March 2012. Built at Crewe Works in 1951, this locomotive was withdrawn from Newton Heath shed (26A/9D) in May 1966.

Robert Arthur Riddles

British Railways (1948–1953)

Robert Riddles was born in 1892 (his place of birth is not recorded) and was a premium apprentice with the London & North Western Railway at Crewe Works between 1909 and 1913. During World War I he was seriously injured while serving with the Royal Engineers in France. Riddles returned to Crewe after the war, where he went on to become head of the production department and was mainly responsible for the reorganisation of the LMS Works in 1925–1927. He repeated this task at Derby before being appointed in 1933 as Chief Assistant to the CME, William Stanier. During this period Riddles was closely involved in the design and building of the 'Coronation' Class 4-6-2s (see page 186), was present on *Coronation*'s record-breaking 114 mph run in 1937 and accompanied the locomotive's tour of North America in 1939.

During World War II, Riddles became Director of Transportation Equipment at the Ministry of Supply, designing the WD 'Austerity' 2-8-0 (see page 196) and 2-10-0 locos. He returned to the LMS in 1943 but was passed over in favour of George Ivatt (see page 204) as CME following Charles Fairburn's sudden death. However, he was appointed Chief Mechanical & Electrical Engineer of the newly formed Railway Executive in 1947 and went on to design three classes of 4-6-2 ('Britannia', 'Clan' and *Duke of Gloucester*), two classes of 4-6-0, three classes of 2-6-0, two classes of 2-6-2T, one class of 2-6-4T (see page 220) and one class of 2-10-0 (see page 222). Probably the most successful of his designs, 251 of the latter type were built and in 1960 No 92220 *Evening Star* became the last steam locomotive to be built for British Railways. A job well done, Riddles retired in 1953 and died in 1983.

Sadly, I missed seeing the 'Brits' on the Western Region as they had all been transferred away before I started trainspotting and they didn't start visiting Gloucester for a brief period until the summer of 1965. My first recorded sightings were on a visit to Crewe Works in August 1962: Nos 70022, 70033 and 70039 were spotted that day. No 70036 was seen at King's Cross station on 4 September 1962. On my trip to Glasgow and Edinburgh on 28/29 March 1964 I spotted No 70019 at Birmingham New Street, No 70050 at Polmadie shed (66A) and No 70003 at Edinburgh Waverley with a train for Carlisle.

On my second trip to Scotland in 1964 I spotted the following 'Brits': No 70003 at Carstairs, Nos 70013 and 70030 at Carlisle station, Nos 70002, 70035, 70037, 70038, 70039 and 70041 at Kingmoor shed (12A), all on 29 July; No 70038 at Perth on 30 July; 70002, 70007,

70037, 70017 and 70039 at Carlisle station and Nos 70008 and 70018 at Upperby shed (12B) on 1 August. I then caught the 'Royal Scot' to Glasgow Central – imagine my surprise when No 70002 *Geoffrey Chaucer* backed onto the train. The next day I spotted Nos 70002, 70013, 70035 and 70037 at Polmadie shed (66A). On 5 August I spotted No 70003 in Glasgow. On 25 May 1965 while on an overnight train trip from Gloucester to Oban I spotted Nos 70021, 70032 and 70052 at Crewe and Nos 70009, 70022, 70033 and 70040 at Carlisle.

My final sightings came in the summer of 1965 near Gloucester, when Oxley-based 'Brits' were employed to haul summer-Saturday holiday trains from the Midlands to the West Country as far as Bristol. Nos 70045 and 70053 were the first of these to be spotted on 10 July, and the last 'Brits' I saw in action.

Specification

Builder	Crewe Works
Wheel arrangement	4-6-2
Build dates	1951–1954
BR power classification	7MT
Cylinders	2 outside
Driving wheels	6 ft 2 in
Tractive effort	32,150 lbs
Boiler pressure	250 psi
Number built	55
BR numbering	70000–70054

The Red Dragon

London (Paddington) to Carmarthen

Compared to the mile-a-minute down 'Pembroke Coast Express', 'The Red Dragon' took a more leisurely journey between London and South Wales. Introduced in 1950, the restaurant car train was soon in the hands of Cardiff Canton's new BR Standard 'Britannia' Pacifics for the journey between Cardiff and London, until these were transferred away to the London Midland Region in 1960. They were replaced by 'Castle' and 'King' Class 4-6-0s until the introduction of 'Hymek' and 'Western' diesel hydraulics in the early 1960s. The summer 1958 timetable shows the up train leaving Carmarthen at 7.30 a.m. and arriving at Paddington at 1 p.m., while the down service, with more stops, left Paddington at 5.55 p.m. and arrived in Carmarthen at 11.48 p.m. – engines were changed at Cardiff while the Carmarthen coaches were attached or detached at Swansea. Strangely, only the down train stopped at Swindon and Badminton, while the up train ran non-stop from Newport to Paddington. It was a very long day for a Carmarthen-based businessperson visiting London for a meeting, but very enjoyable all the same during the days of steam haulage. The train lost its name in 1965.

Cardiff Canton's BR Standard Class '7MT' 4-6-2 No 70019 Lightning waits to depart from Paddington with the down 'The Red Dragon' on 10 September 1960. Built at Crewe Works in 1951, this locomotive was withdrawn from Carlisle Upperby shed (12B) in March 1966.

R obert Riddles (see page 215) developed the LMS Stanier 'Black Five' 4-6-0 (see page 174) for the new BR Standard Class '5' mixed-traffic 4-6-0. His modifications included slightly larger driving wheels, a standard boiler constructed from manganese steel and a high running plate and external pipework to ease maintenance. The first locomotive, No 73000, entered service in April 1951 with the last entering service in June 1957. Nos 73125–73154 were fitted with poppet valves and Caprotti valve gear instead of Walschaerts valve gear.

The Class '5s' are generally acknowledged to be a very successful class of locomotives and their versatility allowed them to haul fast express passenger trains at speeds of over 90 mph or slow, heavy goods trains. The class were widely distributed across the BR network from the Somerset & Dorset Joint Railway and the Southern Region main line out of Waterloo to Bournemouth and Weymouth, to the Scottish Region's Edinburgh/Glasgow to Aberdeen routes, and the London Midland Region and the former Midland main line to Bristol. Twenty of the Southern Region's allocation (Nos 73080–73089 and 73110–73119) received names in 1959 originally carried by 'King Arthur' Class locos (see page 130). The straight nameplates were positioned on the side of the running plate above the centre driving wheel. These Southern Region locos were also fitted with larger water capacity tenders as there were no water troughs on that region.

Withdrawals started in 1964 when fifteen were taken out of service, followed by 43 in 1965, 38 in 1966, 53 in 1967 and the final 23 in 1968. Five members have been preserved, four of which, Nos 73082 *Camelot*, 73096, 73129 (Caprotti valve gear) and 73156 were all rescued from Dai Woodham's scrapyard in Barry. The other, No 73050, (now named *City of Peterborough*) was purchased directly from BR.

Specification

Builders	Derby Works (130)
	Doncaster Works (42)
Wheel arrangement	4-6-0
Build dates	1951–1957
BR power classification	5MT
Cylinders	2 outside
Driving wheels	6 ft 2 in
Tractive effort	26,124 lbs
Boiler pressure	225 psi
Number built	172
BR numbering	73000–73171

BR Standard Class '5s' were a common sight to me living in Gloucester, with Nos 73091, 73092 and 73093 allocated to Barnwood shed (85C) in 1962. Five were also allocated to Bristol Barrow Road (82E), so observing them on the Midland route to Bristol was a daily occurrence. Further afield, five were allocated to Bath Green Park for working over the Somerset & Dorset Joint Railway. Of these, No 73054 hauled my train over the Mendips from Green Park to Templecombe on 3 August 1963 and No 73052 in the reverse direction on 10 August. While trainspotting at Basingstoke on 31 August 1963 I recorded eleven examples, many of them the named Southern Region variety. Also at Basingstoke on 22 August 1964 I spotted twelve examples.

I also recorded many examples of this class on my trainspotting trips to Scotland: nine at Polmadie shed (66A), seven at Corkerhill shed (67A), six at Eastfield shed (65A), and six at St Rollox shed and works, all on 29 March 1964. Again in July/August 1964: four at Carlisle Kingmoor (12A) on 29 July; four at Carlisle station on 1 August; eight at Polmadie shed (66A) on 2 August; three at Eastfield shed (65A), six at St Rollox shed (65B) and seven at Corkerhill shed (67A), all on 5 August.

On 6 September 1965 I travelled on the Somerset & Dorset Joint Railway for the last time – motive power between Bath Green Park and Templecombe was No 73068. Towards the end of 1965, before steam traction ended on the Western Region, my trainspotting notebook records seeing the following at Gloucester Horton Road shed (85B): No 73004 (6 November) and No 73166 (27 November). My nearly final sightings of these fine locos came when I visited Scotland in August 1966: No 73153 at Buchanan Street station, No 73149 at Buchanan Street station with a train to Stirling, and No 73064 at Paisley (23 August). I also saw Nos 73055 and 73057 at Coatbridge scrap yard, Nos 73107 and 73154 at Motherwell shed (66B) and No 73005 cut up at Motherwell scrap yard (all on 25 August). My last ever sighting of a BR Standard Class '5' in action was of No 73160 seen from a Liverpool to Manchester Exchange train on 8 September 1967.

BR Standard Class '5' 4-6-0 No 73062 of Glasgow Polmadie shed (66A) departs from Carlisle Citadel station on 6 July 1964. Built at Derby Works in 1954, this locomotive was withdrawn in June 1965.

One of the twenty BR Standard Class '5' 4-6-0s that carried the names of withdrawn 'King Arthur' Class locomotives (see page 130), No 73116 Iseult is seen here at Eastleigh on 21 April 1963. This locomotive had a very short working life, being built at Doncaster Works in 1956 and withdrawn from Eastleigh shed (71A/70D) in November 1964.

BR Standard Class '4' 2-6-4T

The BR Standard Class '4' 2-6-4T was Robert Riddles' (see page 215) development of the LMS Fairburn 2-6-4T, which in turn was a development of the Stanier and Fowler commuter locomotives of the same wheel arrangement. The class was designed at Brighton Works (see page 49), where the majority were also built. The construction of a further fifteen was cancelled in 1957 due to the onset of dieselisation. Apart from the Western Region, the class were allocated to all of the BR regions. However they are most well known for their work on the non-electrified former LB&SCR routes in Kent and East Sussex, Glasgow commuter services and the London, Tilbury & Southend line commuter service in East London. Closure or electrification of these routes in the 1960s led to their withdrawal after a very short working life although a few eked out their final years allocated to Shrewsbury and Swansea. One was withdrawn in 1962, followed by 31 in 1964, 42 in 1965, 56 in 1966 with the final 25 in 1967.

Fifteen examples have been preserved and all but one (which was bought directly from BR) were rescued from Dai Woodham's scrapyard in Barry.

Specification

Builders	Brighton Works (130)
	Derby Works (15)
	Doncaster Works (10)
Wheel arrangement	2-6-4T
Build dates	1951–1956
BR power classification	4MT
Cylinders	2 outside
Driving wheels	5 ft 8 in
Tractive effort	25,100 lbs
Boiler pressure	225 psi
Number built	155
BR numbering	80000–80154

Built at Brighton Works in 1951, BR Standard Class '4' 2-6-4T No 80010 is seen here in ex-works condition at Eastleigh in September 1957. Its short working life ended in June 1964 when it was withdrawn from Brighton shed (75A).

The BR Standard Class '4' 2-6-4Ts were definitely not a common sight in my hometown of Gloucester, although I did see No 80135 on a Gloucester Central to Hereford train on the last day of services, 31 October 1964. However, they were employed in large numbers on suburban passenger services around Glasgow until the Clydeside Blue electric trains were introduced. My trainspotting notebooks record the following observations made on 29 March 1964 when I visited Scotland: Polmadie shed (66A) – 5; Corkerhill shed (67A) – 14 including No 80000; Eastfield shed (65A) – 3; and St Margarets shed (64A) – 8.

Later that year I visited Scotland again and made the following observations: on 27 July I spotted four at Gourock, six between Gourock and Glasgow Central, three at Stirling shed (65J) and four between Glasgow Central and Gourock. Seven were seen at St Enoch station and three at Dumfries shed (67E) on 28 July. No 80119 was spotted at Stranraer Harbour on the same day with a train for Dumfries. Four were spotted at Carstairs shed (66E), two at Dundee Tay Bridge shed and three at Perth shed (63A) on 29 July. No 80110 hauled me between Glasgow Central and Gourock on 31 July.

No 80120 headed my train from Gourock to Glasgow Central and five were seen at St Enoch station on 1 August. Eleven were spotted at Polmadie shed (66A) and eight at St Margarets shed (64A) on 2 August. Ten were spotted at Corkerhill shed (67A), four at Ardrossan shed (67D) and two at Hurlford shed (67B) on 5 August.

On 6 September 1965 I travelled on the Somerset & Dorset Joint Railway for the last time – motive power between Templecombe and Evercreech Junction was No 80138, and between Evercreech Junction and Bath Green Park was No 80041.

Towards the end of steam haulage on the Western Region my local shed, Horton Road (85B), was host to No 80037 on 6 November 1965 – in my notebook I have written 'very clean' – and it was still there a week later. On my final trainspotting visit to Scotland in 1966 I only saw Nos 80004 and 80086 in action at Glasgow Central during the whole week in August that I was there. The end was nigh!

My final sighting of BR Standard Class '4' tanks in action was at Waterloo station on 31 January 1967 where I recorded Nos 80012, 80085 and 80154 on empty coaching stock duties.

Rush hour at London Bridge station on 15 August 1961. On the left is BR Standard Class '4' 2-6-4T No 80018 of Brighton shed (75A) and on the right is sister engine No 80088 of Three Bridges shed (75E). Both were built at Brighton Works, the former in 1951 and the latter in 1954. They were withdrawn in March 1967 and June 1965 respectively.

A bevy of BR Standard Class '9F' 2-10-0s, including Crosti-boilered
Nos 92028 and 92029, sit in Saltley shed's roundhouse in 1966.

The last steam locomotive built by BR, Standard Class '9F' 2-10-0
No 92220 Evening Star stands at Seaton Junction in September 1964
while hauling an enthusiasts' special. This loco with its unique nameplate
had a very short working life of only 5 years. It has since been preserved
by the National Railway Museum in York.

BR Standard Class '9F' 2-10-0

The BR Standard Class '9F' 2-10-0 was Robert Riddles' (see page 215) swan song and is generally considered to be the most successful of his BR standard locomotive classes. The 251 members of the class were built to haul heavy freight trains unaided at speed over considerable distances, a duty which they excelled at in their short working lives.

Many variations of the '9F' were constructed: Nos 92020–92029 were built with Franco-Crosti boilers but this was not considered a success and they were later modified, although they retained their truly ugly looks until withdrawal; Nos 92060–92066 and 92097–92099 were fitted with Westinghouse pumps to operate the discharging doors on iron ore hopper wagons on the Tyne Dock to Consett line; Nos 92165–92167 were originally fitted with mechanical stokers but this was not a success and they were subsequently removed; No 92250, when built in 1960, was fitted with a Giesl oblong ejector which it retained until withdrawal; No 92079, Nos 92165–92167, No 92178 and Nos 92183–92249 were all fitted with double chimneys, considered to be a very successful modification. The last '9F' to be built, and the last steam locomotive to be built by British Railways, was No 92220 and it emerged new from Swindon Works in March 1960, in lined Brunswick Green livery carrying the name *Evening Star* and sporting a copper-capped chimney.

In addition to their duties hauling heavy goods trains, the '9Fs' were also occasionally pressed into express passenger service where their maximum speed of 90 mph was used to good effect. They could occasionally be seen on the Western Region hauling expresses on the Paddington to South Wales main line and also on the East Coast Main Line to King's Cross. One of their final duties was hauling heavy through passenger trains, including the 'Pines Express', unaided over the Somerset & Dorset Joint Railway's steeply graded route between Bath Green Park and Evercreech Junction, a service which ended on 8 September 1962.

Withdrawals commenced in 1964 when sixteen members were retired, followed by 65 in 1965, 46 in 1966, 106 in 1967 and the final eighteen in 1968. Many of these fine locomotives had a very short working life, with No 92220 being withdrawn only five years after being built.

Nine '9Fs' have been preserved in various conditions including the famous No 92220, which is currently on static display at the National Railway Museum in York. Of the others, four are currently operational on heritage railways.

Sightings of '9Fs' were a daily occurrence to me, living in Gloucester. They could be seen heading heavy freight and mineral trains to and from South Wales as well as on the Midland route to Bristol and the former GWR line to Swindon. In the early 1960s I used to see them hauling the Fawley to Bromford Bridge oil trains on a regular basis. During the final months of steam haulage on the Western Region they were regular visitors to my hometown and Horton Road shed (85B). My trainspotting notebook records these final visitors: 6 December 1965 – No 92084 at 85B; 9 December – No 92250 on goods train at Churchdown; 13 December – No 92224 at 85B; 14 December – Nos 92212 and 92250 at 85B; 15 December – No 92246 on goods train; 1 January 1966 – No 92164 at 85B; 2 January – No 92128 on goods train; 2 January – No 92029 light engine at Cheltenham Lansdown. It was reported to me that a '9F' had visited Gloucester on 29 June 1966, six months after the official end of steam haulage! My final sighting of a '9F' during BR days was of No 92130 at a scrap yard in Motherwell on 25 August 1966.

Specification

Builders	Crewe Works (198)
	Swindon Works (53)
Wheel arrangement	2-10-0
Build dates	1954–1960
BR power classification	9F
Cylinders	2 outside
Driving wheels	5 ft 0 in
Tractive effort	39,667 lbs
Boiler pressure	250 psi
Number built	251
BR numbering	92000–92250

Acknowledgements

Photo credits

t = top; b = bottom; r = right

Alamy Stock Photo: 4t (David Lyons); 10/11 (Maurice Savage); 12 (World History Archive); 15 (Peter Jordon_NE); 16/17 (Science History Images); 20 (Richard Burdon); 22 (Michelle Bridges)

Colour-Rail: 18/19 (B J Swain); 24/25 (N Sprinks); 28/29b; 29t; 30; 31; 32; 33; 37; 44/45 (W H Ashcroft); 47t; 47b; 48t; 48/49b; 50; 52/53t; 52/53b (L F Folkard); 54 (P Chancellor); 55; 59t; 60/61b (P J Hughes); 62/63b; 63t; 64 (G Parry Collection); 65 (P Chancellor); 68t; 68b; 70/71; 72; 73; 74/75; 76/77; 79t (P Chancellor); 80 (P J Hughes); 81; 82b; 85t (T B Owen); 85b; 86; 87; 89t; 90 (R Broughton); 96; 99 (P Chancellor); 100/101; 103; 104; 105 (D C Ovenden); 107t; 108/109; 110; 112; 113 (M J Reade); 116; 118; 124t (N Joseph); 126/127b (T B Owen); 128/129b (P Chancellor); 130/131; 132/133b; 133t (P J Hughes); 134; 137 (P Chancellor); 139 (T B Owen); 142/143 (T B Owen); 144; 149r; 151; 152; 154 (K C H Fairey); 155t (D Woodward); 155b (T B Owen); 157t; 163b (T B Owen); 165b (T B Owen); 166t (M Chapman); 166/167b (D Forsyth); 168/169b (A F H Hudson); 170 (L Hanson); 175t (D Forsyth); 177b; 182/183 (J T Inglis); 184 (P J Hughes); 190; 193t (K C H Fairey); 195 (C C B Herbert); 196/197b (G P Collection); 197t (D C Ovenden); 200/201; 207t (T B Owen); 210/211; 212/213b (P J Hughes); 216/217 (D C Ovenden); 219b; 220 (B J Swain); 221 (L Rowe); 222b

Getty Images: 4b, 23, 26/27, 82t, 111, 146/147b, 160/161, 188/189 (all © Science & Society Picture Library)

Gordon Edgar: front & back endpapers; 5b; 8; 9; 34; 35; 38; 42/43; 57; 67 (A E Durrant); 79b; 91; 92/93; 115b; 117; 123; 127tr; 140/141 (A E Durrant); 148/149b; 153; 158; 163t; 165t; 169t; 172/173b; 175b; 177t; 178t; 178b; 181; 185; 186/187; 192/193b; 198; 202/203b; 204 (Alan Orchard); 206/207b; 209; 214/215; 219t; 222t

John Goss: 51

Julian Holland: 56; 61t; 66; 97; 125br; 129tr; 136; 150; 157b; 159; 162; 164; 173t; 179; 180; 199; 201t; 203t; 205

Peter Hughes: 171, 208

Gavin Morrison: 40/41; 95; 102; 115t; 120/121; 124/125b; 145; 147t; 156; 212t

Science Museum Group: front cover (John Cooper-Smith); 6/7, 13, 21, 58/59b, 88/89b, 106/107b, 119, 135, 176 (all © National Railway Museum)

With thanks for research assistance and advice to:

Gordon Edgar

List of acronyms

The following acronyms appear throughout the book, and are listed here for reference.

ACE	Atlantic Coast Express
B&DJR	Birmingham & Derby Junction Railway
BR	British Railways
CME	Chief Mechanical Engineer
CR	Caledonian Railway
ECML	East Coast Main Line
FR	Ffestiniog Railway
G&SWR	Glasgow & South Western Railway
GCR	Great Central Railway
GER	Great Eastern Railway
GNR	Great Northern Railway
GS&WR	Great Southern & Western Railway
GWR	Great Western Railway
HR	Highland Railway
L&MR	Liverpool & Manchester Railway
L&YR	Lancashire & Yorkshire Railway
LB&SCR	London, Brighton & South Coast Railway
LMR	London Midland Region
LMS	London Midland & Scottish Railway
LNER	London North Eastern Railway
LNWR	London & North Western Railway
LSWR	London & South Western Railway
M&BR	Manchester & Birmingham Railway
MR	Midland Railway
NBL	Northern British Locomotive Company
NBR	North British Railway
NER	North Eastern Railway
NLR	North London Railway
ROD	Railway Operating Division
S&CR	Shrewsbury & Chester Railway
S&DJR	Somerset & Dorset Joint Railway
S&DR	Stockton & Darlington Railway
SDR	South Devon Railway
SE&CR	South Eastern & Chatham Railway
SER	South Eastern Railway
SR	Southern Railway
WCML	West Coast Main Line
WD	War Department
WR	Western Region

Photo captions

FRONT COVER:

Now 100 years old, preserved ex-LNER 'A3' Class 4-6-2 No 60103 Flying Scotsman powers through Settle station with a train on the Settle–Carlisle Line, 4 December 2019. Built as an LNER Class 'A1' at Doncaster Works in 1923 and rebuilt as an 'A3' in 1947, this world-famous locomotive was withdrawn from King's Cross shed (34A) in January 1963 before being sold for preservation to Alan Pegler.

FRONT ENDPAPER:

The Midland Railway '1000' Class Compound 4-4-0 No 1000 was built at Derby Works in 1902 and withdrawn in 1951. As the first of this famous class, it was subsequently preserved and is currently on static display at Barrow Hill Roundhouse where it is seen here on 23 September 2015.

BACK ENDPAPER:

BR 'B1' Class 4-6-0 No 61306 was built by the North British Locomotive Company in 1948 and withdrawn in 1967. It was saved from the scrapheap and privately purchased for preservation, later receiving the name Mayflower which formerly was carried by sister locomotive No 61379. It is seen here at Waterloo station in BR apple green livery with 'The Sunset Steam Express' on 30 July 2019.